Lecture Notebook and Study Guide

Lecture Notebook and Study Guide

to accompany

Biological Psychology

Stephen B. Klein • B. Michael Thorne

Chrystal McChristian
University of Central Arkansas

Billy L. Smith
University of Central Arkansas

WORTH PUBLISHERS

Lecture Notebook and Study Guide
by Chrystal McChristian and Billy L. Smith
to accompany
Klein and Thorne: *Biological Psychology*

ISBN 13: 978-0-7167-7066-4
ISBN 10: 0-7167-7066-0

Printed in the United States of America

Text Design: S. B. Alexander

First Printing

Worth Publishers
41 Madison Avenue
New York, NY 10010
www.worthpublishers.com

◆◆◆ CONTENTS

◆ TO THE STUDENT

Welcome to the field of biological psychology! No doubt you will come to find that a lot is expected of you as a student in a biological psychology course. Most notably, you will be introduced to terminology completely different than what you have been exposed to in other psychology courses and will be asked to analyze biological and anatomical art associated with the various origins of human behavior. To help you navigate one of the more challenging courses in the discipline of psychology, we have created this **Lecture Notebook and Study Guide** in the hopes that you will walk away from this course with a thorough knowledge and appreciation of the biological underpinnings that are so crucial to the study of psychology as a whole.

After years of studying how students learn best, we have created this guide with the expectation that it will not only help you assess how well you are absorbing the material within each chapter but will also serve to acquaint you with material before your instructor even lectures on it.

Many of the features that you will find in this guide will be familiar to you from study guides you may have used in other courses. These are the proven favorites. Beyond these examples, this guide also features a lecture notebook. Because so much of your time will be spent understanding the structures of the brain and the nature of biological reactions, we created the lecture notebook to feature figures and tables from the chapters of your textbook so that you can take your notes directly on the page. This will allow you to spend your time learning the structures of the brain instead of losing time drawing each structure while the lecture continues on. It will also allow you to write your notes next to the relevant piece of art. You will no longer have to jump between your notes and your textbook to find what section of the brain is being discussed. Therefore, our mission is to provide you with a tool that makes your in-lecture learning experience more user-friendly and interactive.

Each chapter of this guide features the following elements:

Chapter Art Lecture Notebook

This notebook features up to 15 pieces of art from each chapter. These selections of labeled pieces were chosen for their relevance to the key concepts in the study of biological psychology. In addition to the labeled art at the beginning of the chapter, you will also be able to quiz yourself on your understanding of these renderings with a series of labeling exercises at the end of each chapter.

Chapter Summary

This section offers an overview of the information covered in each chapter. After you have read the chapter and listened to the lecture, read the summary to make sure that you are comfortable in your understanding of the material.

Key Terms

This section identifies the important concepts and terms presented in the textbook chapters. Read through the list to verify that you recognize and understand each term. If any terms look unfamiliar, you may wish to revisit your text. Be sure that you have a clear sense of how each key term fits into the chapter material.

You should also take special note of the key terms used by your instructor during lectures and make note of them in your study guide. If you're not completely clear on the meaning of each marked term, look it up in the text and write a brief description next to the term.

Labeling Exercises

Each item presented in this section offers an opportunity for you to quiz yourself on your understanding of some of the anatomical art presented in each chapter. If your instructor emphasizes drawings and diagrams on exams, this section will be of particular use to you.

We hope that this **Lecture Notebook and Study Guide** will help every student meet the challenges presented by the biological psychology course. Used in conjunction with the critical thinking, fill-in-the-blank, and multiple-choice questions presented in the Chapter Review section of each textbook chapter, you should be well prepared to excel in your study of this demanding material.

An Introduction to Biological Psychology

1

◆ CHAPTER ART LECTURE NOTEBOOK

The following is a selection of the important figures and tables introduced in Chapter 1. You can take notes during class in the space provided.

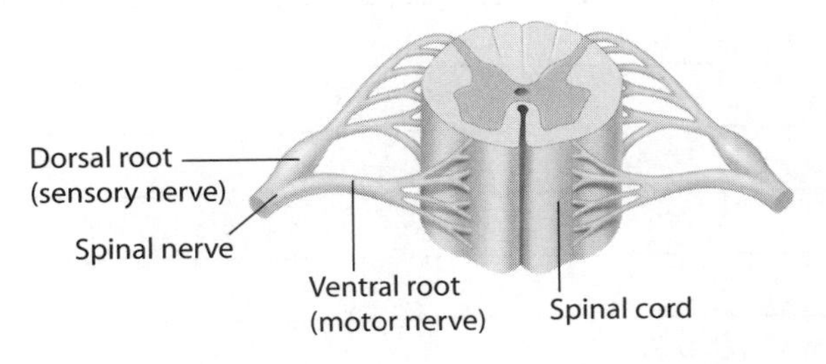

Figure 1.3 A cross-sectional view of part of the spinal cord, p. 5.

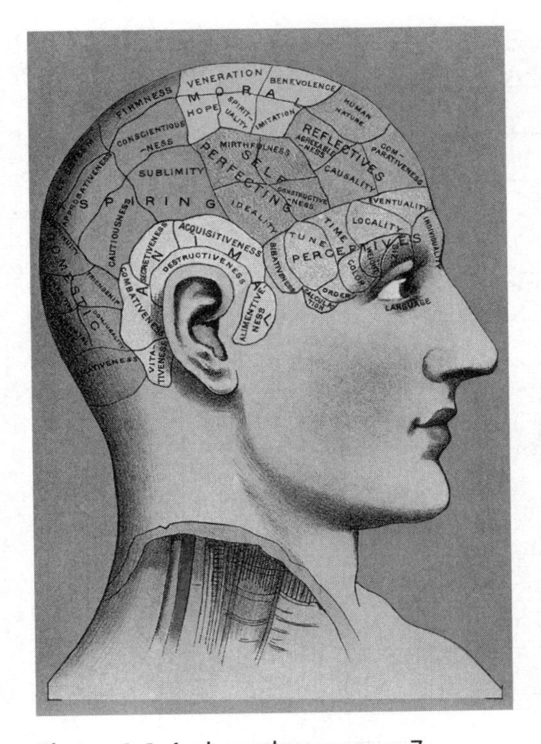

Figure 1.4 A phrenology map, p. 7.

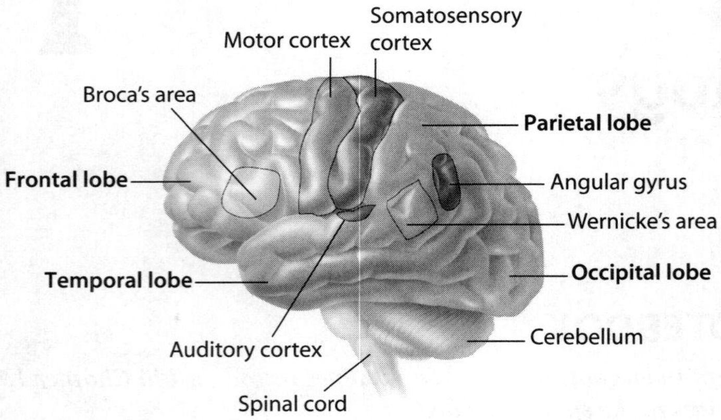

Figure 1.6 The four lobes of the cerebral cortex, p. 9.

Table 1.1
Methods for Studying Brain Function

Method	Purpose	How It Is Done
Ablation, lesion	Destroy neurons in specific area	Cutting or suction, electric current, toxic chemicals
Computerized axial tomography (CT)	Produce static image of nervous system	X-ray imaging with CT scanner
Magnetic resonance imaging (MRI)	Produce static image of nervous system	Radio waves measured with MRI scanner
Electrical recording	Record electrical activity during behavior	Macroelectrode recording of many electrodes; microelectrode recording from single neurons
Positron emission tomography (PET)	Measure metabolic activity in the brain	PET scanner records emission of radioactively charged particles from different brain areas while subject is engaged in particular activity
Functional magnetic resonance imaging (fMRI)	Measuring cerebral blood flow	MRI scanner measures blood flow in different parts of the brain while the subject is engaged in particular activity
Autoradiography	Measure the chemical activity of specific areas of the brain	Target neural tissue is placed against x-ray film to record radioactivity as a measure of chemical absorption by the target area
Microdialysis	Detect presence of specific neurotransmitters in an area of the brain	Neurochemicals diffuse into a fine tube implanted into a brain area and are assessed with an automated chromatograph
Electrical stimulation	Elicit behavior through direct stimulation of brain area	Weak electric current passed through small wire
Chemical stimulation	Elicit behavior through direct stimulation of brain area	Chemical administered to brain through tube called a cannula

Table 1.1 Methods for Studying Brain Function, p. 20.

Table 1.2
Specializations Within Neuroscience

Specialization	Area of Investigation
Behavioral neuroscience	Impact of the nervous system on behavior
Cognitive neuroscience	Relationship between the nervous system and mental processes
Developmental neurobiology	Development of the nervous system
Neuroanatomy	Structure of the nervous system
Neurochemistry	Chemical basis of neural activity
Neuroendocrinology	Influence of hormones on the nervous system and of the nervous system on endocrine (hormone) function
Neuropathology	Disorders of the nervous system
Neuropharmacology	Effects of drugs on the nervous system
Neuropsychology	Behavioral consequences of disorders of the nervous system

Table 1.2 Specializations Within Neuroscience, p. 21.

CHAPTER SUMMARY

Biological psychology is the study of the influences of biological systems, especially the nervous system, on behavior. One of the oldest arguments in biological psychology is the mind/body problem: do both the body and mind exist (dualism) or is there only body or only mind (monism)? Another philosophical concern in biological psychology has been in regards to the location of the mind. For centuries, this location was hypothesized to be many areas, including the heart, brain, and the pineal gland. Localization of function has also been a historically debated topic in biological psychology.

Support for localization became apparent throughout the 19th and 20th centuries with the emergence of the Bell-Magendie law and the doctrine of specific nerve energies. Further support came from other areas of research, such as the study of phrenology, Darwin's theory of evolution, and studies of brain-damaged human subjects. Particularly important was the discovery of Broca's area and Wernicke's area, two specific language areas located in the left hemisphere, and the identification of areas in the brain that control specific sensory systems (occipital lobe controls vision; temporal lobe controls hearing; parietal lobe controls sensation).

One of the greatest neurological discoveries of the 19th century was the identification of the structural unity in the brain responsible for functioning—the neuron. While it was initially believed that the nervous system consists of a network of connected neurons (the nerve net theory), it is now accepted that the nervous system is made up of individual neurons (the neuronal theory). During this time, it was also discovered that information was transmitted across the synapse, or space between individual neurons, by means of chemicals called neurotransmitters.

There are many different methods used to study brain functioning. Computerized axial tomography (CT/CAT scan) employs x-ray imaging to produce a static, cross-sectional image of the brain. Magnetic resonance imaging (MRI) uses radio waves to obtain a picture of the brain. The electroencephalogram (EEG) measures the electrical activity of areas of the brain to provide a graphic record of this activity. Positron emission tomography (PET) measures the metabolic activity of the nervous system in order to assess functional localization. The functional MRI (fMRI) uses rapidly oscillating magnetic fields to measure cerebral blood flow in the brain in order to obtain an image of the brain's neural activity. Autoradiography involves the injection of radioactive chemicals into the bloodstream and the analysis of neural tissue to determine the location of a specific chemical. Microdialysis is a technique to identify a neurotransmitter in a specific area of the nervous system by measuring the chemical constituents of that area.

Biological psychology is part of a larger discipline called neuroscience, the scientific study of the nervous system. Within biological psychology there are five areas of study. Physiological psychology is the investigation of the relationship between the nervous system and behavior. Psychophysiology is the study of the relationship between physiology and behavior through the analysis of the physiological responses of humans engaged in various activities. Psychopharmacology is the study of the effects of psychotropic drugs on behavior. Neuropsychology is the study of the behavioral effects of brain damage. Comparative psychology is the study of the influence of genetics and evolution on behavior through behavioral comparisons of different animal species.

Whether conducting research on human or animal subjects, researchers must adhere to strict ethical guidelines designed to protect subjects and minimize potential risks and pain. Such guidelines have been established by the U.S. Department of Health and Human Services (DHHS), the American Psychological Association, and federal, state, and local laws such as the Animal Welfare Act. Further research can only be conducted when approved by a committee, such as the Institutional Review Board (IRB) or the Institutional Animal Care and Use Committee (IACUC).

KEY TERMS

The following is a list of important terms introduced in Chapter 1. Give the definition of each term in the space provided.

ablation

autoradiography

behavior

behavior genetics

Bell-Magendie law

biological psychology

Broca's area

cerebrum

cognitive neuroscience

comparative psychology

computerized axial tomography (CT)

doctrine of specific nerve energies

dualism

electroencephalogram (EEG)

engram

equipotentiality

ethology

evoked potential

functional MRI (fMRI)

macroelectrode

magnetic resonance imaging (MRI)

mass action

microdialysis

microelectrode

monism

nerve net theory

neuron

neuronal theory

neuropsychology

neuroscience

phrenology

physiological psychology

positron emission tomography (PET)

pressure phosphene

psychoactive drug

psychopharmacology

psychophysiology

reflex

stereotaxic apparatus

synapse

vagusstoff

Wernicke's area

◆ LABELING EXERCISES

1. Instructions: According to the Bell-Magendie law, different parts of the spinal cord carry either sensory or motor information. In the figure below, label the following areas:

spinal nerve	spinal cord
ventral root (motor nerve)	dorsal root (sensory nerve)

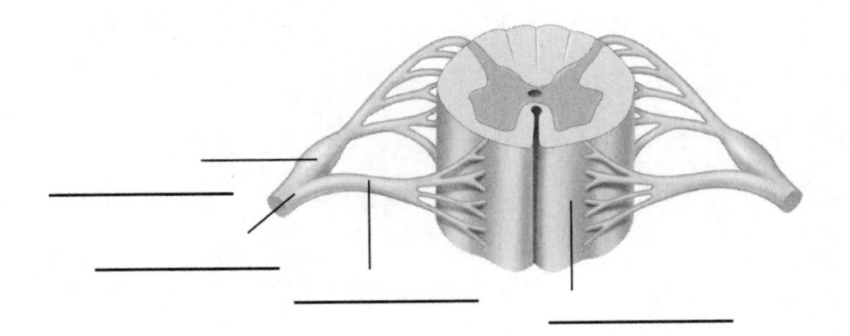

2. Instructions: The cerebral cortex of the brain is divided into four lobes, each of which contain areas responsible for certain functions. Label the following brain areas in the figure below:

parietal lobe	Broca's area
temporal lobe	auditory cortex
occipital lobe	angular gyrus
frontal lobe	spinal cord
somatosensory cortex	Wernicke's area
cerebellum	motor cortex

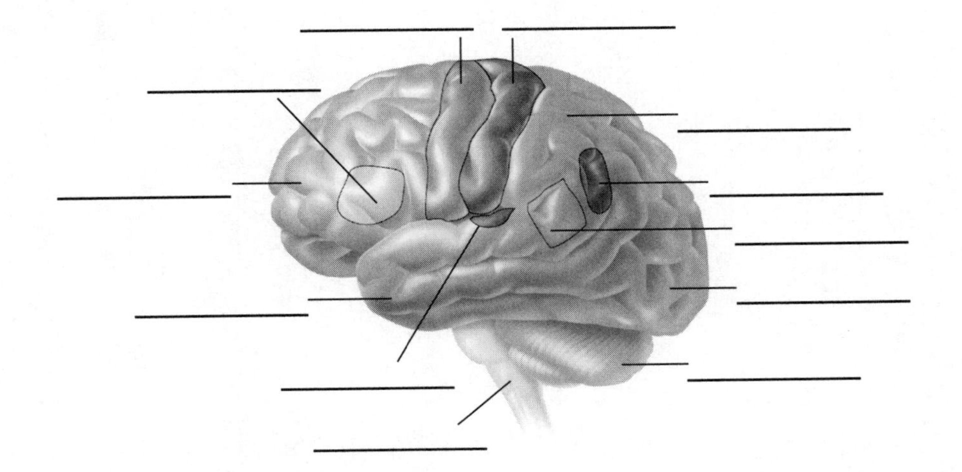

Exploring the Nervous System

2

◆ CHAPTER ART LECTURE NOTEBOOK

The following is a selection of the important figures and tables introduced in Chapter 2. You can take notes during class in the space provided.

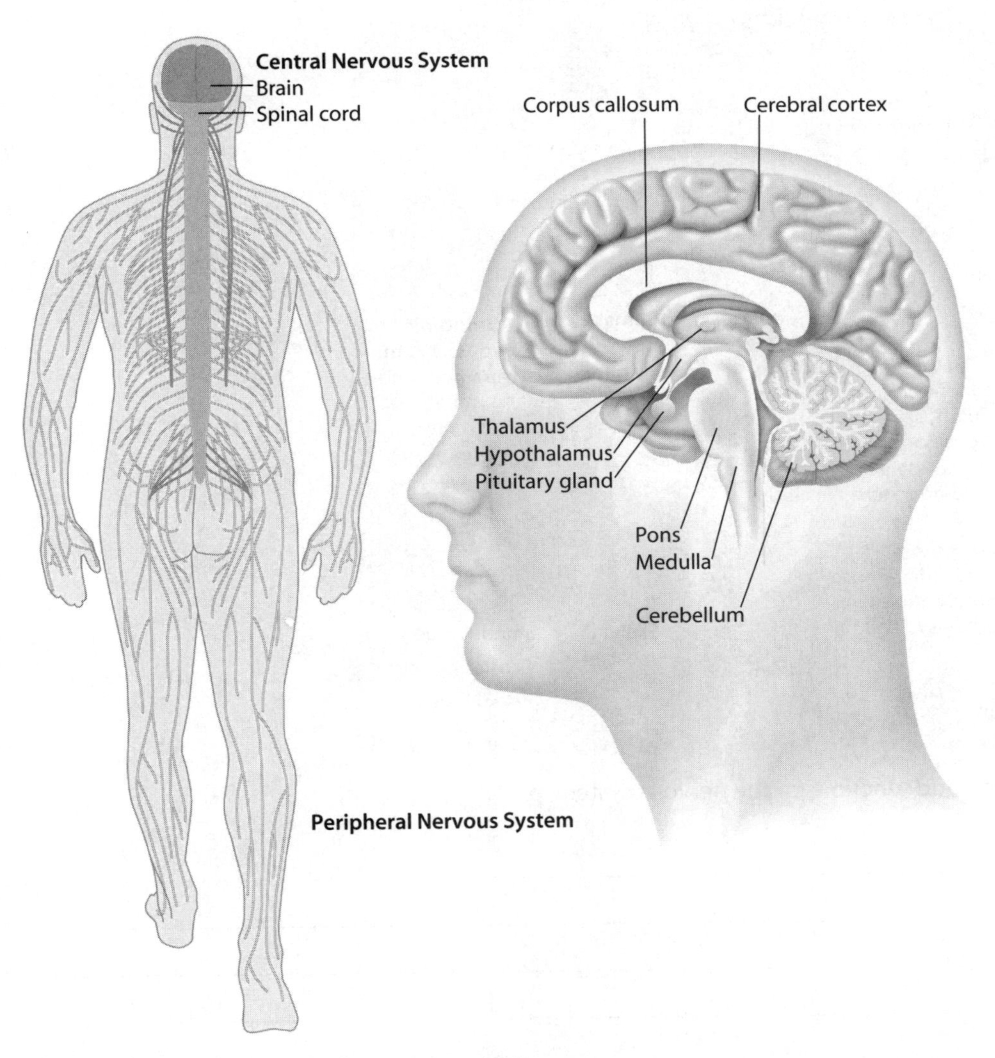

Figure 2.2 The human nervous system, p. 35.

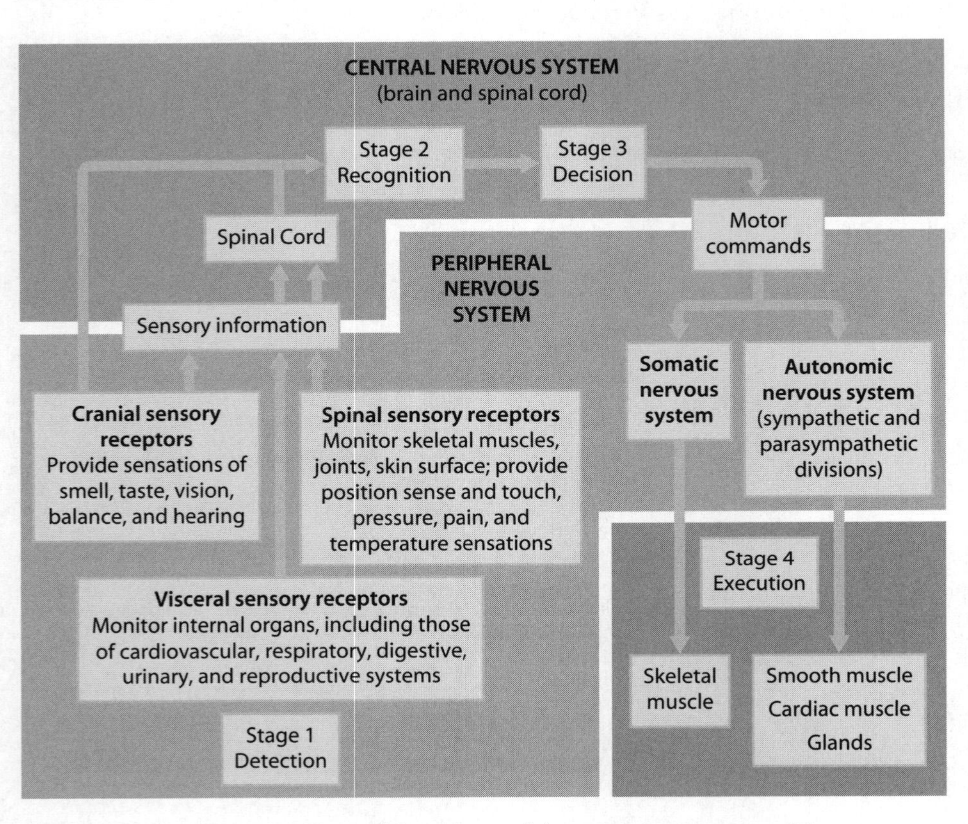

Figure 2.3 The organization and functions of the nervous system, p. 36.

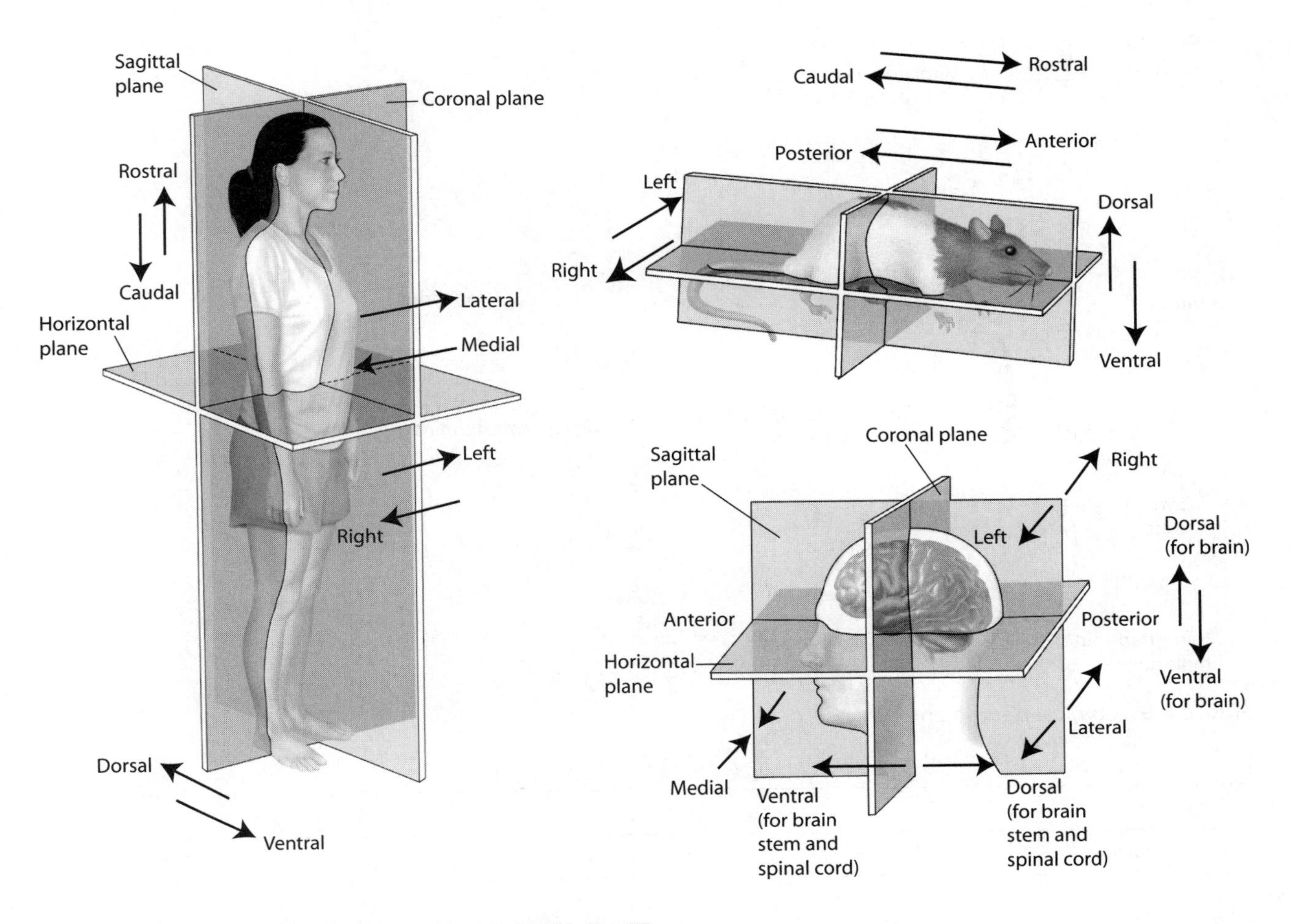

Figure 2.4 Anatomical directions and perspectives, p. 37.

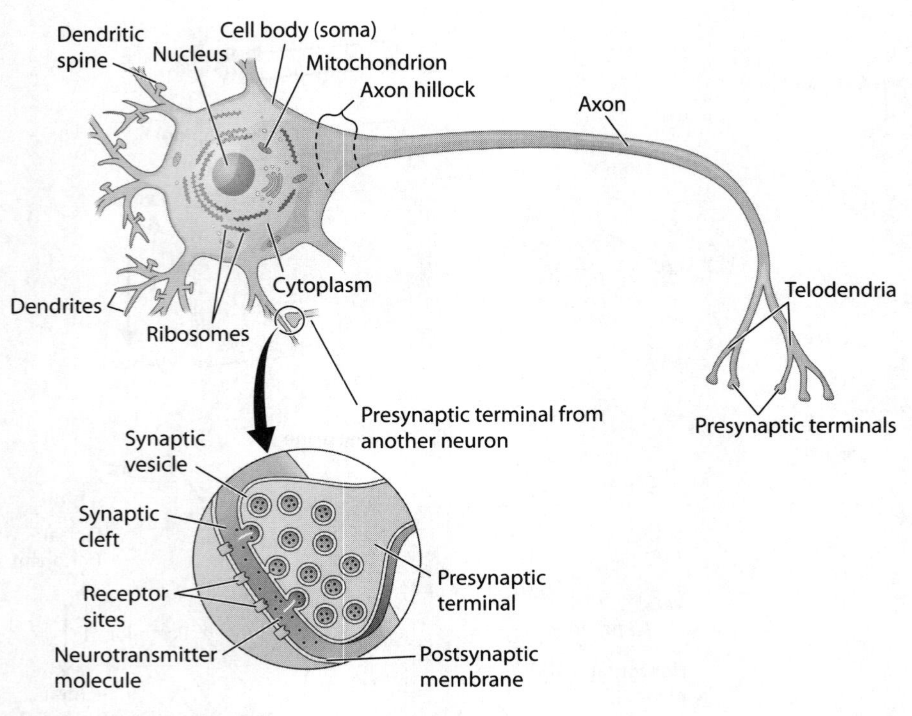

Figure 2.5 A typical neuron and synapse, p. 39.

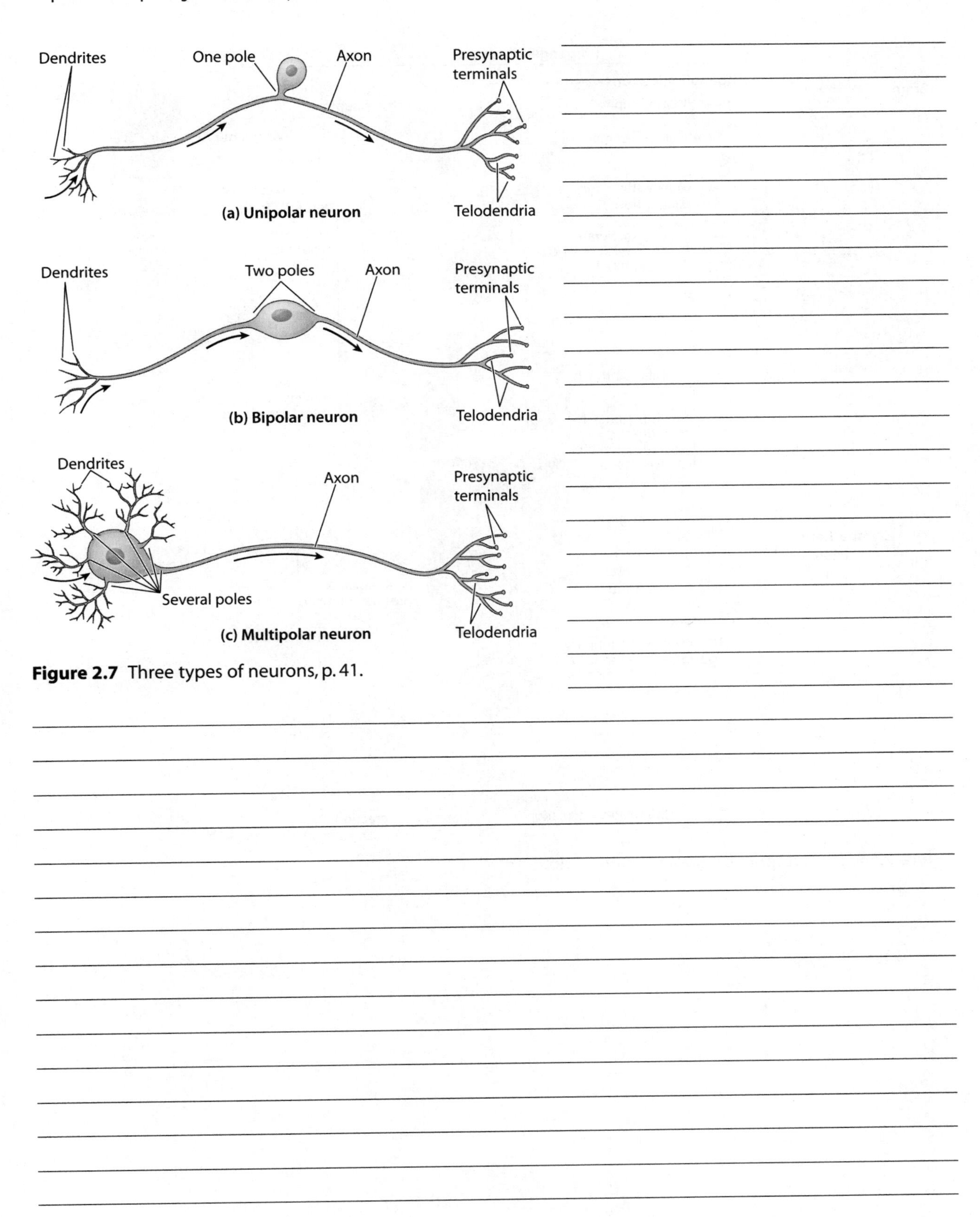

Figure 2.7 Three types of neurons, p. 41.

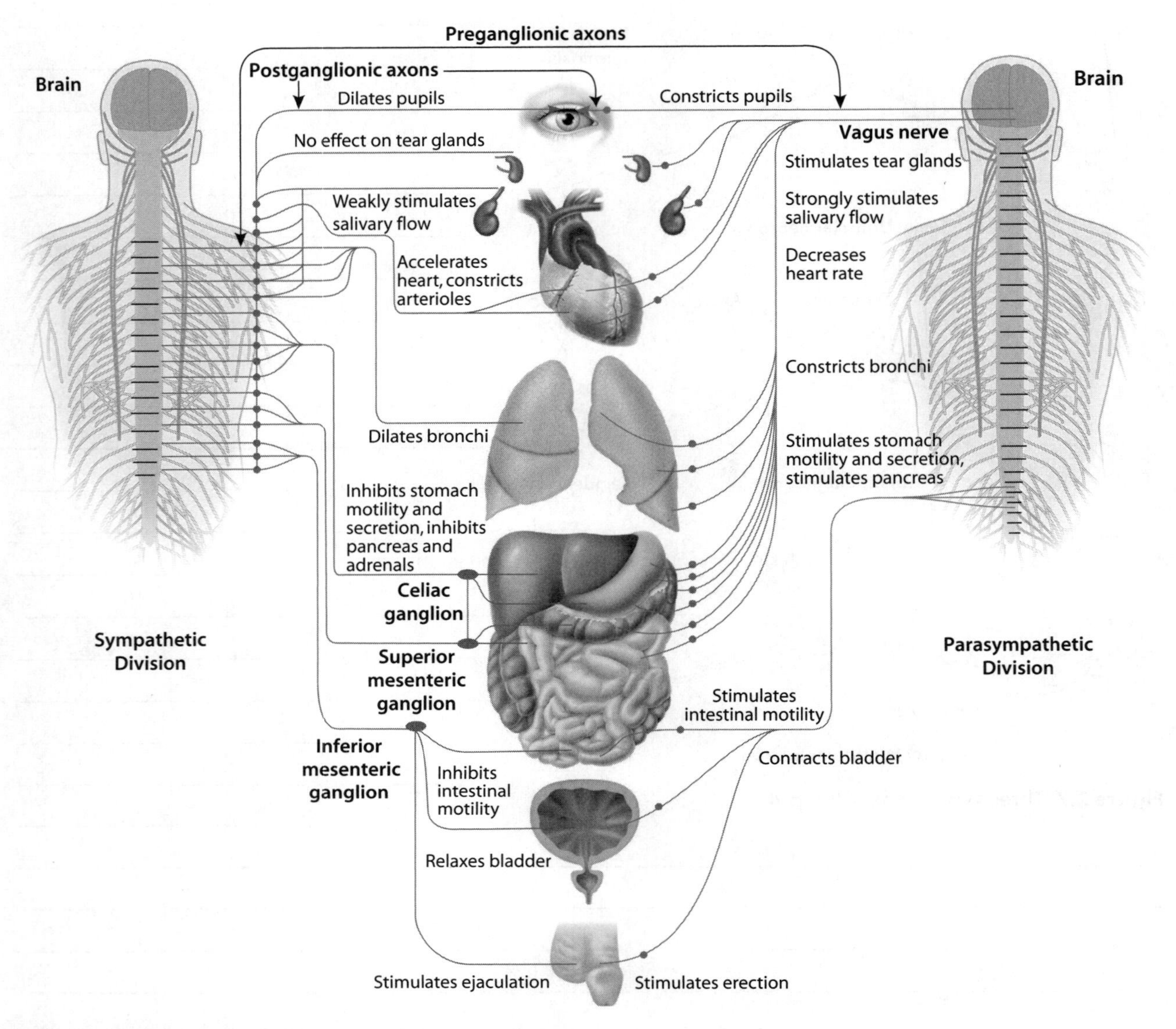

Figure 2.11 The autonomic nervous system, p. 46.

Table 2.2
The Major Structures of the Human Brain and Their Primary Functions

Structure	Primary Function
Hindbrain	
Myelencephalon	
Medulla oblongata	Controls vital functions; relays sensory information to thalamus
Metencephalon	
Cerebellum	Coordinates complex motor responses
Pons	Relays sensory information to cerebellum and thalamus
Raphé system	Controls sleep-wake cycle
Midbrain	
Mesencephalon	
Tectum	
Inferior colliculi	Relay auditory information, auditory localization
Superior colliculi	Mediate visual reflexes, visual localization, gross pattern discrimination
Tegmentum	
Red nucleus	Controls basic body and limb movements
Reticular formation	Controls arousal and consciousness
Substantia nigra	Integrates voluntary movements
Forebrain	
Diencephalon	
Epithalamus	
Habenula	Functions in olfaction
Pineal gland	Coordinates seasonal rhythms
Thalamus	
Lateral geniculate nucleus	Relays visual information to cerebral cortex
Medial geniculate nucleus	Relays auditory information to cerebral cortex
Ventrolateral nucleus	Relays information from cerebellum to motor cortex
Hypothalamus	Detects need states; controls pituitary hormone production and release
Pituitary gland	Controls other glands (anterior lobe); releases oxytocin and vasopressin (posterior lobe)
Telencephalon	
Limbic system	
Amygdala	Controls anger and fear
Cingulate gyrus	Elicits positive and negative emotional responses
Hippocampus	Participates in memory storage and retrieval
Basal ganglia	Integrate voluntary movement; maintain posture and muscle tone
Caudate nucleus }	Corpus striatum
Putamen }	Corpus striatum
Globus pallidus	
Cerebral cortex	
Occipital lobes	Control vision
Parietal lobes	Control skin senses, spatial functions
Temporal lobes	Control audition, language in left hemisphere, visual functions
Frontal lobes	Control motor functions, planning, speech in left hemisphere

Table 2.2 The Major Structures of the Human Brain and Their Primary Functions, p. 55.

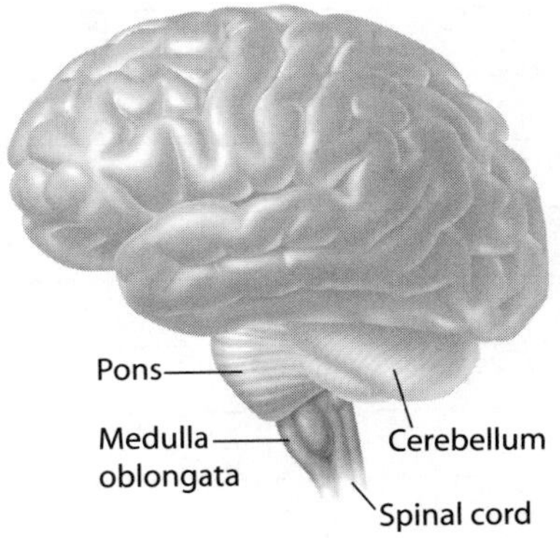

Pons
Medulla oblongata
Cerebellum
Spinal cord

Figure 2.17 The hindbrain, p. 56.

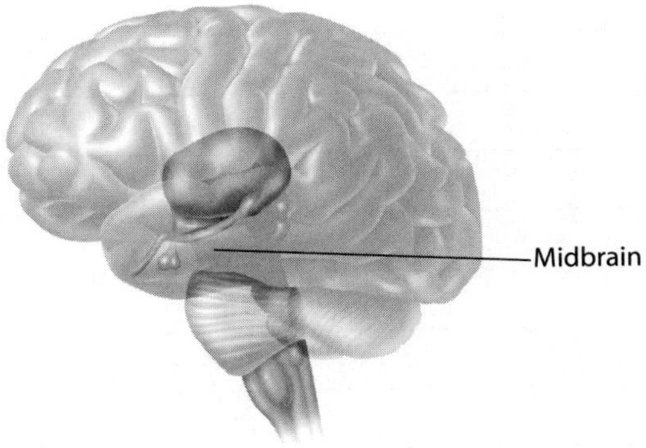

Midbrain

Figure 2.18 The midbrain, p. 57.

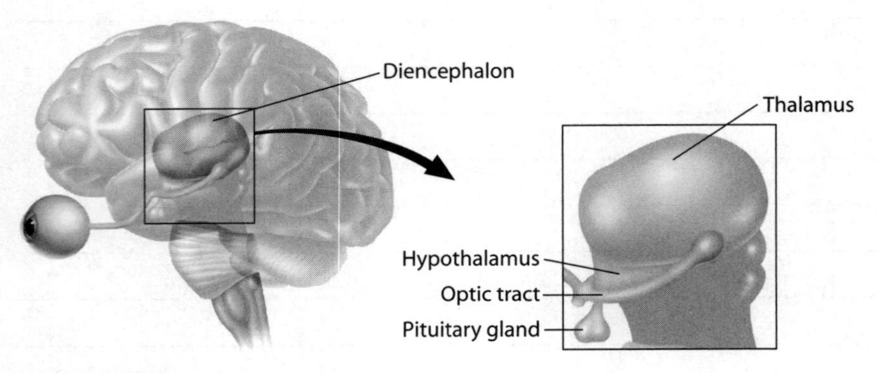

Figure 2.20 The diencephalon, p. 58.

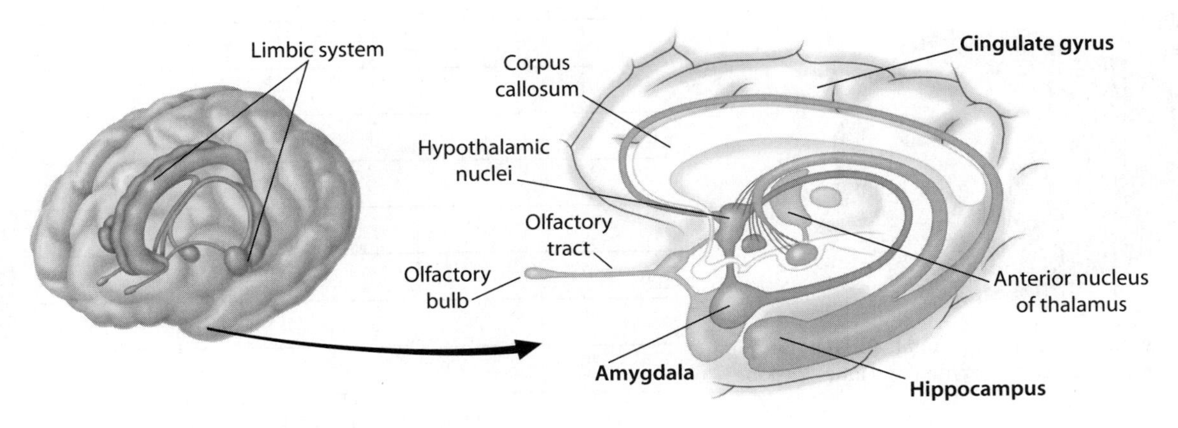

Figure 2.23 The limbic system, p. 61.

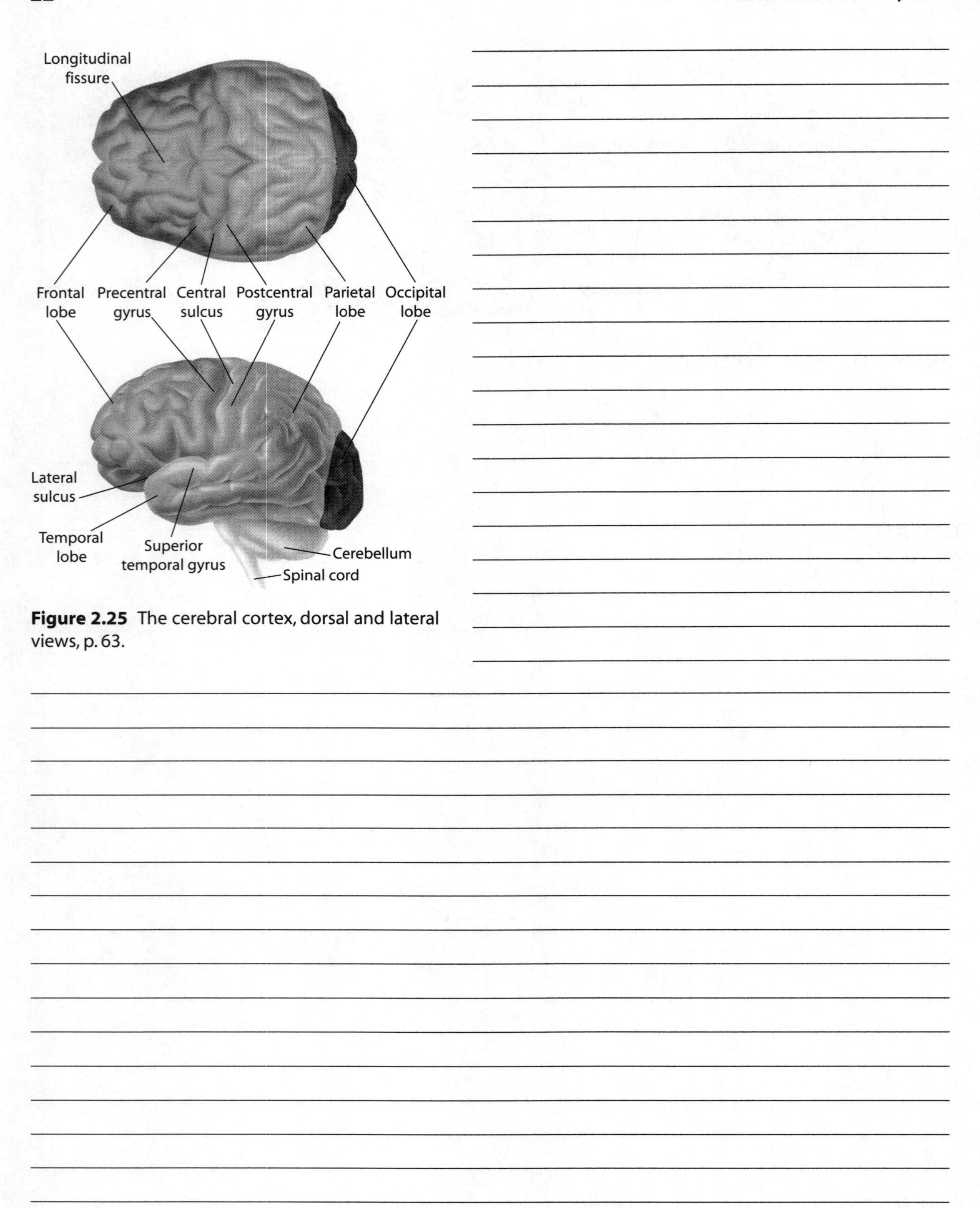

Figure 2.25 The cerebral cortex, dorsal and lateral views, p. 63.

◆ CHAPTER SUMMARY

The nervous system is divided into two systems: the peripheral nervous system (PNS) and the central nervous system (CNS). The PNS consists of the somatic and autonomic nervous systems and the CNS consists of the brain and spinal cord. In order to function properly, all the components of the nervous system must work together.

The nervous system is composed of neurons and glial cells. In order to perform the information-processing and communication functions of the nervous system, neurons communicate with other neurons, blood vessels, muscles, and glands. There are three functional types of neurons: sensory neurons, motor neurons, and interneurons. Sensory neurons detect information from the external and internal environment and transmit it to the CNS. Motor neurons carry information from the CNS to the muscles and glands. Interneurons connect sensory and motor neurons. Additionally, there are three structural forms of neurons: unipolar, bipolar, and multipolar.

Glial cells play a supporting role in the nervous system. There are several types. Astrocytes provide physical support for a neuron, transport nutrients into the neuron, remove waste products from it, and regulate blood flow in the CNS. Microglia remove the debris of dead neurons. Oligodendrocytes and Schwann cells produce myelin to protect and insulate the axons of certain neurons. Recent research has demonstrated that glial cells also help to determine the location of synaptic connections.

The PNS consists of the somatic nervous system and the autonomic nervous system. The somatic nervous system consists of two main types of nerves, spinal and cranial nerves, which receive and send messages from the brain to the skeletal muscles. The autonomic nervous system is made up of the sympathetic and parasympathetic systems. These systems act in opposition of each other and prepare the body for "fight or flight"—preparing the body to cope with danger and stress; and conserving and replenishing energy when the danger and stress is over.

The CNS is protected by several structures. The hard, bony composition of the skull and vertebral column protect the soft tissue of the CNS, including the brain and spinal cord. The meninges are three layers of tissue that separate the skull and brain and the vertebral column and spinal cord. The ventricular system is a series of interconnected hollow chambers that contain cerebrospinal fluid (CSF), which cushions, nourishes, and protects the brain and spinal cord.

The brain is divided into three major sections: the hindbrain, the midbrain, and the forebrain. The hindbrain contains the medulla oblongata, the pons, the cerebellum, and the raphé system. It controls the basic functions essential to life, such as breathing, heart rate, reflexive responses, sleep, and arousal. The midbrain includes the tectum and tegmentum, which are responsible for integrating voluntary movements and relaying visual and auditory information. The forebrain has two divisions: the diencephalon and the telencephalon. The diencephalon contains the epithalamus, thalamus, hypothalamus, and the pituitary gland. These structures are responsible for relaying sensory information, regulating hunger, thirst, and sex, and regulating hormones and glandular activity. The telencephalon consists of the limbic system (important in emotional experience and regulation), the basal ganglia (integration of voluntary movements), and the cerebral cortex.

The cerebral cortex is divided into two hemispheres, each of which has four lobes. The occipital lobe analyzes visual information. The parietal lobe analyzes sensory information. The temporal lobe analyzes auditory information, as well as, visual object recognition. The frontal lobe controls voluntary body movement and complex intellectual functions, such as planning and sequencing behavior, as well as, attention and emotional processing.

◆ KEY TERMS

The following is a list of important terms introduced in Chapter 2. Give the definition of each term in the space provided.

adrenocorticotropic hormone (ACTH)

afferent neuron

amygdala

anterior

anterior pituitary gland

antidiuretic hormone (ADH)

arachnoid mater

astrocyte

autonomic nervous system

axoaxonic synapse

axodendritic synapse

axon

axon hillock

axosomatic synapse

basal ganglia

brain

brain stem

caudal

cell body (soma)

cell membrane

central canal

central nervous system (CNS)

central sulcus

cerebellum

cerebral commissure

cerebral cortex

cerebrospinal fluid (CSF)

choroid plexus

cingulate gyrus

congenital disorder

contralateral control

coronal section

corpus callosum

cranial nerve

cytoplasm

dendrite

dendrodendritic synapse

dermatome

deoxyribonucleic acid (DNA)

diencephalon

dorsal

dura mater

efferent neuron

epithalamus

forebrain

frontal lobe

ganglion

glial cell

gonadotropin

gray matter

habenula

hindbrain

hippocampus

horizontal section

hydrocephalus

hypothalamus

inferior

inferior colliculus

interneuron

lateral

lateral geniculate nucleus (LGN)

lateralization of function

lateral sulcus

limbic system

longitudinal fissure

medial

medial geniculate nucleus (MGN)

medulla oblongata

melatonin

meninges

metencephalon

microglial cell

midbrain

motor cortex

motor neuron

myelencephalon

myelin

nerve

neuromuscular junction

neurotransmitter

nucleus (of cell)

nucleus (of CNS)

occipital lobe

oligodendrocyte

oxytocin

parasympathetic nervous system

parietal lobe

peripheral nervous system (PNS)

pia mater

pineal gland

pituitary gland

pons

posterior

posterior pituitary gland

postsynaptic membrane

prefrontal cortex

prefrontal lobotomy

presynaptic membrane

presynaptic terminal

primary auditory cortex

primary visual cortex

raphé system

red nucleus

reticular formation

ribonucleic acid (RNA)

rostral

sagittal section

Schwann cell

sensory neglect

sensory neuron

skull

soma

somatic nervous system

somatosensory cortex

somatotropin

spinal cord

spinal nerve

spinal reflex

subarachnoid space

substantia nigra

superior

superior colliculus

sympathetic nervous system

synapse

synaptic cleft

synaptic vesicle

tectum

tegmentum

telencephalon

telodendron

temporal lobe

thalamus

thyroid-stimulating hormone (TSH)

tract

tumor

ventral

ventricle

ventricular system

ventrolateral nucleus

vertebral column

white matter

◆ LABELING EXERCISES

1. In a neuron, many structures are involved in the transmission of information within the neuron and between neurons. In the following figure of a neuron and synapse, label these structures:

axon	cytoplasm
cell body (soma)	presynaptic terminals
dendrites	presynaptic terminal from another neuron
nucleus	synaptic cleft
telodendria	synaptic vesicle
mitochondrion	neurotransmitter molecules
ribosomes	postsynaptic membrane
dendritic spine	receptor sites
axon hillock	

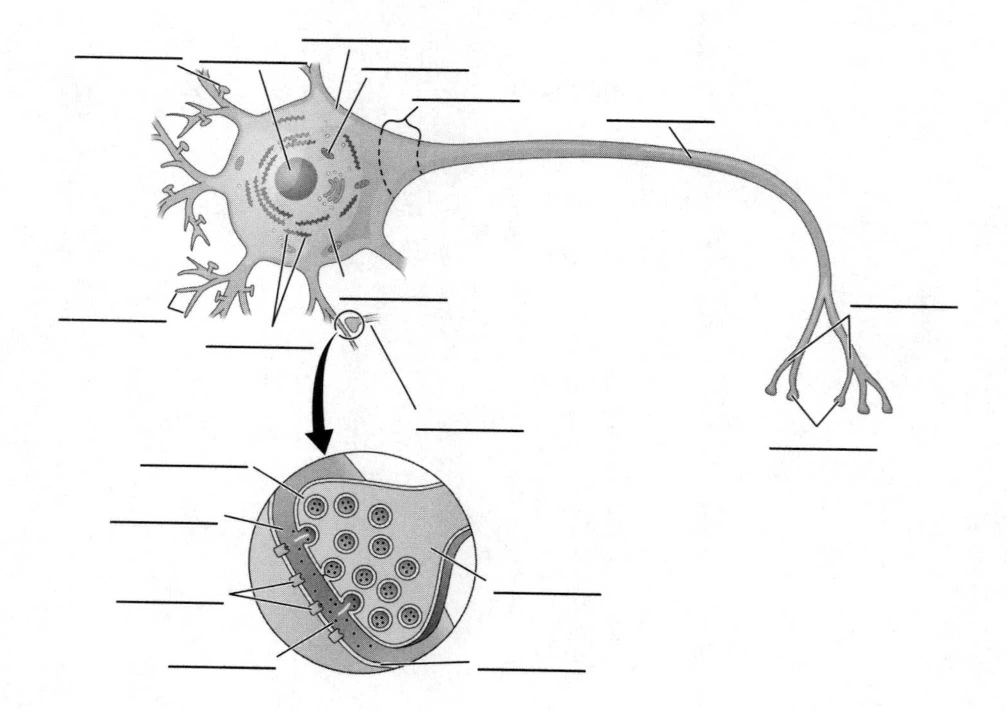

2. The two cerebral hemispheres are separated and connected by several different structures, as are the four lobes of the brain. Label the following brain structures in the figure below:

frontal lobe	longitudinal fissure
parietal lobe	central sulcus
occipital lobe	lateral sulcus
temporal lobe	precentral gyrus
spinal cord	postcentral gyrus
cerebellum	superior temporal gyrus

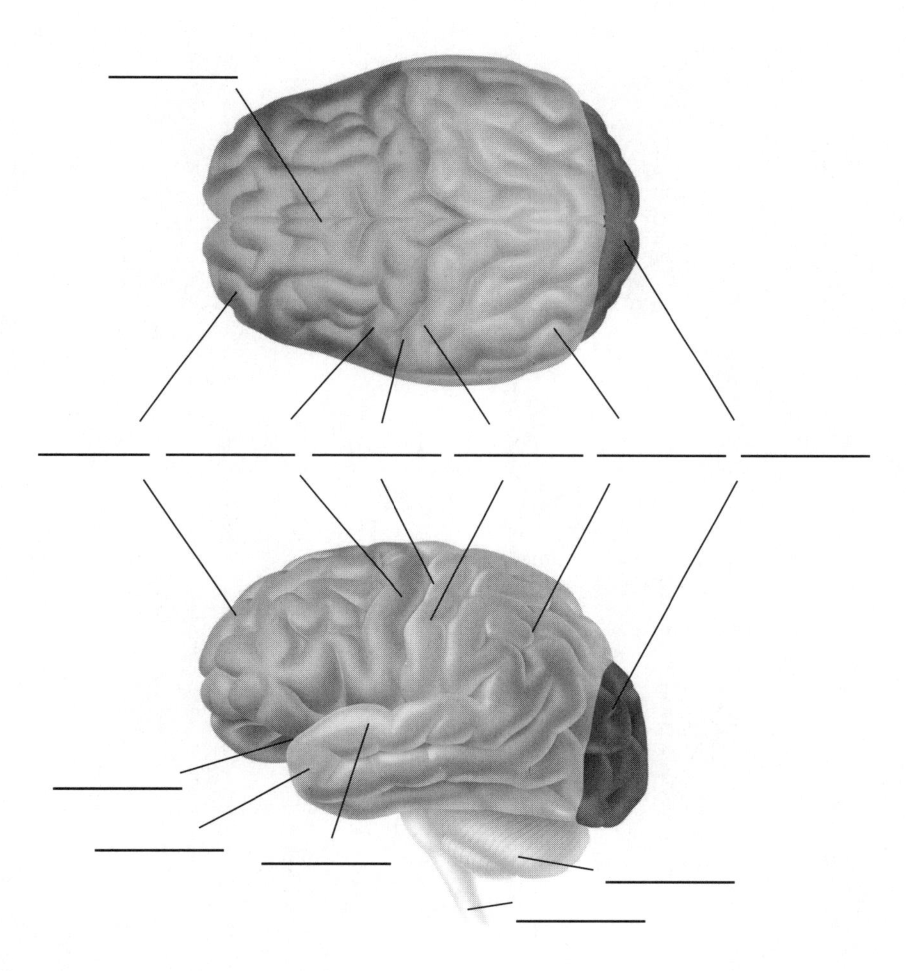

The Development and Plasticity of the Nervous System

3

◆ CHAPTER ART LECTURE NOTEBOOK

The following is a selection of the important figures and tables introduced in Chapter 3. You can take notes during class in the space provided.

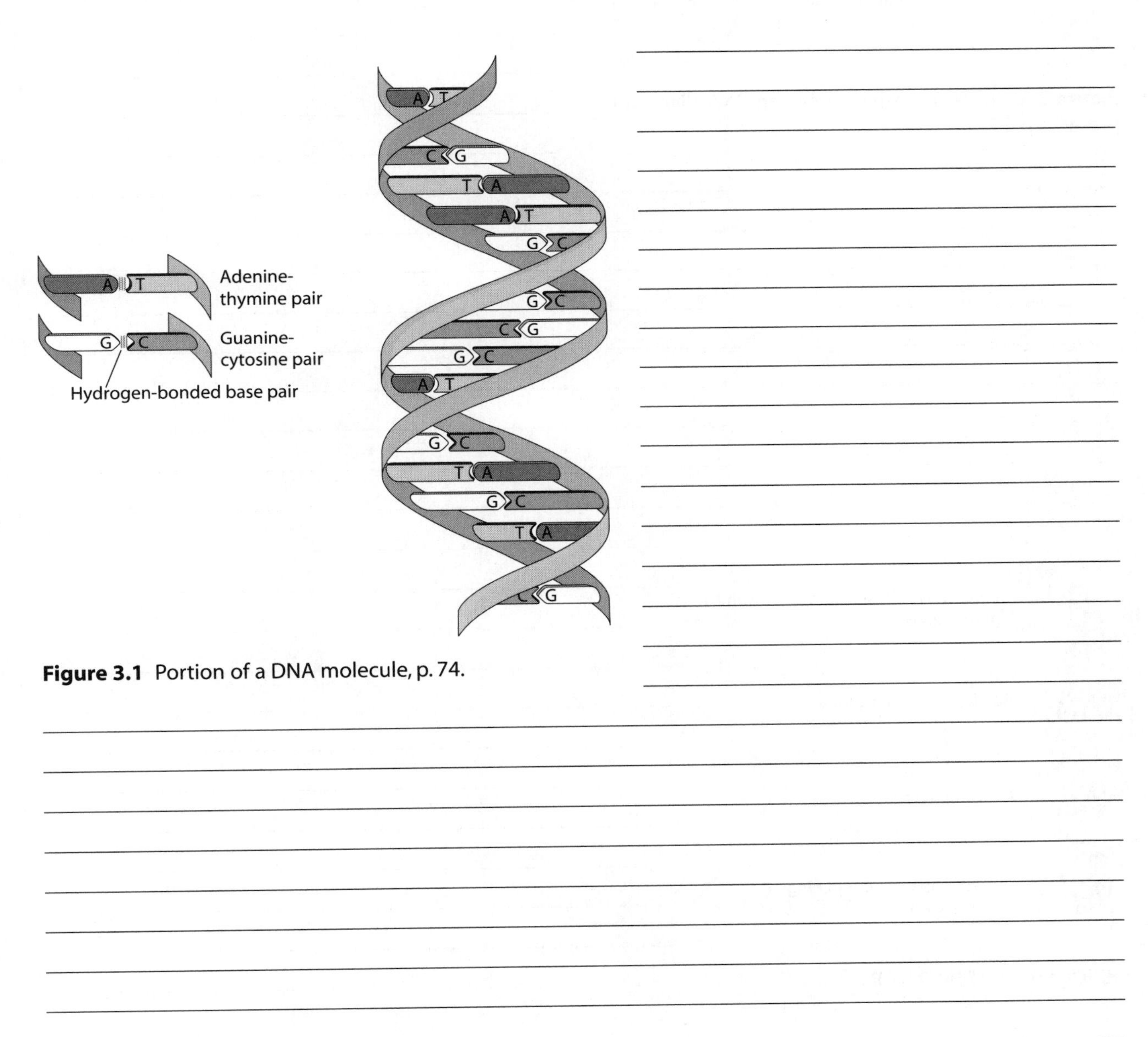

Figure 3.1 Portion of a DNA molecule, p. 74.

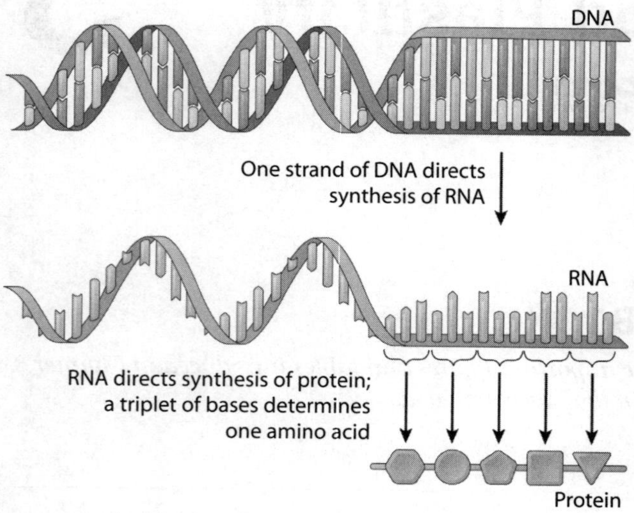

Figure 3.2 The relationships between DNA, RNA, and proteins, p. 75.

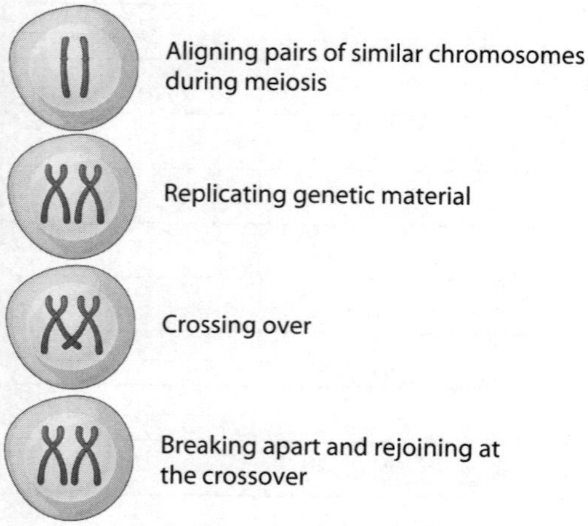

Figure 3.4 Crossing over, p. 76.

Figure 3.5 The inheritance of freckles, p. 77.

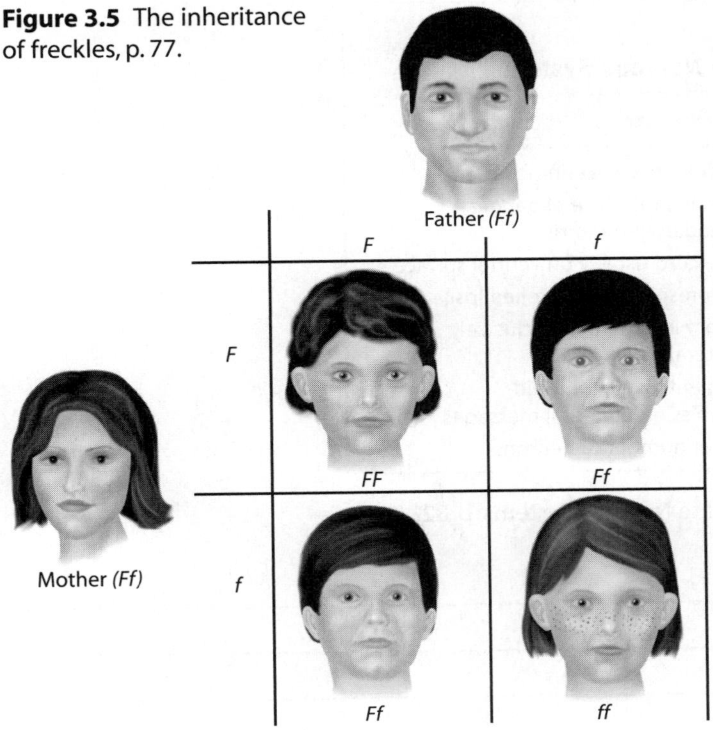

Father *(Ff)*

	F	*f*
F	*FF*	*Ff*
f	*Ff*	*ff*

Mother *(Ff)*

Table 3.1
Comparison of Vertebrate and Invertebrate Nervous Systems

Vertebrate	Invertebrate
Protective covering over CNS	No protective covering over CNS
Cell bodies inside bony coverings; axons outside	Axons in inner core of ganglia; cell bodies in outer ring
CNS located on dorsal surface	Nerve cord usually on ventral surface
Motor responses controlled contralaterally	Motor responses controlled ipsilaterally
Sensory information contralateral and ipsilateral	Sensory information exclusively ipsilateral
Myelinated axons for rapid transmission of neural messages	Few giant axons for rapid transmission of neural messages
Larger number of neurons	Smaller number of neurons

Table 3.1 Comparison of Vertebrate and Invertebrate Nervous Systems, p. 82.

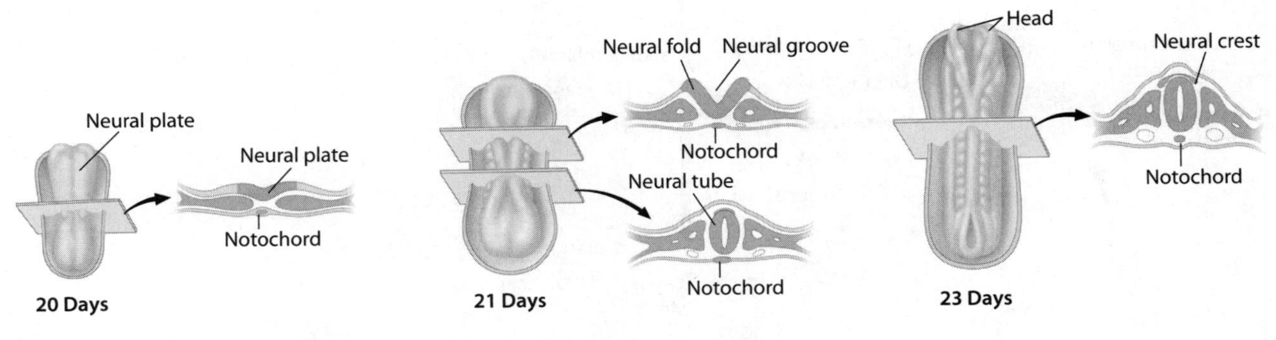

Figure 3.14 Formation of the neural tube and central nervous system in the human embryo, p. 84.

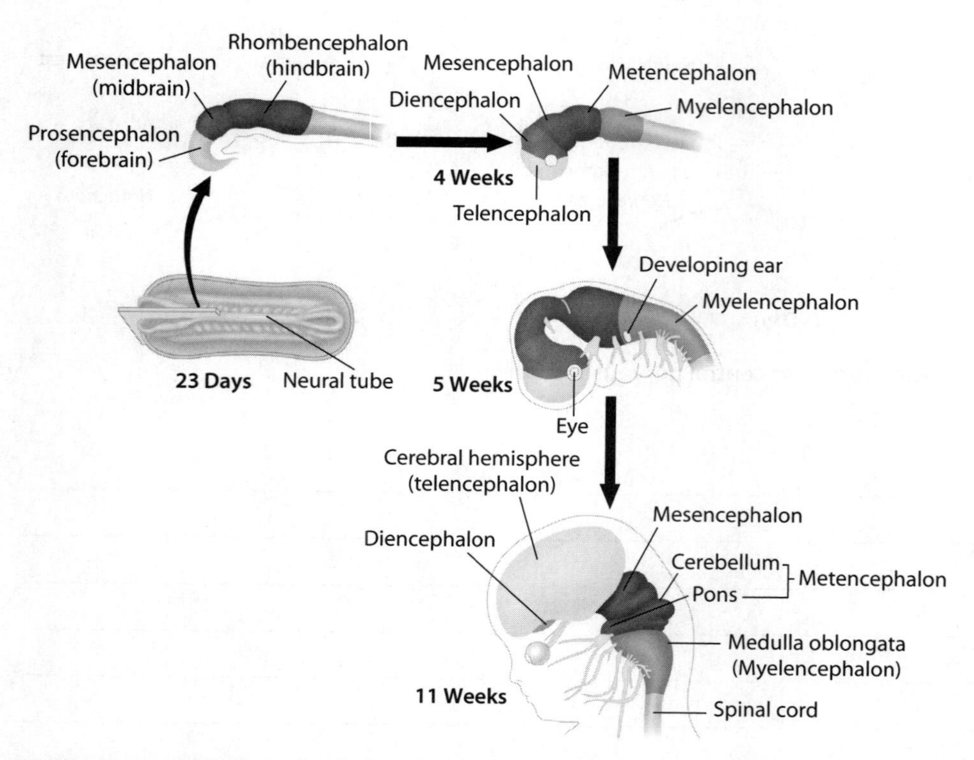

Figure 3.16 Development of the neural tube into the spinal cord and brain of the human embryo, p. 86.

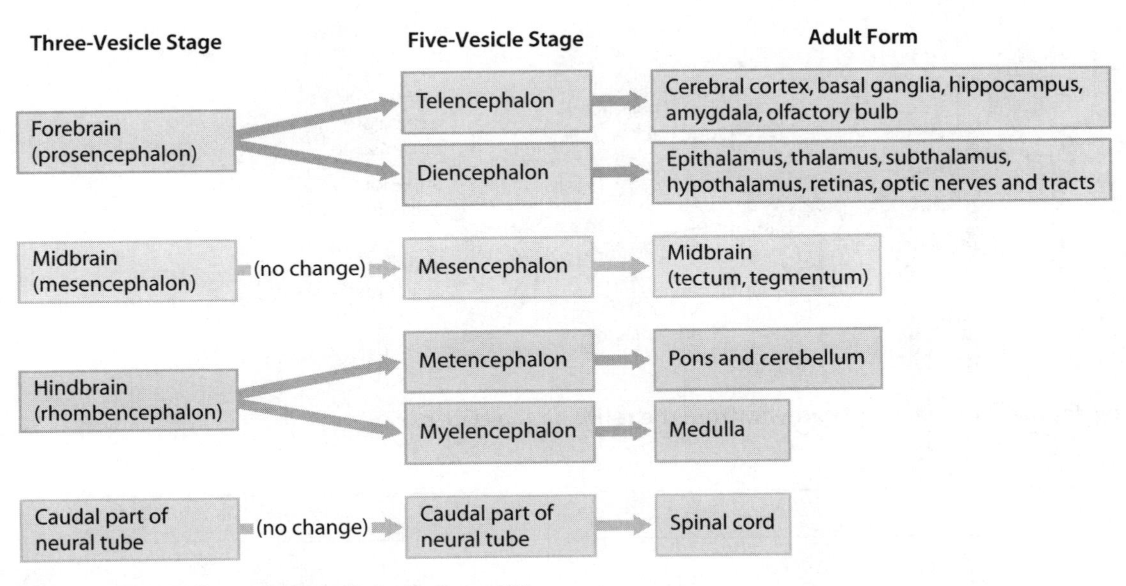

Figure 3.17 Differentiation of the brain, p. 86.

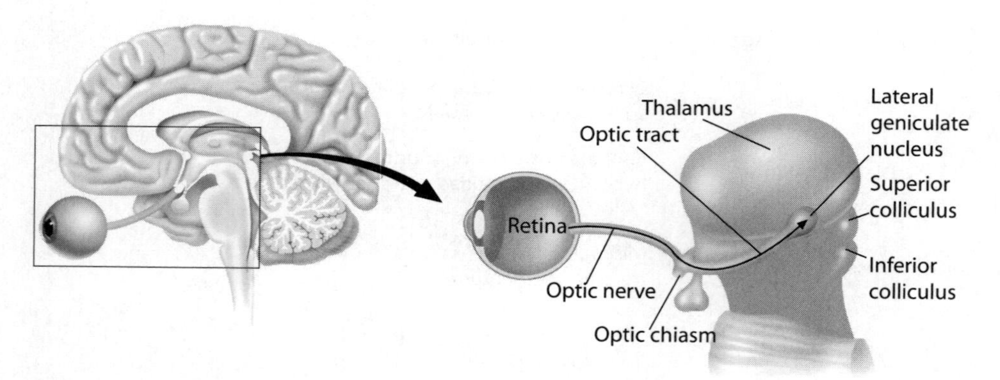

Figure 3.25 Development of the visual pathway from the retina to the LGN, p. 92.

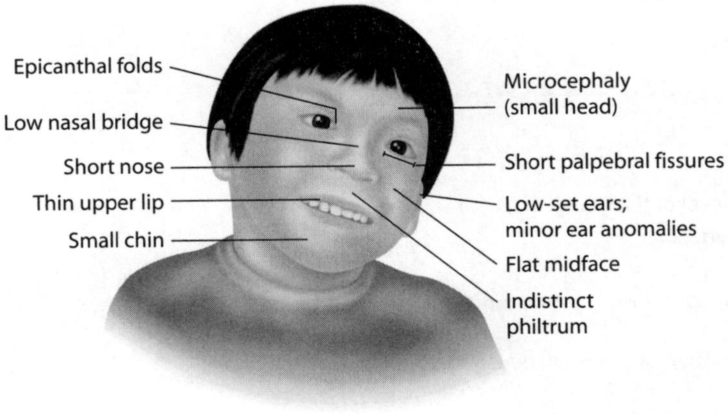

Figure 3.30 Fetal alcohol syndrome, p. 97.

Table 3.2
Failures of Neural Development

Type of Defect	Characterized by
Developmental defect	
Spina bifida	Paralysis below the level of the defect
Anencephaly	Failure in all major functions
Genetic defect	
Down syndrome	Altered facial features, decreased mental functioning, organ abnormalities
Phenylketonuria	If untreated, accumulation of phenylalanine and severe mental retardation
Fragile X syndrome	Abnormal facial features, mild to severe mental retardation
Defect from external factors	
Malnutrition	Decreased birth weight and increased mortality, low performance on tests of mental capacity
Fetal alcohol syndrome	Low birth weight, diminished height, distinctive facial features, hyperactivity and irritability, mental retardation

Table 3.2 Failures of Neural Development, p. 97.

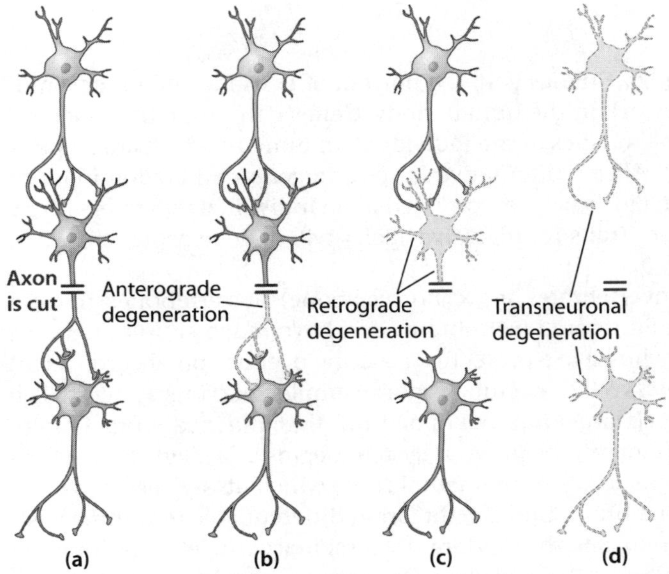

Figure 3.31 Degeneration of a neuron or neurons following damage to an axon, p. 99.

CHAPTER SUMMARY

Genetics, the science of heredity, studies genes, a portion of DNA located on chromosomes in the nucleus of every cell in the human body. Genes determine the inherited physical and behavioral characteristics of the individual. In humans, there are 23 pairs of chromosomes (46 in total). Alleles, alternative forms of a gene, can be dominant or recessive. Traits for dominant alleles will be expressed in an individual regardless of the trait carried by the other allele. Traits for recessive alleles will only be expressed when both alleles are recessive.

Animals can be either invertebrates (have no backbone) or vertebrates (have a backbone). Most animals on Earth are invertebrates and have much simpler nervous systems. Vertebrate animals, who have a protective covering over its spinal cord (vertebral column) and brain (bony skull), have much more complex nervous systems. The vertebrate brain also has a much larger number of neurons than the invertebrate brain.

During embryonic development, the nervous system begins as a single layer of ectodermal cells along the inner surface of the neural tube, which also gives rise to the central nervous system and the brain. Initially, the brain differentiates into three vesicles—the forebrain, the midbrain, and the hindbrain. The spinal cord develops from the dorsal portion of the neural tube, or the alar plate. Once a neuron migrates to its destination, it begins to establish connections. To do so, filopodia extend from the growth cones of the axons and pull the growing axons toward target cells. The filopodia are attracted by neurotrophins released by target cells in a process called chemotropism. Because the path an axon takes to reach its target cell may be long, guidepost cells redirect axonal growth toward the target cell.

Developmental and genetic defects, such as Down syndrome, PKU, and fragile X syndrome, can lead to failures in any or all major functions and result in impaired neural development. Environmental factors, such as malnutrition and alcohol consumption, can also adversely affect development. The nervous system can suffer damage in many ways. If damage to a neuron involves the cell body, the neuron will die. Damage to the axon, however, leads to degenerative changes that may or may not kill the neuron. Whether or not regeneration of damaged neurons occurs depends on the location of the damage to the nervous system and the age at which the damage occurs. Several areas of research hold promise for treating damaged neurons in adults, including the promotion of collateral sprouting, axon growth-inhibitory protein antibodies, fetal tissue implantation, embryonic stem cell implantation, and rehabilitation.

KEY TERMS

The following is a list of important terms introduced in Chapter 3. Give the definition of each term in the space provided.

alar plate

allele

anencephaly

anterograde degeneration

basal plate

cell-autonomous differentiation

cephalization

chemotropism

chromatolysis

chromosome

collateral sprouting

conception

cortical plate

crossing over

deoxyribonucleic acid (DNA)

diencephalon

differentiation

dominant allele

Down syndrome

ectoderm

embryo

endoderm

evolution

fertilization

fetal alcohol syndrome (FAS)

fetus

filopodia

fragile X syndrome

ganglion

gene

genetics

glycoprotein

growth cone

guidepost cell

heterozygous

homozygous

Huntington's disease

induction

invertebrate

locus

meiosis

mesencephalon

mesoderm

metencephalon

myelencephalon

neural crest

neural fold

neural groove

neural plate

neural regeneration

neural tube

neurogenesis

neuroplasticity

neurotrophin

phenylketonuria (PKU)

prosencephalon

radial glial cell

recessive allele

rehabilitation

retrograde degeneration

rhombencephalon

ribonucleic acid (RNA)

spina bifida

subventricular layer

supraesophageal ganglion

target cell

telencephalon

transneuronal degeneration

ventricular layer

vertebrate

zygote

◆ LABELING EXERCISES

1. During embryonic development, the major subdivisions of the central nervous system are formed. Given the major adult form brain structures in the figure below, label the following three-vesicle stage and five-vesicle stage brain structures:

mesencephalon	diencephalon
hindbrain (rhombencephalon)	metencephalon
caudal part of neural tube *(place two times)*	telencephalon
forebrain (prosencephalon)	myelencephalon
	midbrain

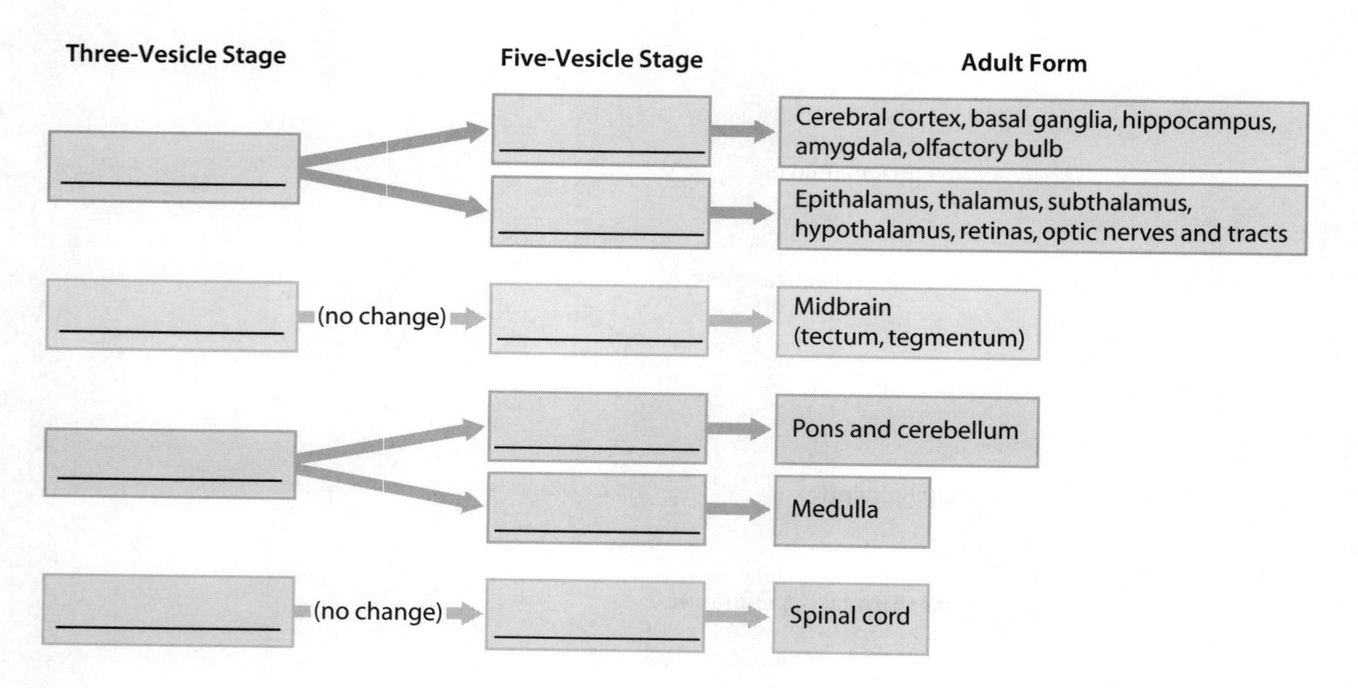

Communication Within the Nervous System

4

CHAPTER ART LECTURE NOTEBOOK

The following is a selection of the important figures and tables introduced in Chapter 4. You can take notes during class in the space provided.

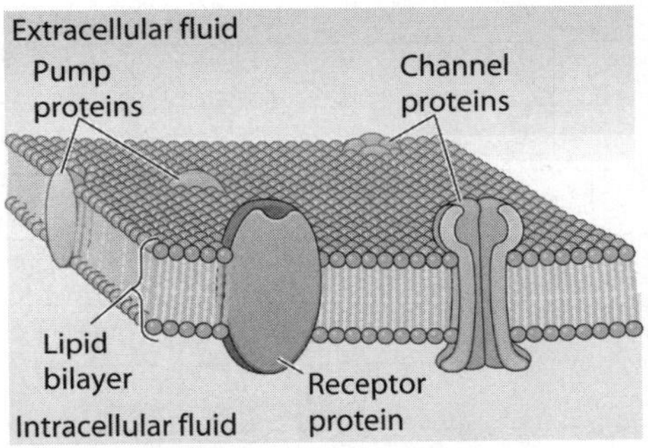

Extracellular fluid
Pump proteins
Channel proteins
Lipid bilayer
Receptor protein
Intracellular fluid

Figure 4.1 The cell membrane, p. 111.

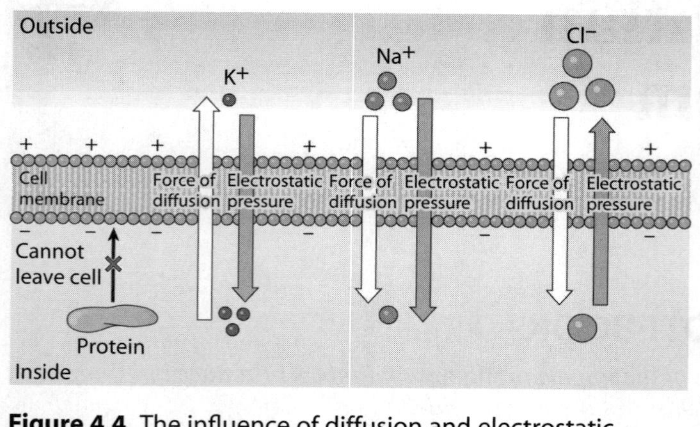

Figure 4.4 The influence of diffusion and electrostatic pressure on the movement of ions into and out of the neuron, p. 112.

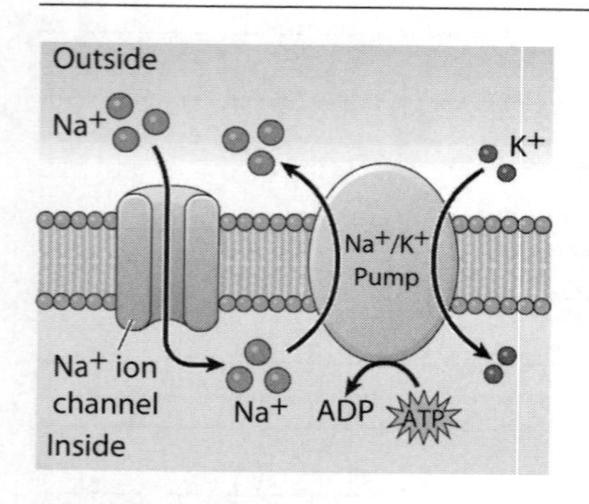

Figure 4.5 The sodium-potassium pump, p. 113.

A. **K^+ ion** concentration is higher inside the cell so diffusion tends to push K^+ out. But the inside of the cell is more negative than the outside, so electrostatic pressure tends to pull K^+ in. Because the force of diffusion is slightly greater than the electrostatic pressure, some K^+ leaves the cell and is returned by the sodium-potassium pump.

B. **Cl^- ion** concentration is higher outside the cell, so diffusion tends to pull Cl^- in. But because the inside of the cell is more negative than the outside, electrostatic pressure tends to push Cl^- out.

C. **Negatively charged protein molecules** cannot leave the cell; they create a negative charge inside the cell.

D. **Na^+ ion** concentration is higher outside the cell, and the inside of the cell is more negative than the outside, so both diffusion and electrostatic pressure tend to pull Na^+ in. But the sodium-potassium pump actively transports Na^+ out.

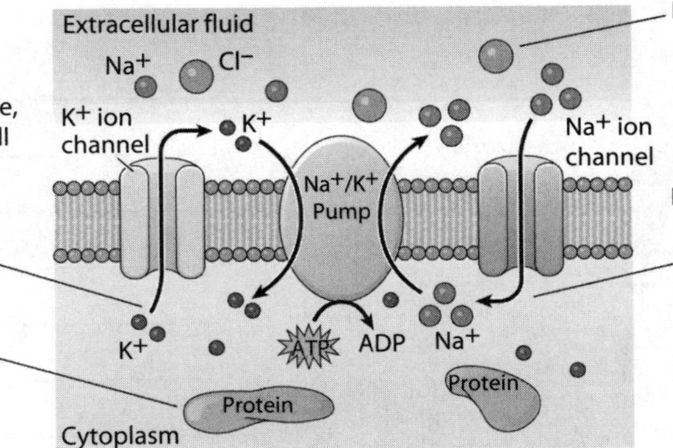

Figure 4.6 The neuron at rest, p. 113.

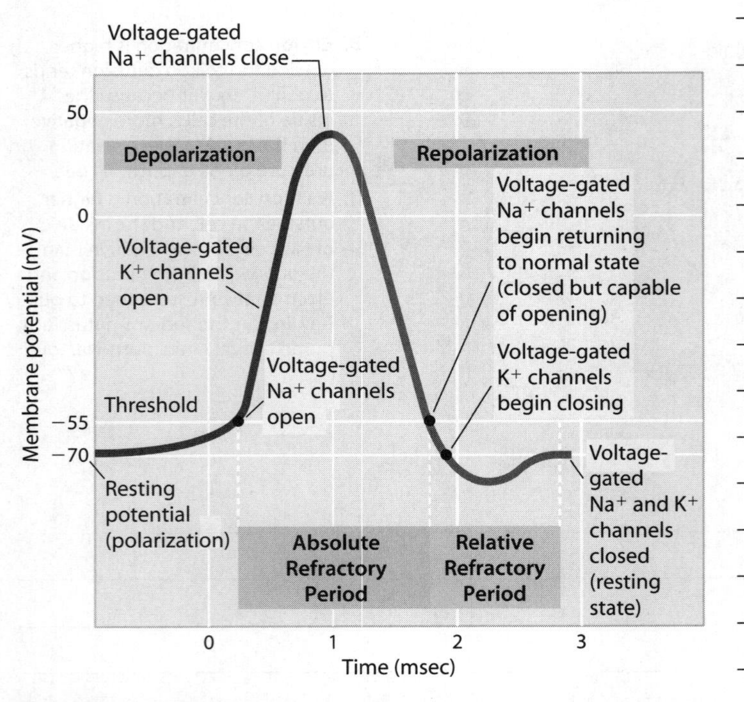

Figure 4.7 Changes in the membrane potential during the action (spike) potential, p. 114.

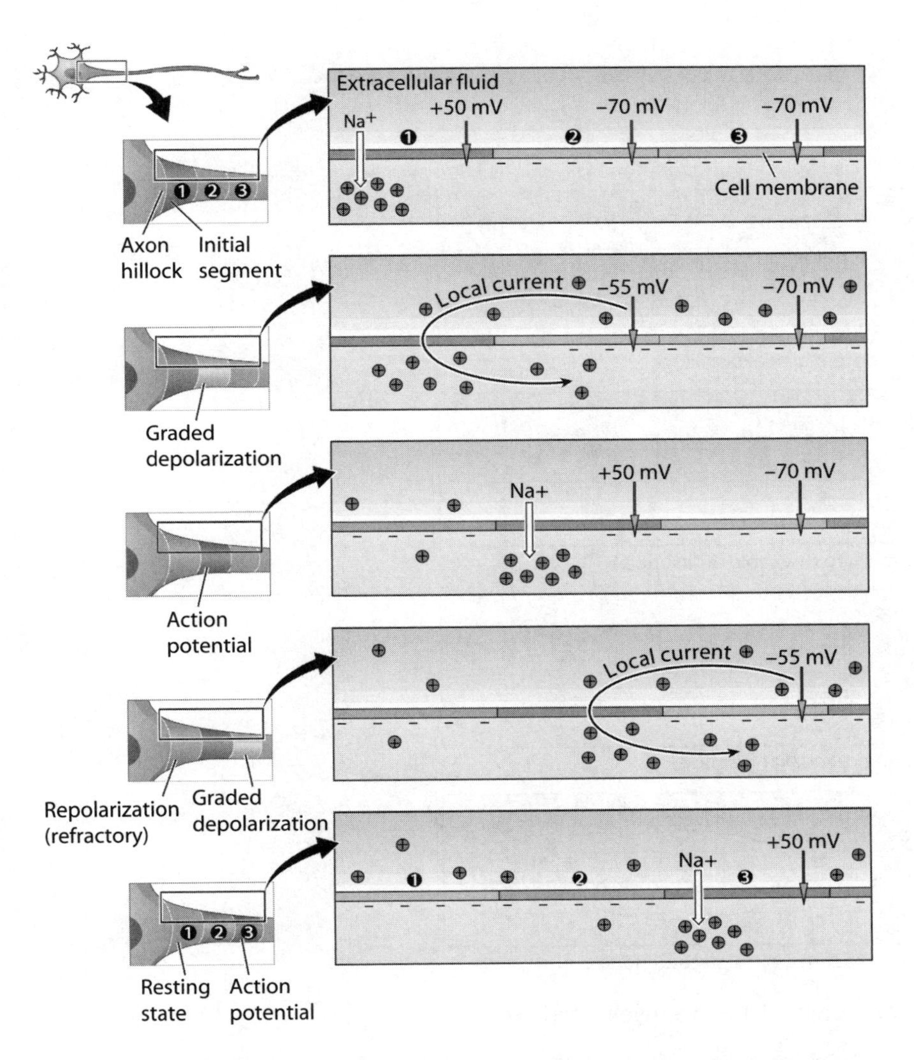

Figure 4.9 Propagation of the action potential along an unmyelinated axon, p. 118.

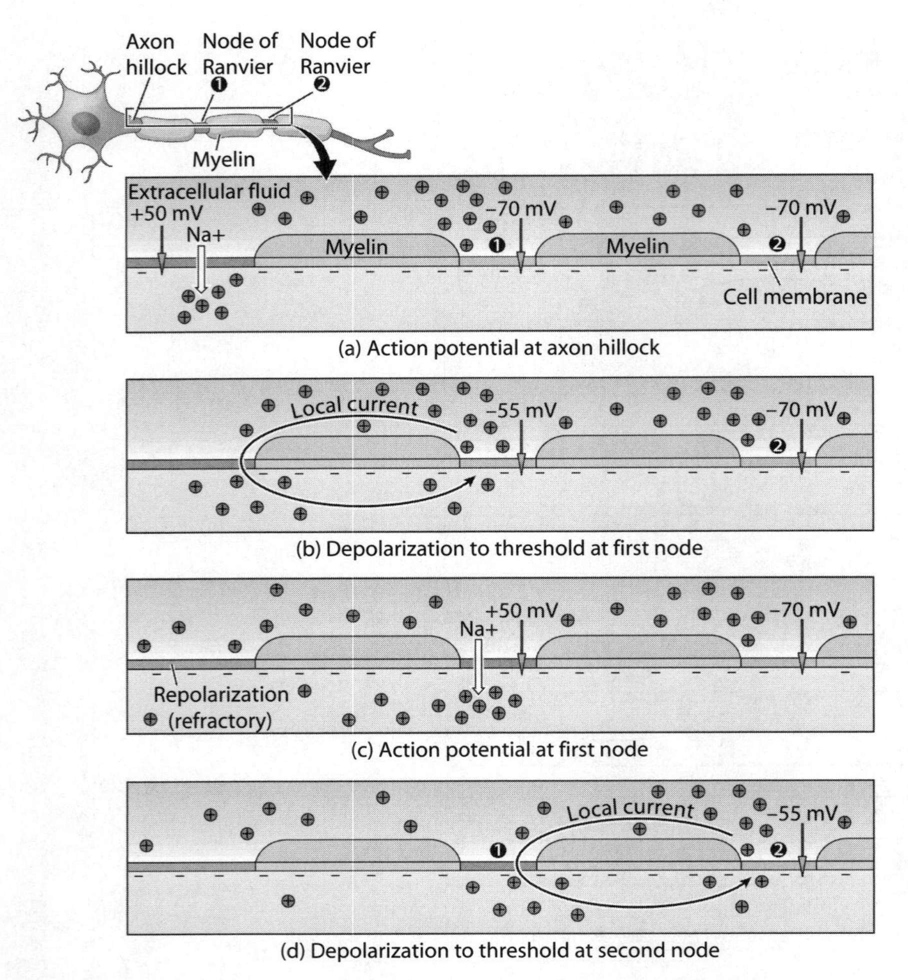

Figure 4.10 Propagation of the action potential along a myelinated axon, p. 119.

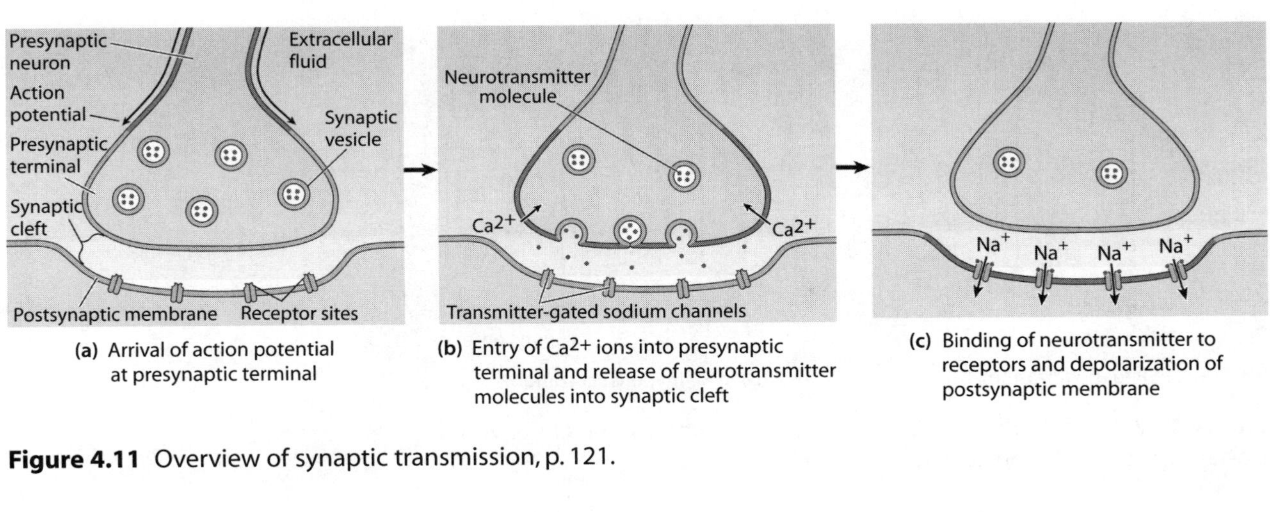

(a) Arrival of action potential at presynaptic terminal

(b) Entry of Ca^{2+} ions into presynaptic terminal and release of neurotransmitter molecules into synaptic cleft

(c) Binding of neurotransmitter to receptors and depolarization of postsynaptic membrane

Figure 4.11 Overview of synaptic transmission, p. 121.

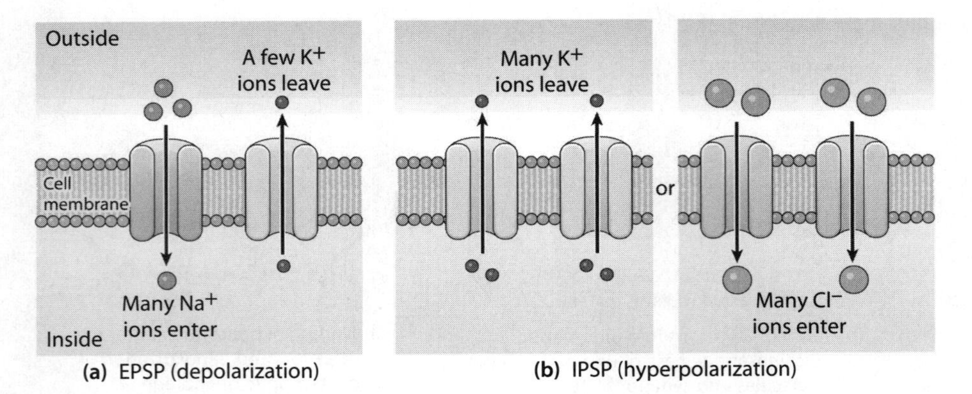

Figure 4.12 Ionic changes caused by neurotransmitters interacting with the postsynaptic membrane, p. 122.

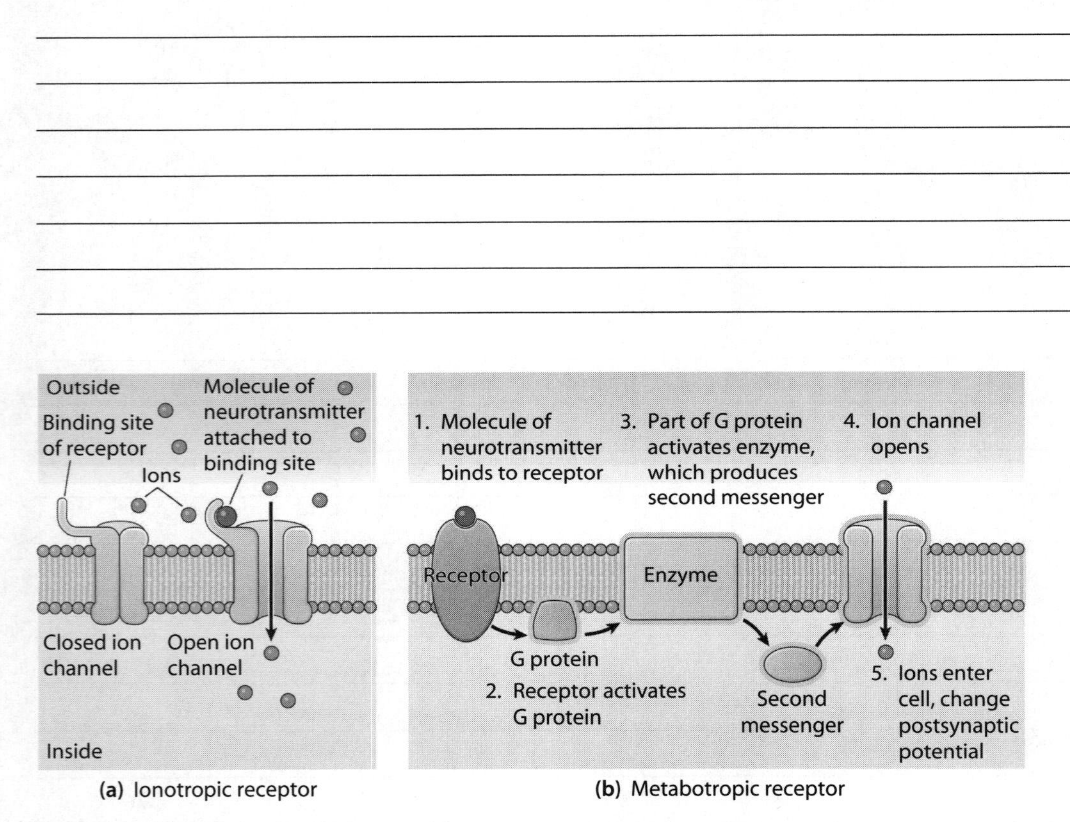

Figure 4.17 Ionotropic and metabotropic receptors, p. 125.

Table 4.1
Differences Between Ionotropic and Metabotropic Receptors

Ionotropic Receptors	Metabotropic Receptors
Ion channels open directly	Ion channels open indirectly
Effect begins and ends rapidly	Effect begins and ends relatively slowly
Only first messenger (neurotransmitter) is involved	Both neurotransmitter and a second messenger (another chemical) are involved

Table 4.1 Differences Between Ionotropic and Metabotropic Receptors, p. 126.

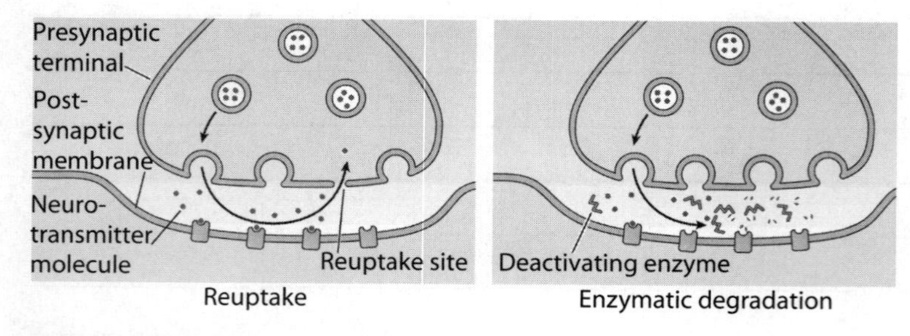

Figure 4.18 Termination of neural transmission, p. 127.

Table 4.2
Classification of Neurotransmitters, With Some Examples

Small-molecule neurotransmitters

- Amino acids
  - Glutamate
  - Gamma-amino butyric acid (GABA)
  - Aspartate
  - Glycine
- Monoamines
  - Catecholamines
    - Epinephrine (adrenalin)
    - Norepinephrine (noradrenalin)
    - Dopamine
  - Indoleamines
    - Serotonin
    - Melatonin
- Soluble gases
  - Nitric oxide
  - Carbon monoxide
- Acetylcholine

Large-molecule neurotransmitters

- Endogenous opioids
- Substance P
- Oxytocin
- Antidiuretic hormone (ADH)
- Cholecystokinin (CCK)

Table 4.2 Classification of Neurotransmitters, With Some Examples, p. 128.

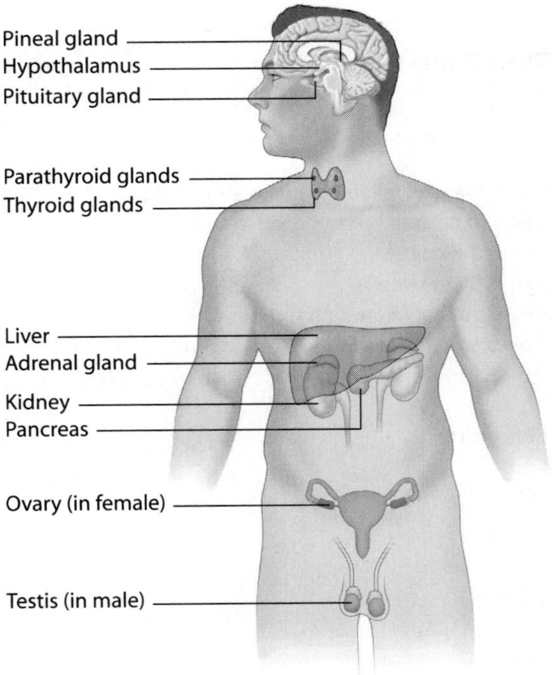

Figure 4.25 The location of major endocrine glands, p. 136.

Table 4.3

Major Endocrine Glands, the Hormones They Secrete, and Their Principal Functions

Gland	Hormone	Function
Adrenal gland		
Cortex	Aldosterone	Retention of sodium and excretion of potassium by kidneys
	Androstenedione	Growth of pubic and underarm hair, sex drive (women)
	Cortisol	Metabolism; response to stress
Medulla	Epinephrine, norepinephrine	Metabolism; response to stress
Hypothalamus*	Releasing hormones	Control of anterior pituitary hormone secretion
Pancreas	Insulin, glucagon	Regulation of glucose use and storage as glycogen
Pineal	Melatonin	Regulation of circadian rhythms
Pituitary gland		
Anterior	Adrenocorticotropic hormone (ACTH)	Control of adrenal cortex
	Gonadotropic hormones: follicle-stimulating hormone (FSH) and luteinizing hormone (LH)	Control of testes and ovaries
	Somatotropin or growth hormone (STH or GH)	Growth; control of metabolism
	Prolactin (PRL)	Milk production
	Thyroid-stimulating hormone (TSH)	Control of thyroid gland
Posterior	Antidiuretic hormone (ADH)**	Retention of water by kidneys
	Oxytocin	Release of milk, contraction of uterus, contraction of prostate gland
Ovaries	Estrogen	Maturation of female reproductive system; secondary sex characteristics
	Progesterone	Maintenance of uterine lining; facilitation of pregnancy
	Inhibin	Control of FSH release
Testes	Androgens	Maturation of male reproductive system; sperm production; secondary sex characteristics; sex drive (men)
	Inhibin	Control of FSH release
Thyroid gland	Thyroxine, triiodothyronine	Energy metabolism; growth and development
	Calcitonin	Helps regulate the level of calcium in the blood
Parathyroids	Parathyroid hormone	Helps regulate the level of calcium in the blood

*The hypothalamus, although it is part of the brain, secrets hormones; thus, it can be considered an endocrine gland.

**These hormones are produced by the hypothalamus but are transported to and released from the posterior pituitary gland.

Table 4.3 Major Endocrine Glands, the Hormones They Secrete, and Their Principal Functions, p. 137.

CHAPTER SUMMARY

The neuron is uniquely suited to receive information from other neurons and from the external and internal environment. It is embedded with protein molecules that move in and out of the cell through channel proteins and pump proteins. Because of charged particles called ions, the cell membrane is electrically charged. In its resting state, the inside of the cell is negatively charged relative to the outside. This is referred to as the resting membrane potential and is −70 mV (the inside is 70 mV more negatively charged than the outside). This resting potential is maintained by three mechanisms: diffusion, electrostatic pressure, and the sodium-potassium pump.

When the neuron receives information, the inside of the cell becomes depolarized (more negative). This results in an action potential and the transmission of a neural impulse along the axon. An action potential occurs in an all-or-none manner, that is, if the cell is depolarized enough so that the threshold is reached, an action potential is generated; if the cell is not depolarized enough, an action potential is not generated. The axons of many neurons are covered in segments by a myelin sheath, which allows the action potential to transmit faster down the axon than with unmyelinated axons. This is called saltatory conduction. Once the action potential reaches the presynaptic terminals, Ca^{2+} ions enter the cell, causing synaptic vesicles to release neurotransmitters into the synaptic cleft.

The amount of neurotransmitter released can be influenced by several processes, including presynaptic inhibition, presynaptic facilitation, and the stimulation of autoreceptors. Once these neurotransmitters are released into the synaptic cleft, they bind to receptor sites on the postsynaptic membrane, causing either an excitatory (EPSP) or inhibitory (IPSP) effect. Neurotransmitter effects on the postsynaptic membrane involve either ionotropic receptors or metabotropic receptors. Binding of neurotransmitters to ionotropic receptors directly affect ion channels, whereas binding to metabotropic receptors produce metabolic changes in the cell that indirectly affect ion channels through the production of second messengers.

Neurotransmitters can be classified as small-molecule (amino acids, monoamines, soluble gases, and acetylcholine) and large-molecule (neuropeptides) neurotransmitters. Amino acid neurotransmitters include glutamate (the most common excitatory neurotransmitter), GABA (the most common inhibitory neurotransmitter), aspartate, and glycine. Monoamines are divided into two subclasses: catecholamines, which include epinephrine, dopamine, and norepinephrine; and indoleamines, which include serotonin and melatonin. Soluble gases include nitric oxide and carbon monoxide. These neurotransmitters do not affect postsynaptic receptors, as they are quickly inactivated upon release. Acetylcholine (ACh) is widespread throughout both the CNS and PNS. It has two receptors: nicotinic receptors (activated by nicotine) and muscarinic receptors (activated by muscarine). Neuropeptides include endogenous opioids, substance P, oxytocin, antidiuretic hormone (ADH), and cholecystokinin (CCK).

The endocrine system releases hormones into the bloodstream, which carries them to distant target organs. These hormones are a slower means of communication than neurotransmitters and have more widespread effects. Many of these hormones are controlled by the brain through feedback loops. Positive feedback loops promote further release of that hormone, whereas negative feedback loops inhibit further release of that hormone. The ability of the nervous system to process and respond efficiently to the environment depends on a balance between the fluid outside and inside the neuron. This balance is maintained by the blood-brain barrier, which prevents the free flow of substances from the bloodstream into the brain. This helps prevent many harmful substances from entering the brain. However, it also keeps out many beneficial substances, such as nutrients, vitamins, and amino acids.

◆ KEY TERMS

The following is a list of important terms introduced in Chapter 4. Give the definition of each term in the space provided.

absolute refractory period

acetylcholine (ACh)

acetylcholinesterase (AChE)

action potential

adrenergic

all-or-none law

anaxonic neuron

autoreceptor

axon hillock

blood-brain barrier

catecholamines

channel protein

cholinergic

connexon

dendrodendritic transmission

depolarization

diffusion

dopamine

dopaminergic

electrical synapse

electrostatic pressure

endocrine system

endogenous opioid

enzymatic degradation

epinephrine

excitatory postsynaptic potential (EPSP)

experimental allergic encephalomyelitis (EAE)

GABAergic

gamma-aminobutyric acid (GABA)

gap junction

glutamate

glutamatergic

graded potential

hormone

hyperpolarized

indoleamine

inhibitory postsynaptic potential (IPSP)

ion

ionotropic receptor

metabotropic receptor

monoamine

monoamine oxidase (MAO)

monoamine oxidase inhibitor (MAOI)

multiple sclerosis (MS)

myelin sheath

negative feedback loop

neural impulse

neuromodulator

neuropeptide

neurotransmitter reuptake

nitric oxide (NO)

node of Ranvier

noradrenergic

norepinephrine

pheromone

positive feedback loop

presynaptic facilitation

presynaptic inhibition

pump protein

rate law

receptor protein

relative refractory period

repolarization

resting membrane potential

saltatory conduction

second messenger

selective serotonin reuptake inhibitor (SSRI)

serotonergic

serotonin

sodium-potassium pump

soluble gas

spatial summation

temporal summation

threshold

transmitter-gated ion channel

tricyclic compound

voltage-gated ion channel

◆ LABELING EXERCISES

1. When a neural impulse arrives at the synapse, a series of events occur to transmit that impulse to the adjacent neuron. During this synaptic transmission, several structures are involved. Label the following structures in the figure below:

neurotransmitter molecule	transmitter-gated sodium channels
synaptic vesicle	action potential
presynaptic neuron	postsynaptic membrane
synaptic cleft	extracellular fluid
receptor sites	presynaptic terminal

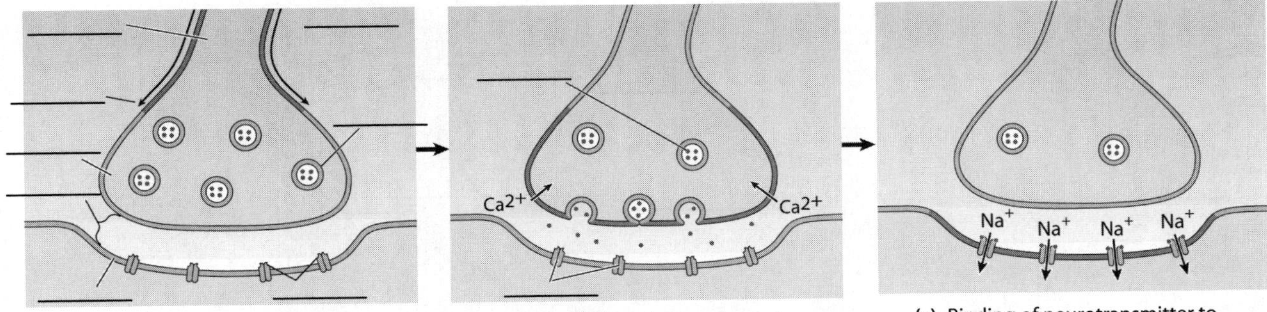

(a) Arrival of action potential at presynaptic terminal

(b) Entry of Ca^{2+} ions into presynaptic terminal and release of neurotransmitter molecules into synaptic cleft

(c) Binding of neurotransmitter to receptors and depolarization of postsynaptic membrane

2. For more widespread communication, the endocrine system releases hormones that travel throughout the body via the bloodstream. The major endocrine glands are shown in the figure below; label them using the following terms:

pituitary gland	hypothalamus
thyroid glands	pancreas
adrenal gland	ovary (in female)
pineal gland	parathyroid glands
testis (in male)	kidney
liver	

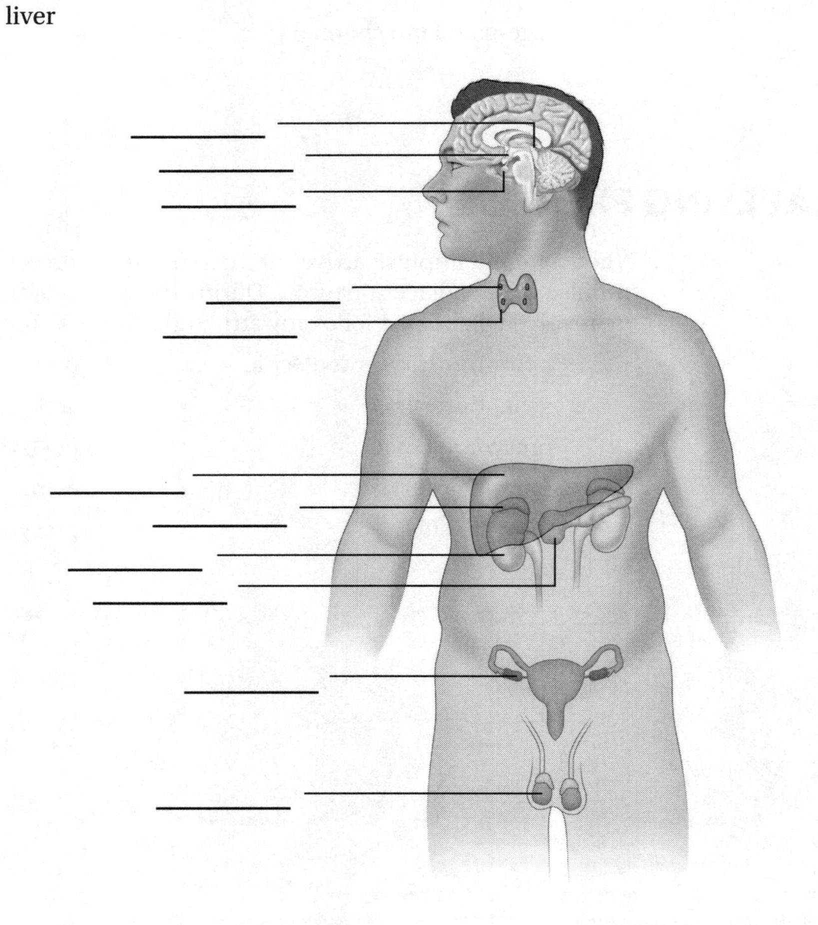

The Effects of Psychoactive Drugs

5

◆ CHAPTER ART LECTURE NOTEBOOK

The following is a selection of the important figures and tables introduced in Chapter 5. You can take notes during class in the space provided.

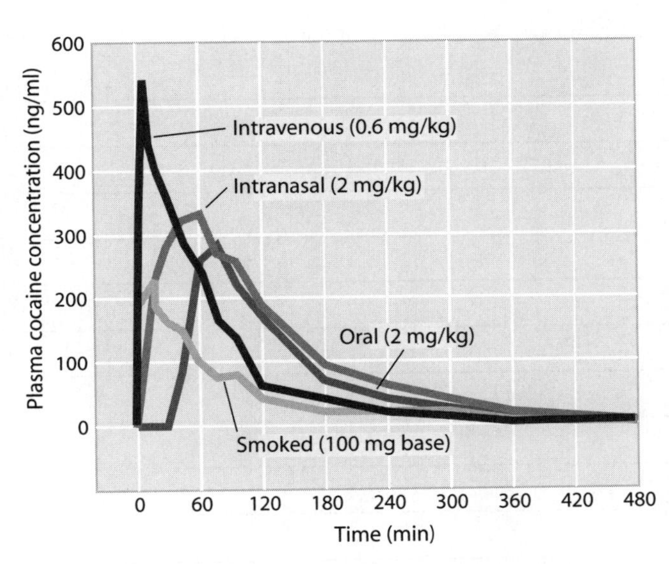

Figure 5.1 The blood plasma concentration of cocaine after different methods of administration, p. 150.

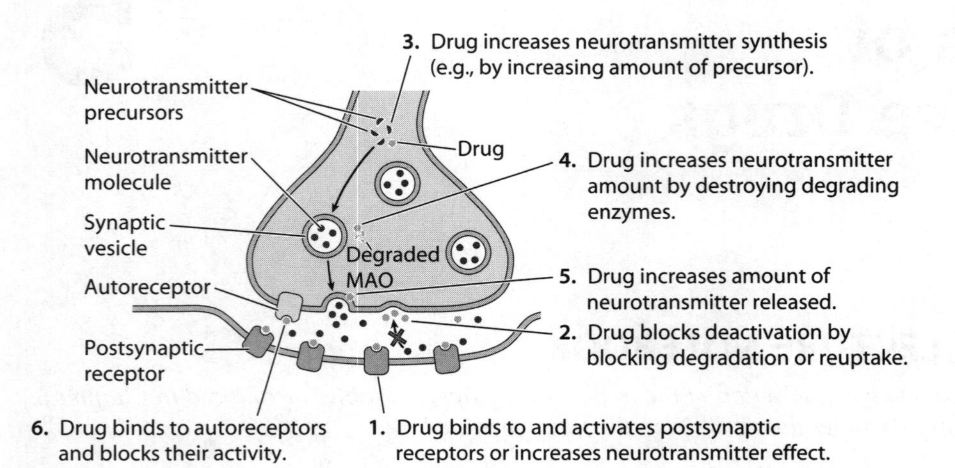

Figure 5.2 The actions of agonist drugs, p. 152.

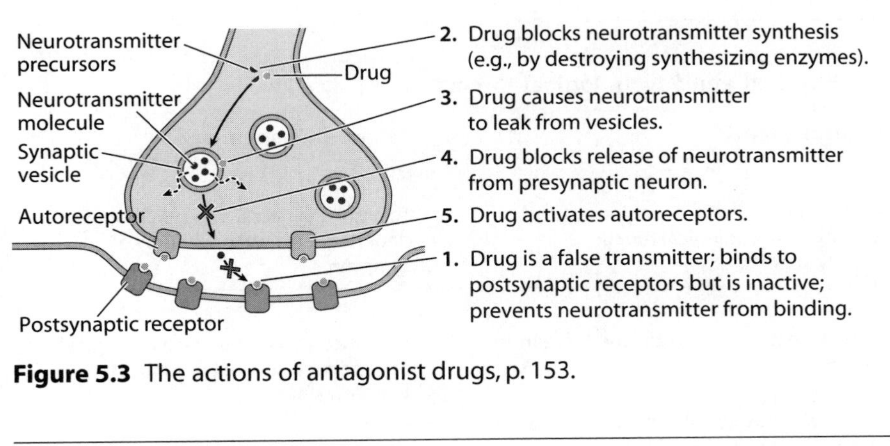

Figure 5.3 The actions of antagonist drugs, p. 153.

Table 5.1
The Psychoactive Drugs and Their Physical and Psychological Effects

Category	Typical Effects	Tolerance/Dependence
Opioids		
Codeine, heroin, morphine, meperidine, opium	Analgesia, euphoria, drowsiness, a rush of pleasure, psychological functions mostly spared	Tolerance, physical and psychological dependence, severe withdrawal symptoms
Depressants		
Alcohol	**Low doses:** decreased alertness, feelings of relaxation	Tolerance, physical and psychological dependence, severe withdrawal symptoms
	Moderate doses: mild sedation, impairment of sensory-motor functions	
	High doses: severe motor disturbances, unconsciousness, coma, death	
Barbiturate and nonbarbiturate sedative-hypnotic drugs Pentobarbital (Nembutal), methaqualone (Quaalude)	Calming effect, muscle relaxation; reduced tension, anxiety, and irritability; sleep-inducing, anesthetic, anticonvulsant effects	Tolerance, psychological and physical dependence, withdrawal symptoms
Benzodiazepines and nonbenzodiazepine anxiolytics Diazepam (Valium), zolpidem (Ambien)	Reduced nervousness, anxiety, or fear	Tolerance, low physical and high psychological dependence, withdrawal symptoms
Psychostimulants		
Amphetamine, cocaine	Increased alertness, euphoria, sense of well-being; sleeplessness; appetite suppression	Tolerance, psychological and physical dependence, withdrawal symptoms
Caffeine, nicotine	Increased alertness, sleeplessness, more rapid reaction times, increased metabolism	Tolerance, physical and psychological dependence, withdrawal symptoms
Psychedelic Drugs		
Peyote	Visual hallucinations	None known
Psilocybin, psilocin	Illusions, hallucinations, distortions in time perception, loss of contact with reality	None known
LSD	Illusions, hallucinations, distortions in time perception, loss of contact with reality	None known
PCP	Illusions, hallucinations, distortions in time perception, loss of contact with reality	Psychological dependence
MDMA (Ecstasy)	Euphoric mood state, mild hallucinations	Tolerance, withdrawal symptoms
Marijuana		
Marijuana, hashish, THC	Euphoria, relaxed inhibitions, increased vividness of experiences, increased appetite, mild hallucinations, possible disorientation, impaired motor coordination, decreased reaction time, distortions in time perception	Psychological dependence

Table 5.1 The Psychoactive Drugs and Their Physical and Psychological Effects, p. 155.

Table 5.2
Some Psychoactive Drugs and Their Effects on Synaptic Transmission

Category	Main Effect(s)	Effect on Synaptic Transmission
Opioids		
Heroin, morphine	Stimulate endorphin receptors	Direct agonist
Depressants		
Alcohol	Binds to endorphin and $GABA_A$ receptors	Direct agonist
Barbiturate and nonbarbiturate sedative-hypnotic drugs	Binds to $GABA_A$ receptors	Direct agonist
Thiopental (Pentothal)		
Phenobarbital (Luminal)		
Benzodiazepines and nonbenzodiazepine anxiolytics	Binds to $GABA_A$ receptors	Direct agonist
Alprazolam (Xanax)		
Chlordiazepoxide (Librium)		
Diazepam (Valium)		
Meprobamate (Miltown)		
Psychostimulants		
Amphetamine	Stimulates dopamine and norepinephrine release and blocks reuptake of both	Indirect agonist
Cocaine	Blocks dopamine and norepinephrine reuptake	Indirect agonist
Caffeine	Blocks adenosine release	Indirect antagonist
Nicotine	Stimulates ACh receptors and increases dopamine, ACh, and glutamate release	Direct and indirect agonist
Psychedelic Drugs		
LSD	Stimulates 5-HT receptors	Direct agonist
PCP	Inhibits NMDA receptors	Direct antagonist
MDMA	Stimulates D_2 and serotonin receptors	Direct agonist
Marijuana		
Marijuana	Binds to THC receptors	Direct agonist

Table 5.2 Some Psychoactive Drugs and Their Effects on Synaptic Transmission, p. 157.

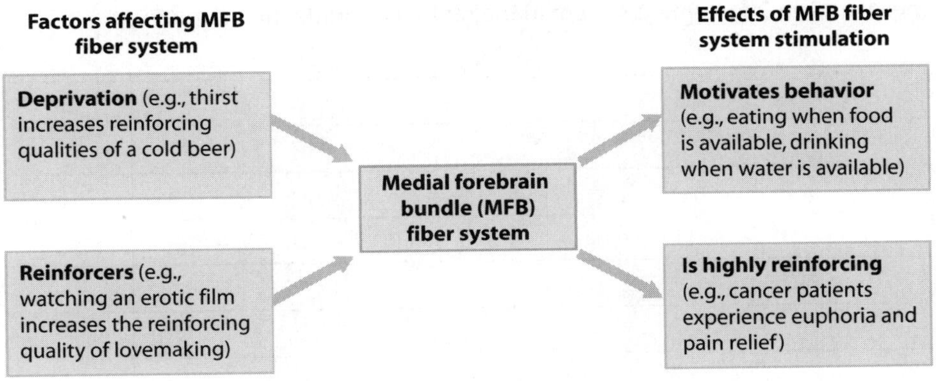

Figure 5.14 The medial forebrain bundle (MFB) fiber system and reinforcement, p. 178.

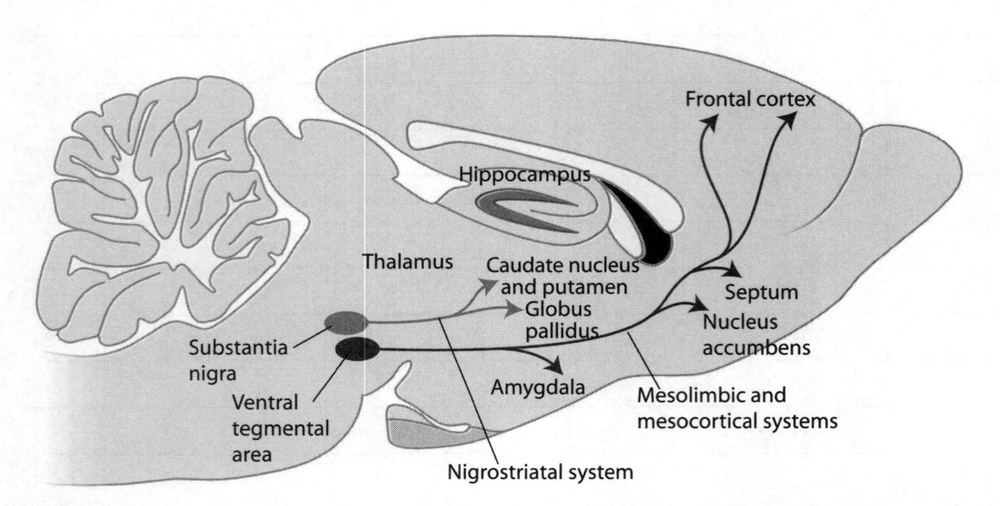

Figure 5.15 Structures of the mesolimbic reinforcement system in the rat brain (sagittal plane), p. 179.

CHAPTER SUMMARY

A drug is any substance taken into the body that has the power to functionally or structurally change the body. A psychoactive drug is a substance that affects mental functioning. The study of the effects of drugs on behavior is called psychopharmacology. Drugs can be administered through several routes: oral ingestion, injection (intramuscular, intraperitoneal, intravenous, subcutaneous, intracerebral, and intraventricular), inhalation, or absorption. The long-term effects of drug use include substance abuse, substance dependence (addiction), tolerance, and withdrawal symptoms. Drugs can either facilitate or inhibit the transmission of neural impulses. Agonists are drugs that mimic or enhance the activities of a neurotransmitter; antagonists are drugs that block or inhibit the activities of a neurotransmitter.

There are several classifications of psychoactive drugs: opioids, depressants, psychostimulants, psychedelic drugs, and marijuana. Opioids, including opium, codeine, heroin, and morphine, are highly addictive psychoactive drugs used for analgesia (pain relief), inducing sleep, and euphoria (feelings of well-being). Depressants, or sedative-hypnotic drugs, include alcohol, barbiturate and nonbarbiturate drugs, and benzodiazepine and nonbenzodiazepine sedative-hypnotics. These drugs slow down mental and physical functioning, produce relaxation, drowsiness, and sleep, and decrease anxiety.

Psychoactive drugs, including amphetamines, cocaine, caffeine, and nicotine, produce increased alertness, reduced appetite, and increased energy. Tolerance to these drugs occurs very quickly, with users commonly experiencing a craving for the drug. Psychedelic drugs, such as peyote, LSD, PCP, and MDMA, are also referred to as hallucinogens. They profoundly alter a person's state of consciousness and the way in which a person thinks, feels, and perceives. Marijuana has a weak sedative effect and, at high doses, often produces experiences compared to those of psychedelics (e.g., panic, depressive reactions, and mild paranoia). Its psychoactive ingredient, THC, has also been used medically to treat nausea and to stimulate appetite.

Research has suggested that the medial forebrain bundle (MFB) is the "reinforcement center" of the brain. It is part of the larger mesolimbic reinforcement system (MRS), which mediates the influence of reward on behavior. Other important structures involved in reinforcement include the ventral tegmental area and the nucleus accumbens. Additionally, because dopamine controls the activity of neurons in the MRS, it also plays a major role in the behavioral effects of reinforcement. One hypothesis suggests that a defect in the dopaminergic system causes a person to abuse certain substances in order to obtain greater stimulation of their dopaminergic reward system. This suggests that addiction may have a genetic component and be inherited.

KEY TERMS

The following is a list of important terms introduced in Chapter 5. Give the definition of each term in the space provided.

agonist

alcohol

alcoholism

amphetamine

anandamide

antagonist

anxiolytic

barbiturate

benzodiazepine

caffeine

cocaine

codeine

depressant

false transmitter

half-life

heroin

inhalation

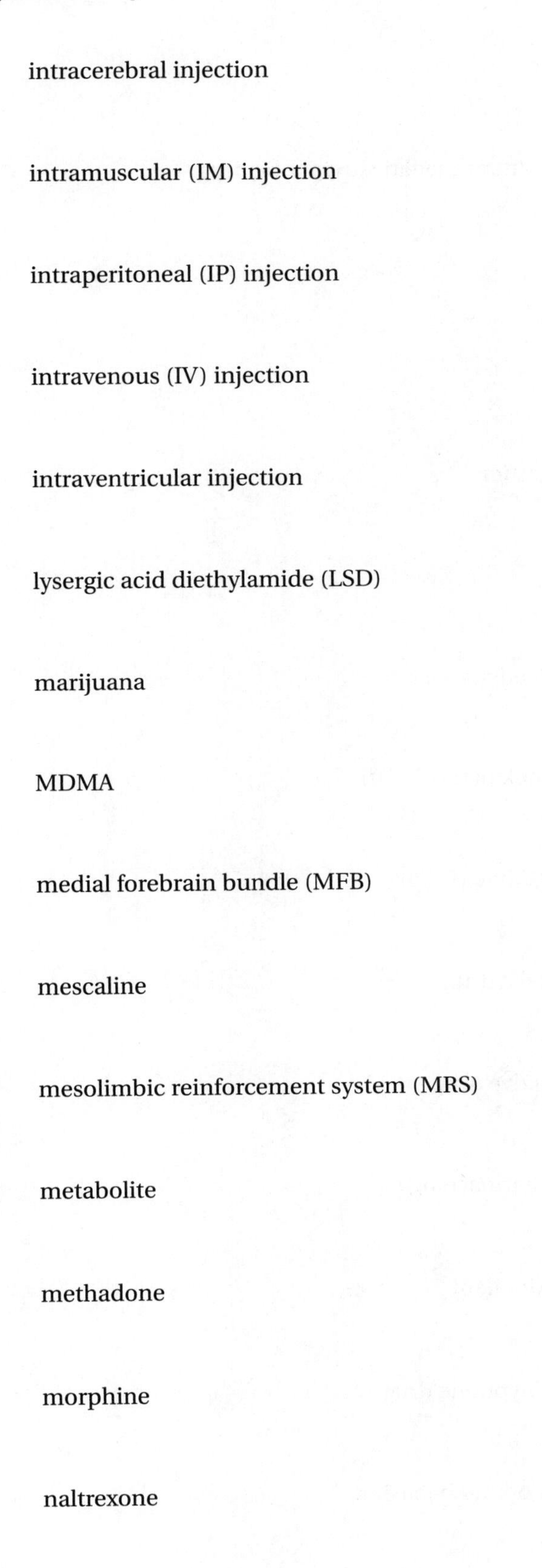

intracerebral injection

intramuscular (IM) injection

intraperitoneal (IP) injection

intravenous (IV) injection

intraventricular injection

lysergic acid diethylamide (LSD)

marijuana

MDMA

medial forebrain bundle (MFB)

mescaline

mesolimbic reinforcement system (MRS)

metabolite

methadone

morphine

naltrexone

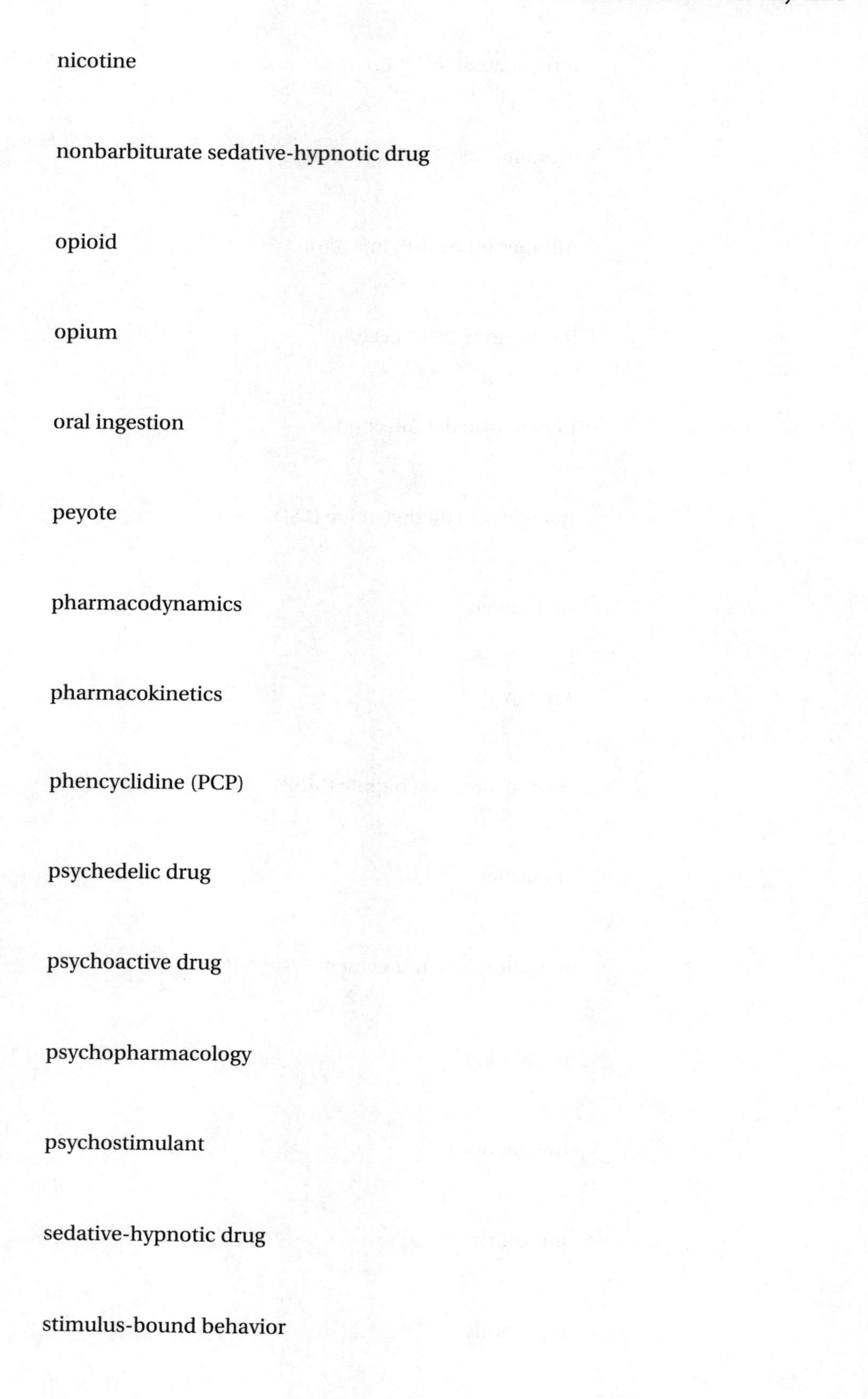

nicotine

nonbarbiturate sedative-hypnotic drug

opioid

opium

oral ingestion

peyote

pharmacodynamics

pharmacokinetics

phencyclidine (PCP)

psychedelic drug

psychoactive drug

psychopharmacology

psychostimulant

sedative-hypnotic drug

stimulus-bound behavior

subcutaneous (SC) injection

substance abuse

substance dependence

THC

tolerance

withdrawal symptom

◆ LABELING EXERCISES

1. Agonist drugs can enhance synaptic transmission in six ways. In the figure below, label the six actions of an agonist drug.

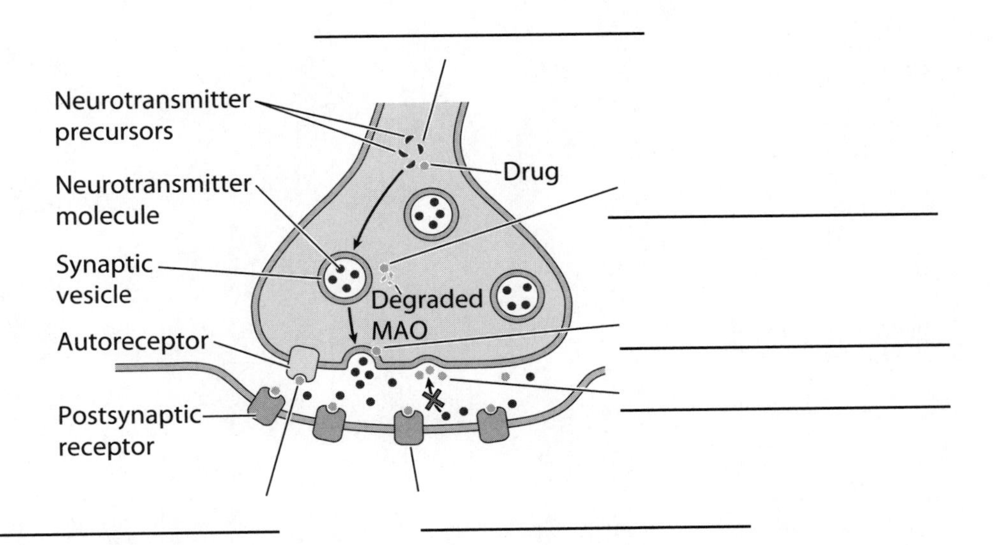

2. Antagonistic drugs can reduce synaptic transmission in five ways. In the figure below, label the five actions of an antagonist drug.

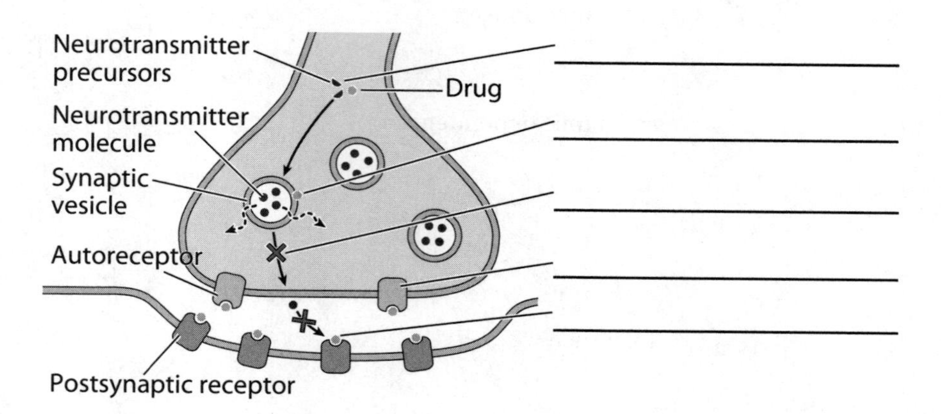

Vision

6

CHAPTER ART LECTURE NOTEBOOK

The following is a selection of the important figures and tables introduced in Chapter 6. You can take notes during class in the space provided.

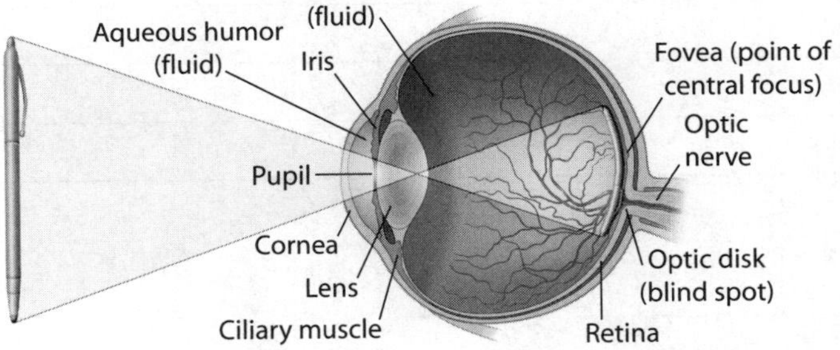

Vitreous humor (fluid)
Aqueous humor (fluid)
Iris
Fovea (point of central focus)
Optic nerve
Pupil
Cornea
Lens
Ciliary muscle
Optic disk (blind spot)
Retina

Figure 6.1 A cross-sectional view of the human eye, p. 194.

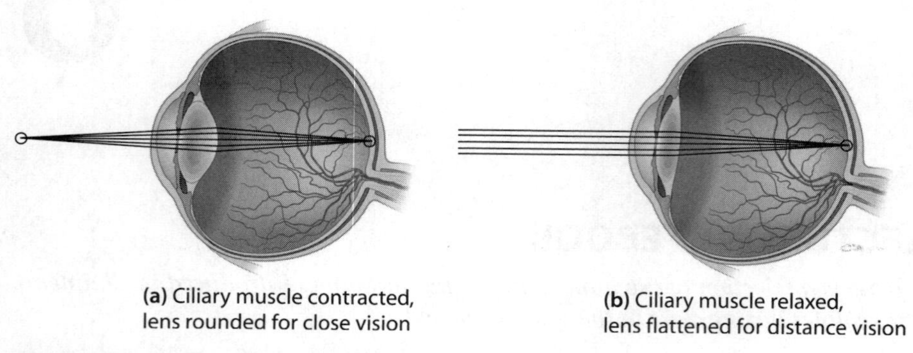

Figure 6.2 Accommodation, p. 195.

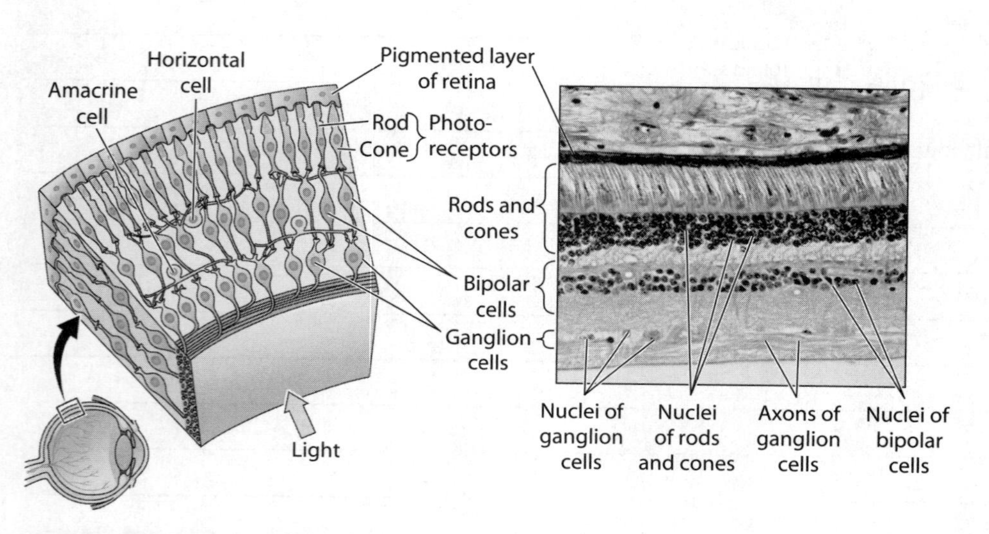

Figure 6.3 Cellular organization of the retina, p. 195.

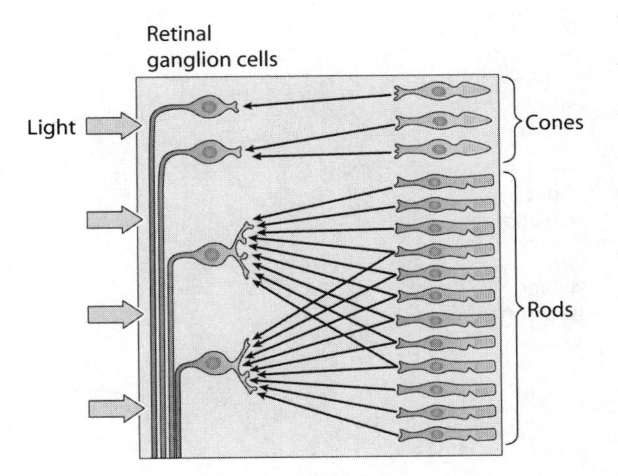

Figure 6.4 The convergence of cones and rods onto ganglion cells, p. 196.

Table 6.1

The Duplex Theory: Differences Between Rods and Cones

Rods	Cones
Located mostly in the periphery of the retina	Located mostly in the center of the retina
Relatively sensitive to light	Relatively insensitive to light
Operate under low light levels (at night)	Operate under high light levels (during the day)
Achromatic (colorless) vision	Chromatic (color) vision
Low visual acuity	High visual acuity
120 million in each retina (in humans)	6 million in each retina (in humans)
High convergence of information	Low convergence of information

Table 6.1 The Duplex Theory: Differences Between Rods and Cones, p. 197.

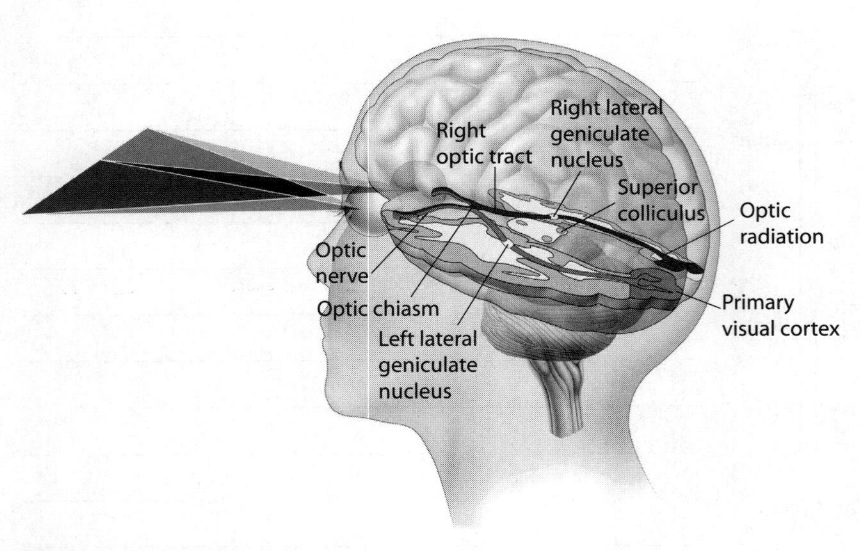

Figure 6.6 Pathways to the primary visual cortex, p. 198.

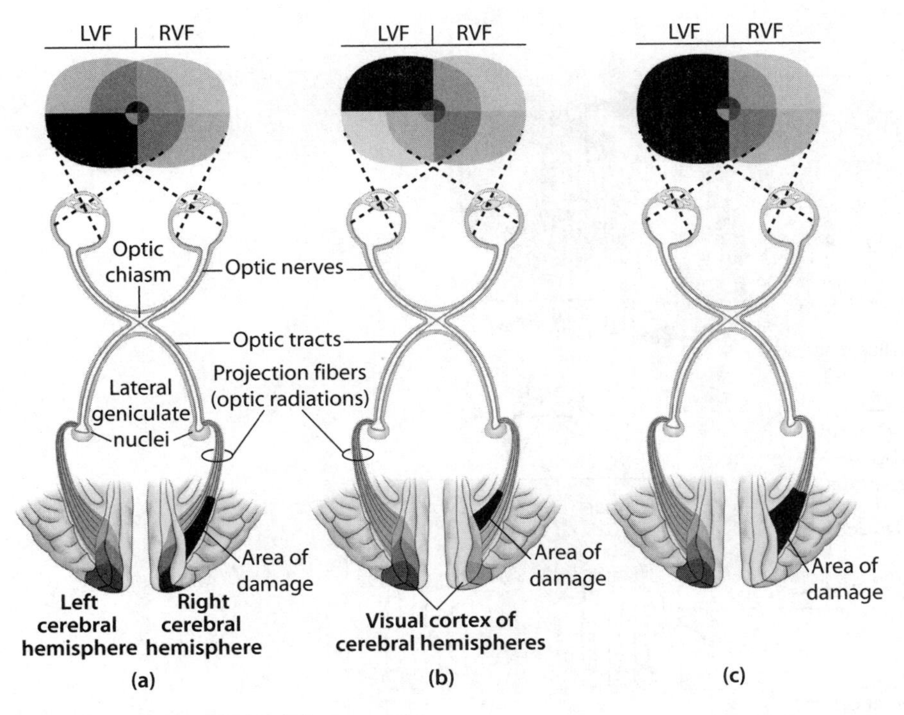

Figure 6.7 Visual field deficits, p. 201.

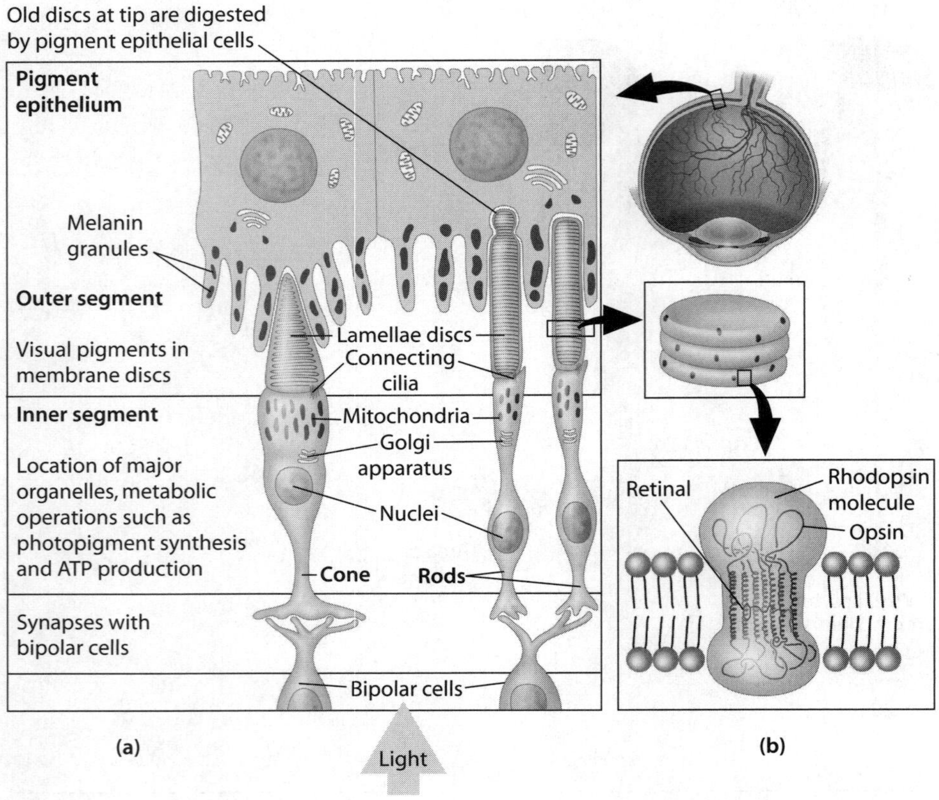

Figure 6.10 Photoreceptors, p. 203.

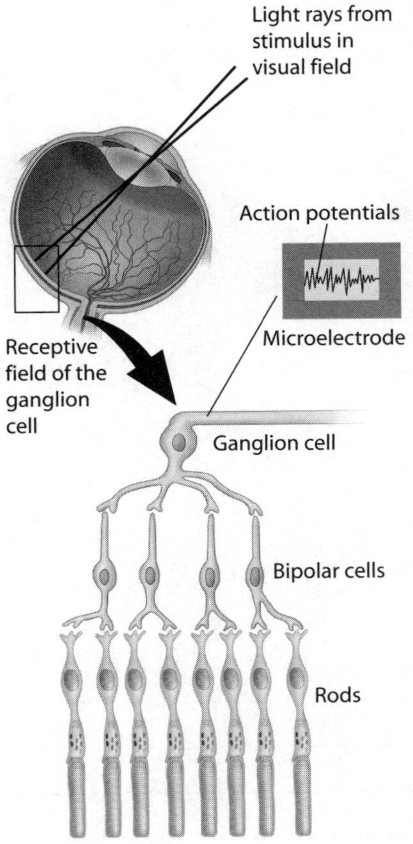

Light rays from stimulus in visual field

Action potentials

Microelectrode

Receptive field of the ganglion cell

Ganglion cell

Bipolar cells

Rods

Figure 6.13 The receptive field of a ganglion cell in the periphery of the retina, p. 207.

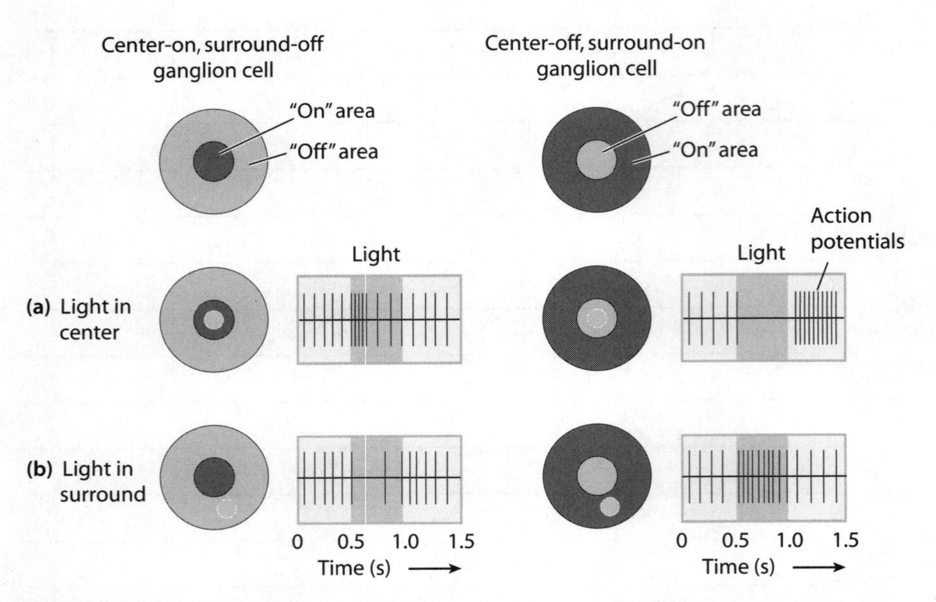

Figure 6.14 The receptive fields of center-on, surround-off and center-off, surround-on ganglion cells, p. 207.

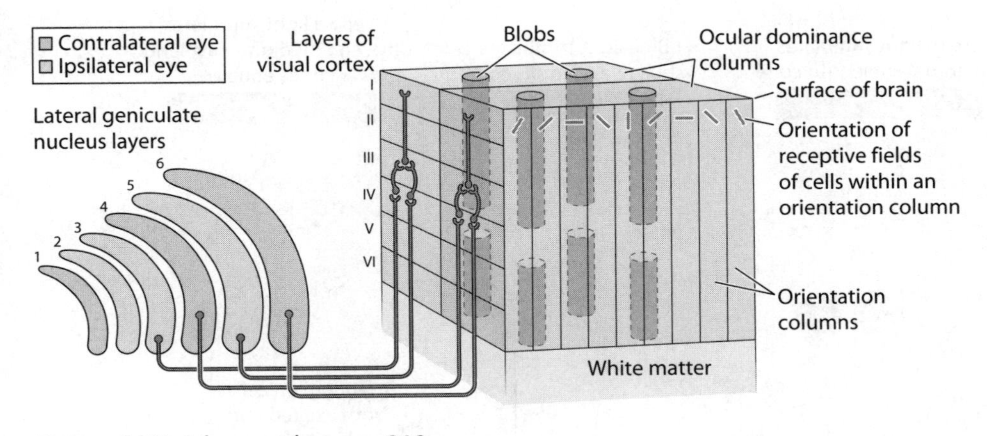

Figure 6.18 A hypercolumn, p. 210.

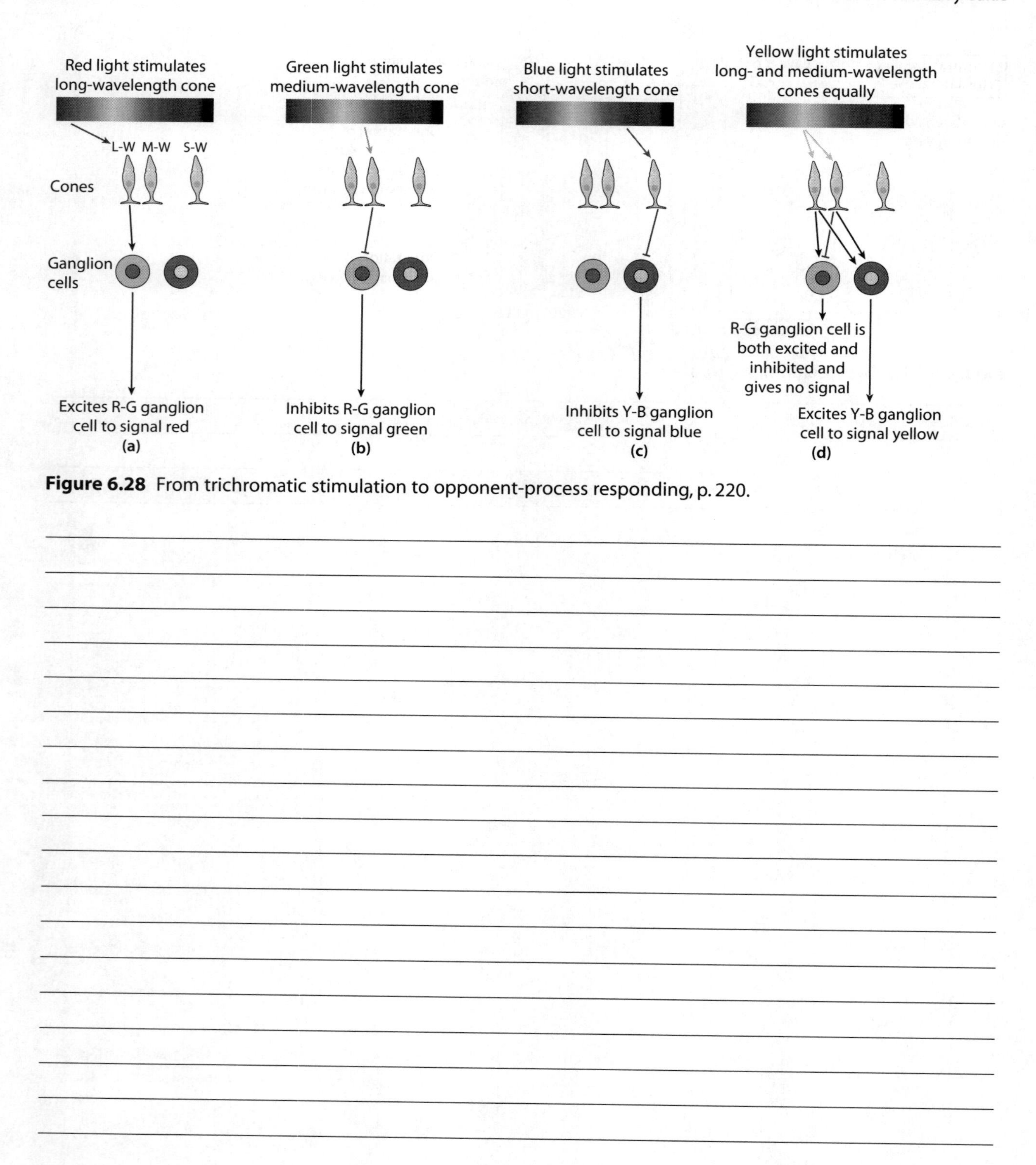

Figure 6.28 From trichromatic stimulation to opponent-process responding, p. 220.

CHAPTER SUMMARY

A sense is the mechanism of the nervous system that is used for detecting specific sets of stimuli. Sensory receptors perform three basic functions—absorption, transduction, and coding. In order to see an object, the stimulus must be detected by receptor cells, called photoreceptors, located at the back of the eye. To get there, light passes through the cornea (the outer layer of the eye), the pupil, and the lens, which focuses an image of the object on the retina. This image is upside down and reversed. It is in the retina that photoreceptors (rods and cones), bipolar cells, and ganglion cells are contained. Rods are located at the periphery of the retina and allow for the detection of stimuli under dim lighting conditions; cones are located in the central part of the retina (the fovea) and allow for the detection of color and the details of daytime vision. From the photoreceptors, light passes to the bipolar cells, then the ganglion cells, which come together at the optic disk to form the optic nerve.

In humans, 50% of the optic nerve fibers cross at the optic chiasm—those that originate in the nasal half of each retina cross to the opposite side of the brain, whereas those that originate in the lateral half of each retina stay on the same side. This means that input from the right visual field is processed by the left hemisphere and vice versa. Beyond the optic chiasm, optic nerves are called optic tracts, most of which project to the lateral geniculate nucleus (LGN) and then the primary visual cortex (area V1). Information from area V1 travels by three pathways to the secondary visual cortex (area V2) for analysis.

Light varies along three physical dimensions: wavelength (hue), intensity (brightness), and purity (saturation). Photoreceptors transduce light into neural impulses. They contain photopigment, made up of a protein opsin and a lipid retinal, which absorbs light and is split by the light. At this point, the photoreceptor membrane becomes hyperpolarized and less neurotransmitter is released, leading to depolarization of the bipolar cells. This has an excitatory influence on ganglion cells, which exhibit the following response pattern: on ganglion cells respond when a light is turned on; off ganglion cells respond when a light is turned off; on-off ganglion cells respond when a light stimulus begins and ends.

Object recognition is aided by lateral inhibition, which sharpens the edges between an object and its background, and receptive fields, regions of the retina that, when stimulated, cause a change in the activity of the cell. The receptive fields of bipolar cells, ganglion cells, LGN cells, and cortical cells have a center-surround configuration, with one region (central vs. peripheral) being excitatory and the other being inhibitory.

There are several types of cells in the visual cortex. Simple cells, found only in area V1, respond to lines or edges with a specific orientation and location in the visual field. Complex cells, found in areas V1 and V2, are sensitive to a specific line stimulus that moves in a particular direction occurring anywhere in the receptive field. Hypercomplex cells are similar to complex cells, except the length of the line stimulus is critical (they do not respond if it is too long). Several types of cues provide information about the spatial location of a stimulus (depth perception), including monocular cues and binocular depth cues. Two types of neurons detect the movement of stimuli: component direction-selective neurons and pattern direction-selective neurons.

To explain color perception, two main theories have been proposed. The Young-Helmhotz trichromatic theory suggests that there are three different types of receptors in the eye, each responding to a different color (one red, one green, one blue/violet). The opponent-process theory proposed that three receptors operate in opponent fashion: blue-yellow, green-red, and white-black. Parts of both theories have been proven correct—cones can be classified into three types as predicted by the Young-Helmholtz theory, whereas ganglion and LGN cells respond to color as predicted by the opponent-process theory.

KEY TERMS

The following is a list of important terms introduced in Chapter 6. Give the definition of each term in the space provided.

accommodation

across-fiber pattern coding

amacrine cell

aqueous humor

Balint's syndrome

binding problem

binocular depth cue

bipolar cell

blindsight

blind spot

blob

brightness

center-off, surround-on ganglion cell

center-on, surround-off ganglion cell

ciliary muscle

coding

color constancy

complex cell

component direction-selective neuron

cone

cornea

duplex theory

feature detector

fovea

fusiform face area

ganglion cell

horizontal cell

hue

hypercomplex cell

iris

labeled-line coding

lamella

lateral geniculate nucleus (LGN)

lateral inhibition

lens

magnocellular layer

monocular depth cue

negative afterimage

ocular dominance column

off ganglion cell

on ganglion cell

on-off ganglion cell

opponent-process theory

opsin

optic chiasm

optic disk

optic nerve

optic tract

orientation column

parvocellular layer

pattern direction-selective neuron

photopigment

photoreceptor

primary visual cortex

prosopagnosia

pupil

pursuit movement

receptive field

retina

retinal

retinal image

rhodopsin

rod

rod opsin

saccadic movement

saturation

secondary visual cortex

sense

simple cell

sine-wave grating

spatial-frequency theory

transduction

visual agnosia

visual field deficit

vitreous humor

X ganglion cell

Y ganglion cell

Young-Helmholtz trichromatic theory

◆ LABELING EXERCISES

1. There are several components of the visual system that allow us to see the world around us. One important part of this system is the human eye. In the figure below, label the following structures of the human eye:

pupil	lens
optic nerve	aqueous humor (fluid)
vitreous humor (fluid)	cornea
iris	optic disk (blind spot)
fovea	ciliary muscle
retina	

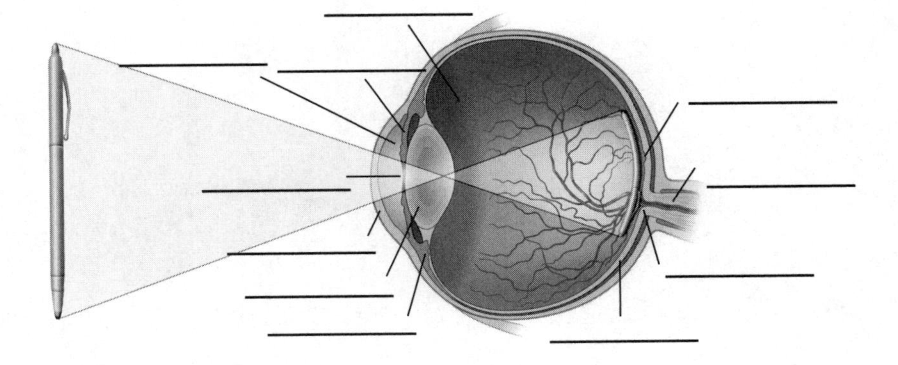

2. Beyond the primary visual cortex, there are several structures that are responsible for detecting different types of visual stimuli. Label these structures in the figure below:

   primary visual cortex (striate cortex)

   secondary visual cortex (prestriate cortex)

   inferotemporal cortex

   posterior parietal cortex

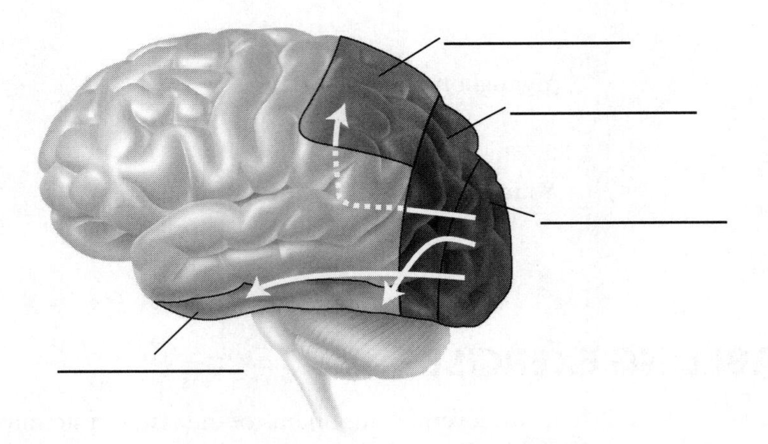

Hearing, Balance, and the Cutaneous and Chemical Senses

7

◆ CHAPTER ART LECTURE NOTEBOOK

The following is a selection of the important figures and tables introduced in Chapter 7. You can take notes during class in the space provided.

Table 7.1
Amplitude and Damaging Effects of Various Sounds

Typical Decibel Level	Example	Exposure That Can Damage Hearing
0	Lowest audible sound	
30	Quiet library; soft whisper	
40	Quiet office; living room; bedroom away from traffic	
50	Light traffic at a distance; refrigerator; gentle breeze	
60	Air conditioner at 20 feet; conversation; sewing machine in operation	
70	Busy traffic; noisy restaurant	Some damage if continuous
80	Subway; heavy city traffic; alarm clock at 2 feet; factory noise	More than 8 hours
90	Truck traffic; noisy home appliances; shop tools; gas lawnmower	Less than 8 hours
100	Chain saw; boiler shop; pneumatic drill	2 hours
120	"Heavy metal" rock concert; sandblasting; thunderclap nearby	Immediate danger
140	Gunshot; jet plane	Immediate danger
160	Rocket launching pad	Hearing loss inevitable

Source: Martini, F. H. (1998). *Fundamentals of anatomy and physiology* (4th ed.). Upper Saddle River, NJ: Prentice-Hall.

Table 7.1 Amplitude and Damaging Effects of Various Sounds, p. 229.

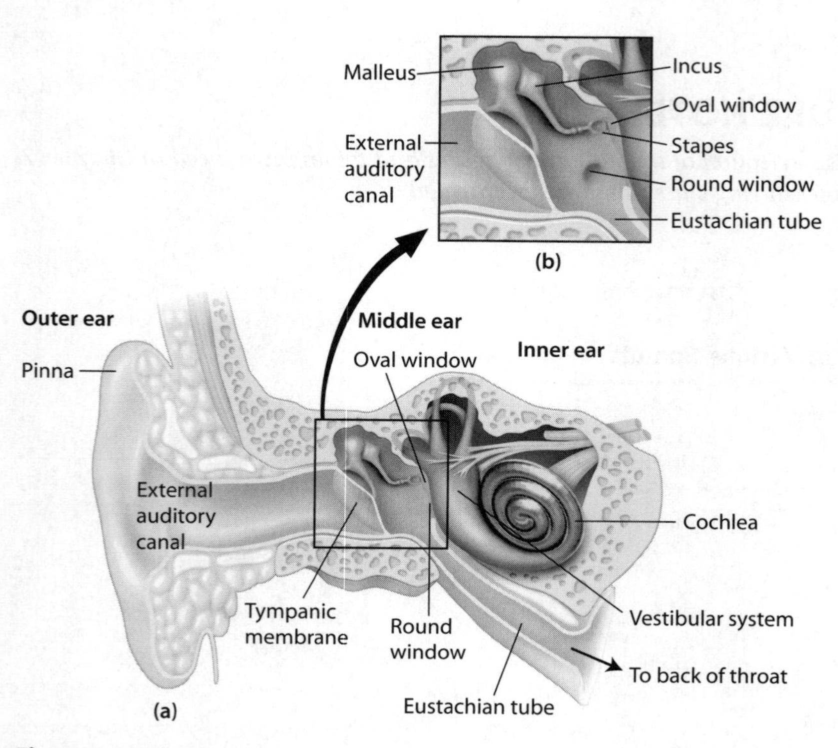

Figure 7.2 The ear, p. 229.

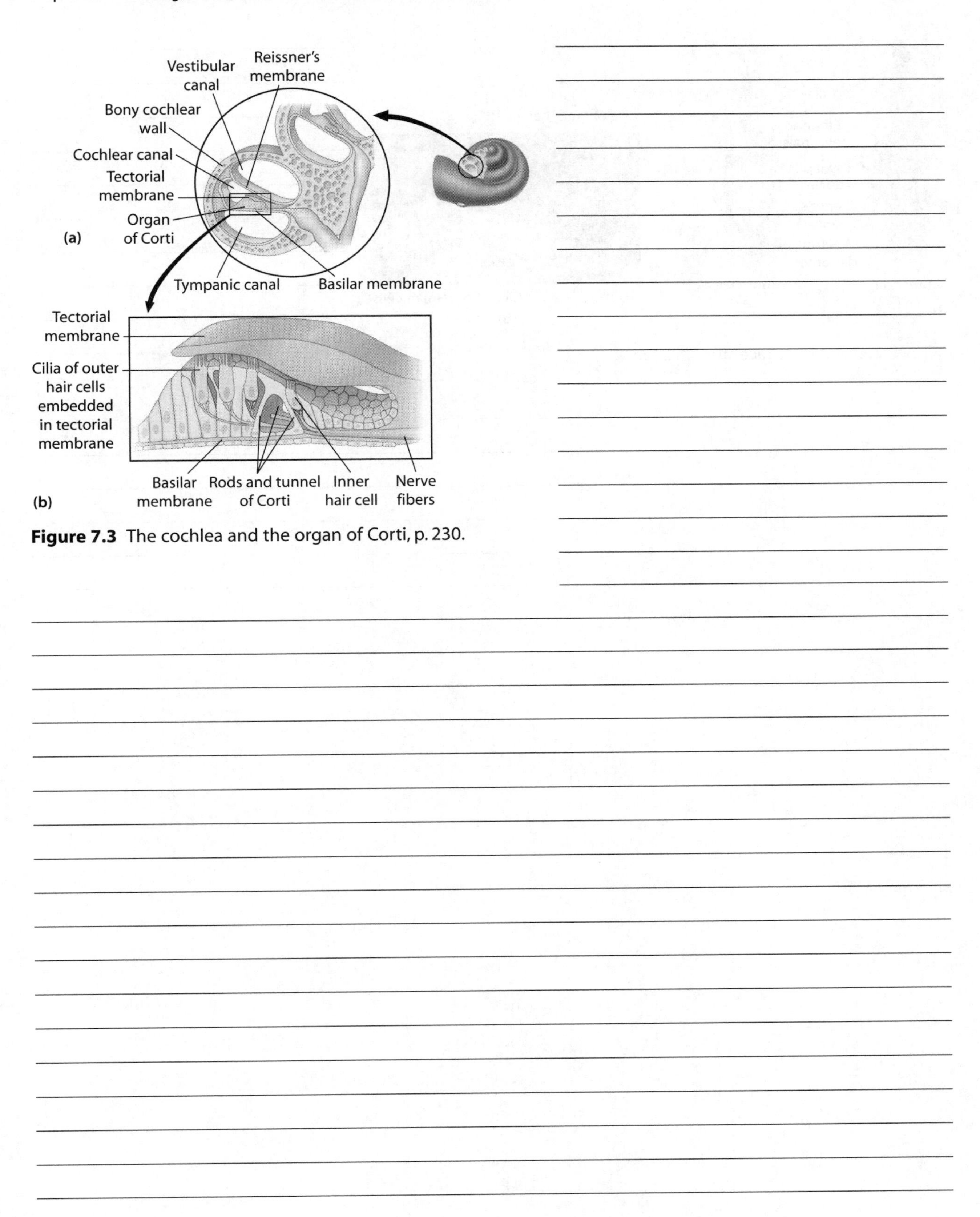

Figure 7.3 The cochlea and the organ of Corti, p. 230.

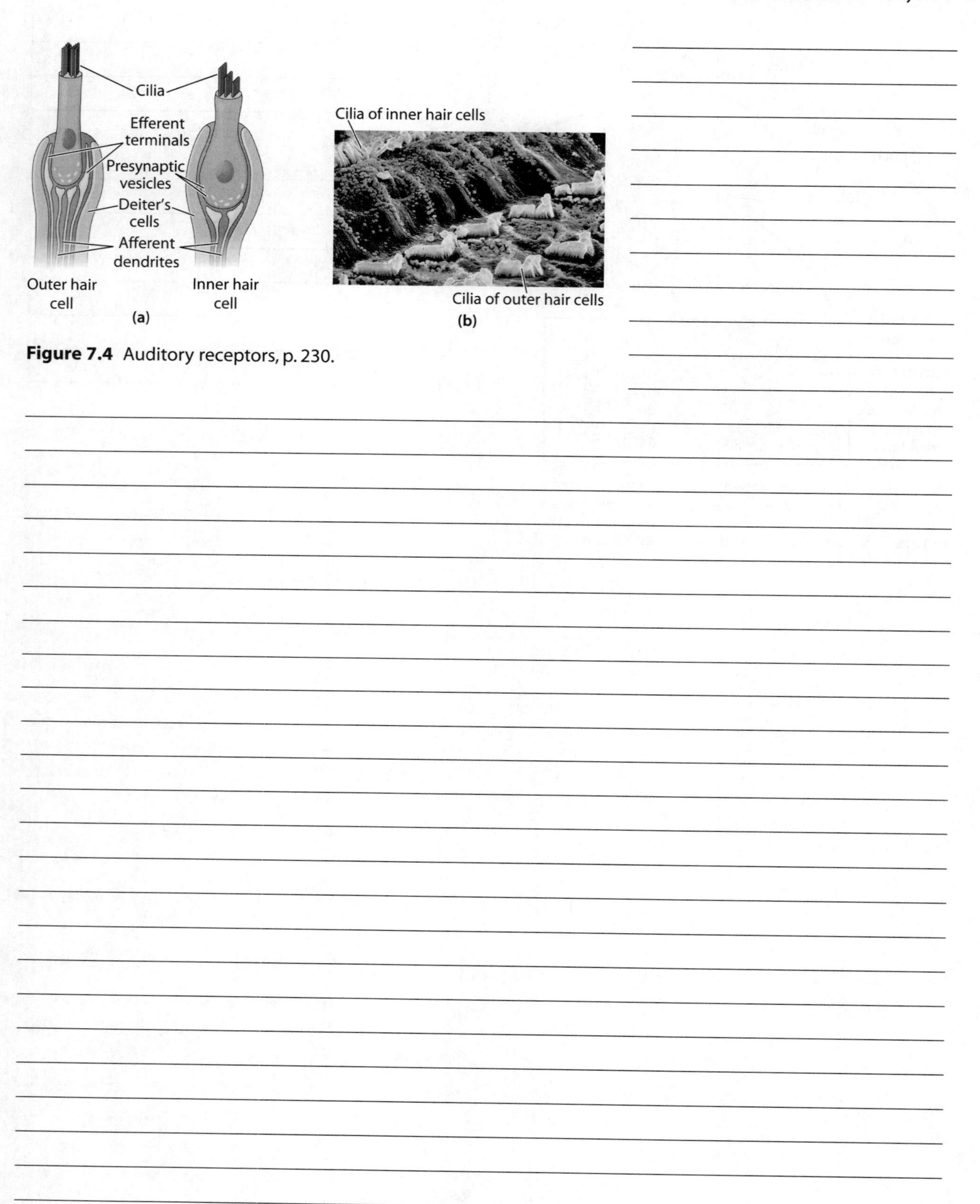

Figure 7.4 Auditory receptors, p. 230.

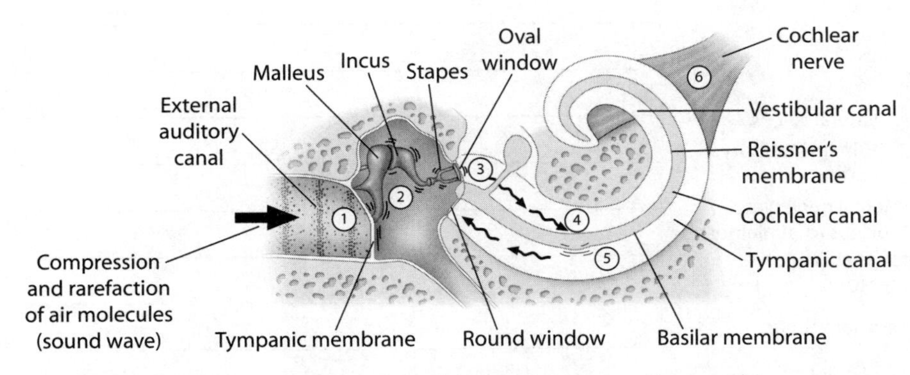

Figure 7.6 Steps in the production of an auditory sensation, p. 231.

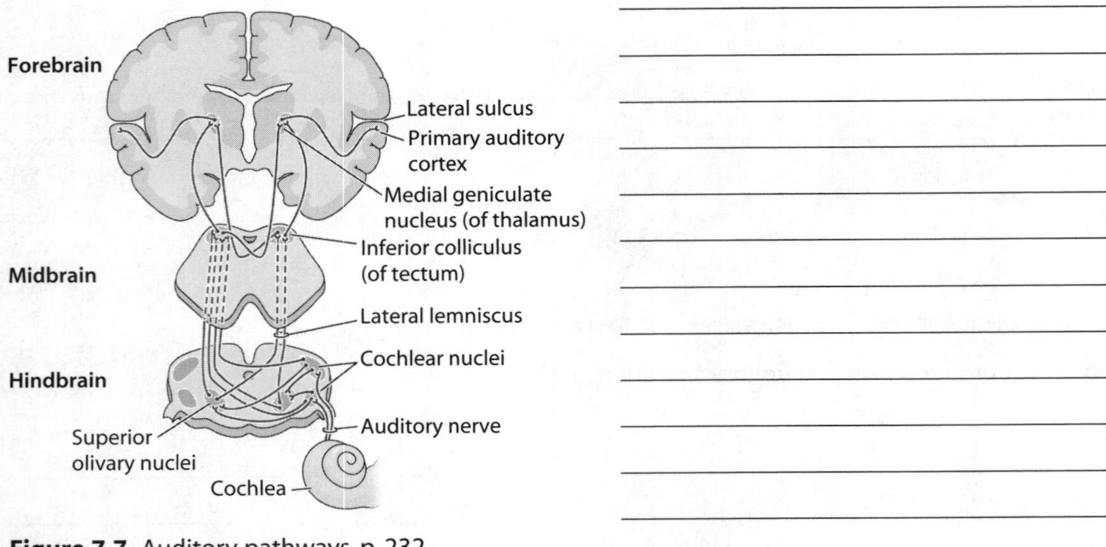

Figure 7.7 Auditory pathways, p. 232.

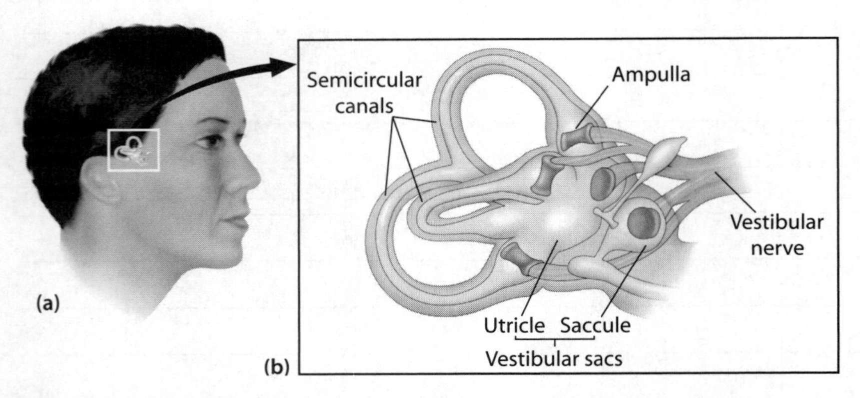

Figure 7.14 Components of the vestibular system, p. 240.

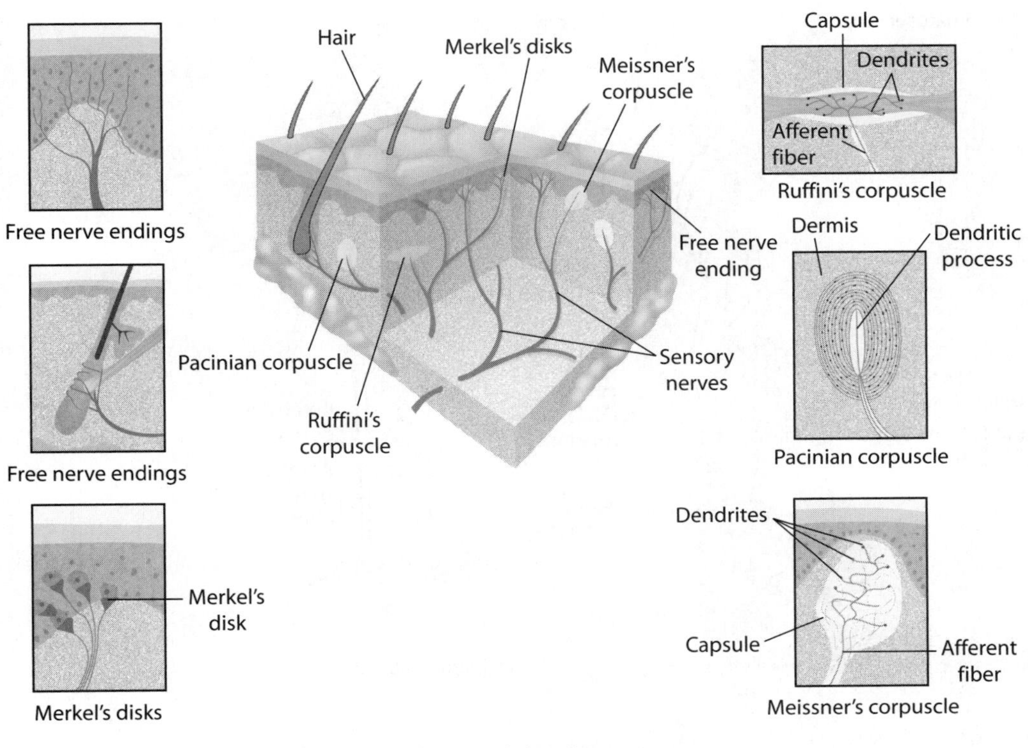

Figure 7.16 The somatosensory receptors of the skin, p. 244.

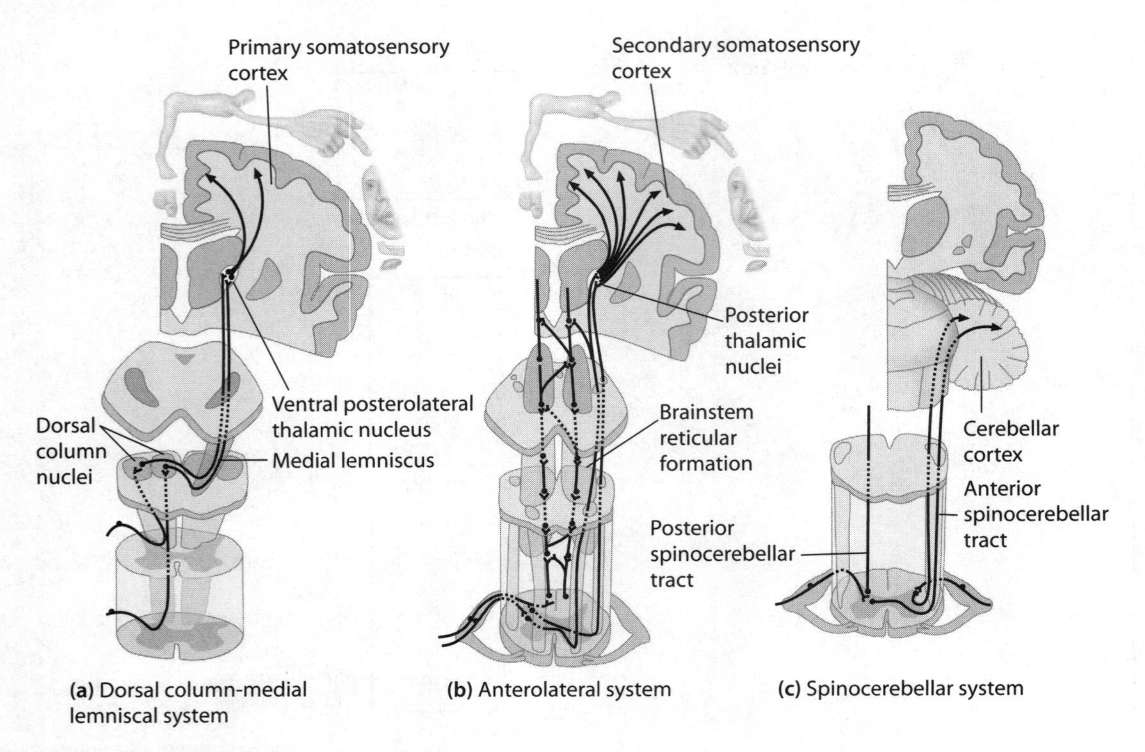

Figure 7.18 Somatosensory pathways, p. 246.

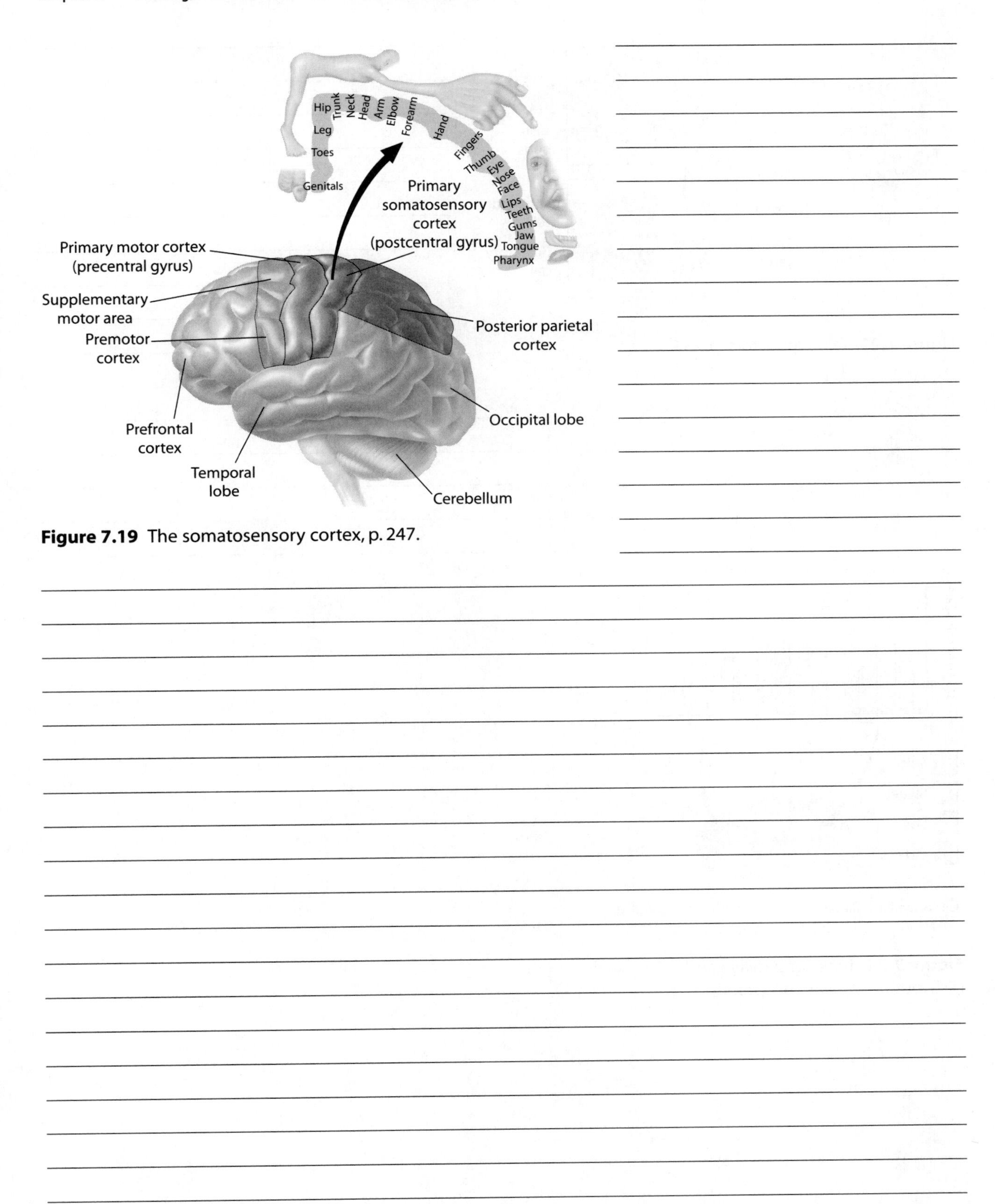

Figure 7.19 The somatosensory cortex, p. 247.

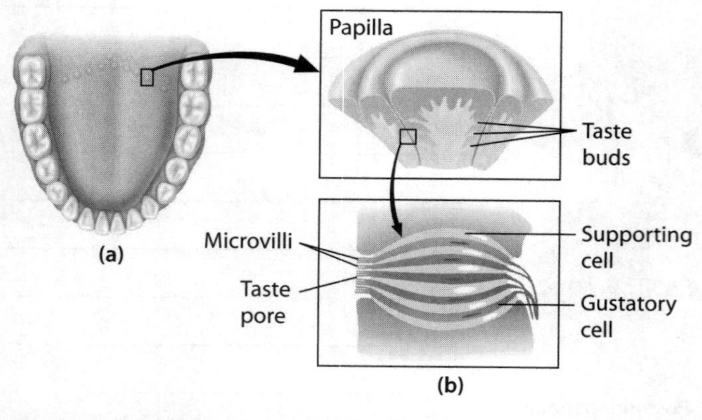

Figure 7.23 Taste receptors, p. 253.

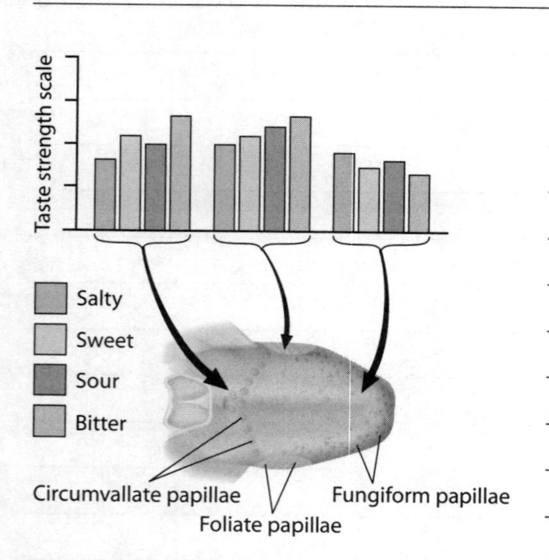

Figure 7.24 Types of papillae and distribution of taste receptors, p. 253.

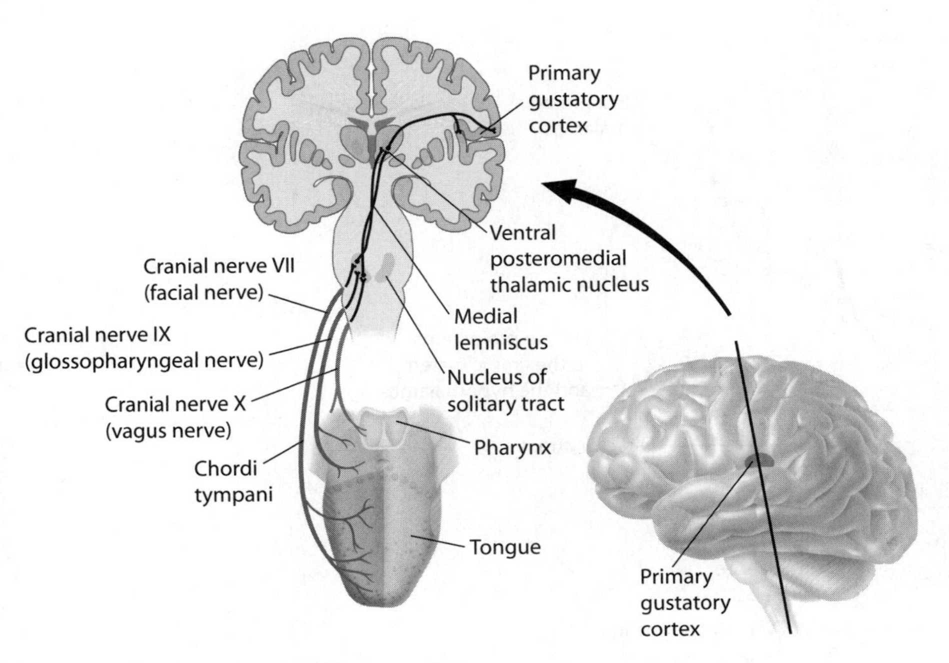

Figure 7.25 Gustatory pathways, p. 255.

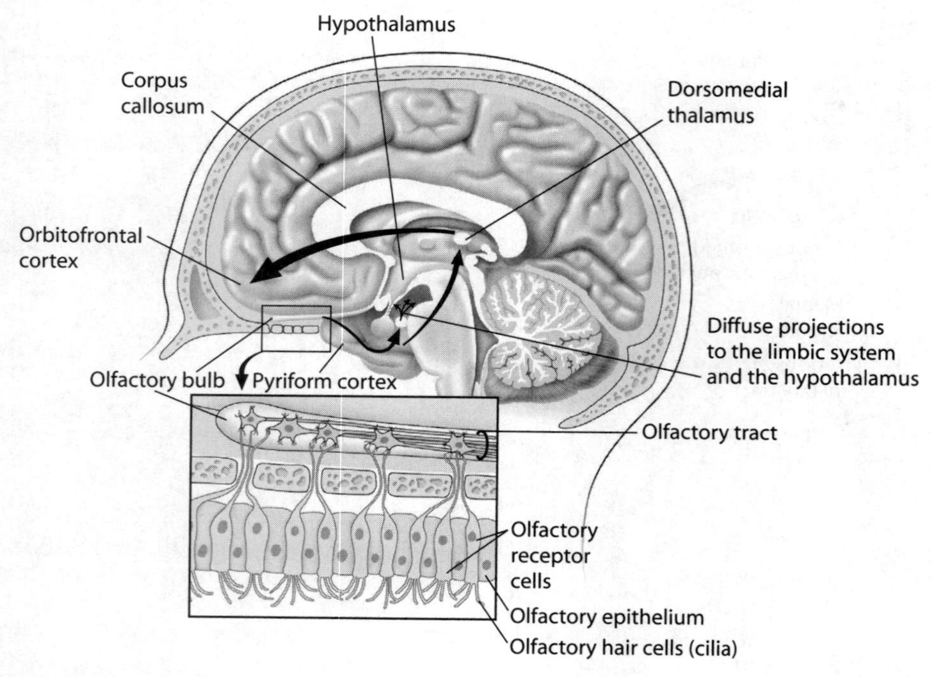

Figure 7.26 Olfactory receptors and pathways, p. 259.

CHAPTER SUMMARY

The auditory system detects sound waves produced by objects vibrating in a material medium. Sound waves vary along three dimensions: frequency (perceived as pitch and measured in hertz); intensity (perceived as loudness and measured in decibels); and complexity (perceived as timbre). Sound waves enter the pinna (outer ear) and travel down the external auditory canal to the tympanic membrane (eardrum), which vibrates in response. These vibrations are transmitted by the bones of the middle ear to the oval window, then the cochlea, and round window. In the inner ear, fluid movement causes vibrations in the basilar and tectorial membranes, bending the cilia, which act as auditory receptors. These receptors synapse with cochlear nerve neurons that project to the cochlear nuclei of the medulla. Axons leaving the cochlear nuclei synapse with the superior olivary nucleus. The auditory pathways continue by way of the lateral lemniscus to the inferior colliculus, then to the MGN of the thalamus, and finally to the primary auditory cortex for recognition of auditory patterns.

Pitch perception depends on the frequency of vibration of the material medium. There have been two main theories of pitch perception: the place theory of pitch perception (proposed by Helmholtz and supported by Von Békésy) and Rutherford's frequency theory of pitch perception and volley principle. The current view of pitch perception is a combination of these theories. There are two mechanisms for determining the intensity, or loudness, of a stimulus. For low-frequency sounds, loudness is encoded by the number of neurons firing; for high-frequency sounds, loudness is encoded by the rate of responding (a higher rate for higher-intensity sounds). Pure, or simple, tones are sounds of only one frequency, while complex sounds have two or more frequencies. The combination of frequencies produces what we perceive as the timbre of a particular sound. Sound localization depends on time-of-arrival cues, intensity differences, and phase differences.

The vestibular system is responsible for maintaining balance, keeping the head in an upright position, and adjusting eye movements to compensate for head movements. It consists of the vestibular sacs and the semicircular canals. The vestibular nerve is activated when head movement causes the cilia in the vestibular sacs to bend. These nerve fibers project to the medulla and pons, which coordinate head and eye movements, to the spinal cord and cerebellum, which coordinate balance, body position, and body movement, and to the temporal cortex, which may produce conscious awareness of dizziness and imbalance.

Somatosense refers to the skin sensations of touch, pain, temperature, and proprioception. There are several types of skin receptors: Pacinian corpuscles, free nerve endings, Meissner's corpuscles, Merkel's disks, and Ruffini's corpuscles. Skin receptor fibers project to the CNS through the cranial or spinal nerves and information travels along one of three pathways: the dorsal column-medial lemniscal system (transmits information about touch and proprioceptive sensations); the anterolateral system (transmits information about temperature and pain sensations); or the spinocerebellar system (transmits information about proprioception). The somatosensory cortex is organized topographically, with adjacent areas of the skin represented by adjacent areas of the somatosensory cortex. There have been two main theories of pain perception: the gate-control theory of pain and the neuromatrix theory of pain (which explains phenomena such as phantom limb pain).

The gustatory system distinguishes among four basic tastes: sweet, sour, bitter, and salty. Taste receptors are found in taste buds located near or within papillae in the tongue, palate, pharynx, and larynx. Genetic differences in the number of taste buds on the tongue determine whether people are supertasters, medium tasters, or nontasters.

Taste is associated with the reward areas of the brain and with such neurotransmitters as dopamine and the endogenous opioids.

The olfactory sense (sense of smell) is an important part of our daily life and is sensitive to airborne molecules of volatile substances. Mapping of the human genome indicates that about half of the odor receptor (OR) genes are pseudogenes (genes with no function), which may be indicative of the evolution of the decreased olfactory sense in primates (as opposed to New World and Old World monkeys). Axons of olfactory receptors synapse with cells in the olfactory bulbs, whose fibers form the olfactory tracts, which project to the primary olfactory cortex. Olfactory messages pass from this cortex to the hypothalamus and to the dorsomedial thalamus. The orbitofrontal cortex receives information from the dorsomedial thalamus and seems to be important for odor identification.

◆ KEY TERMS

The following is a list of important terms introduced in Chapter 7. Give the definition of each term in the space provided.

anterolateral system

auditory agnosia

auditory nerve

basilar membrane

capsaicin

chorda tympani

cochlea

cochlear implant

cochlear nerve

cochlear nucleus

dorsal column-medial lemniscal system

dorsal column nucleus

eustachian tube

fast pain

free nerve ending

frequency theory of pitch perception

gate-control theory of pain

gustatory sense

hair cell

incus (anvil)

inferior colliculus

intensity difference

loudness

malleus (hammer)

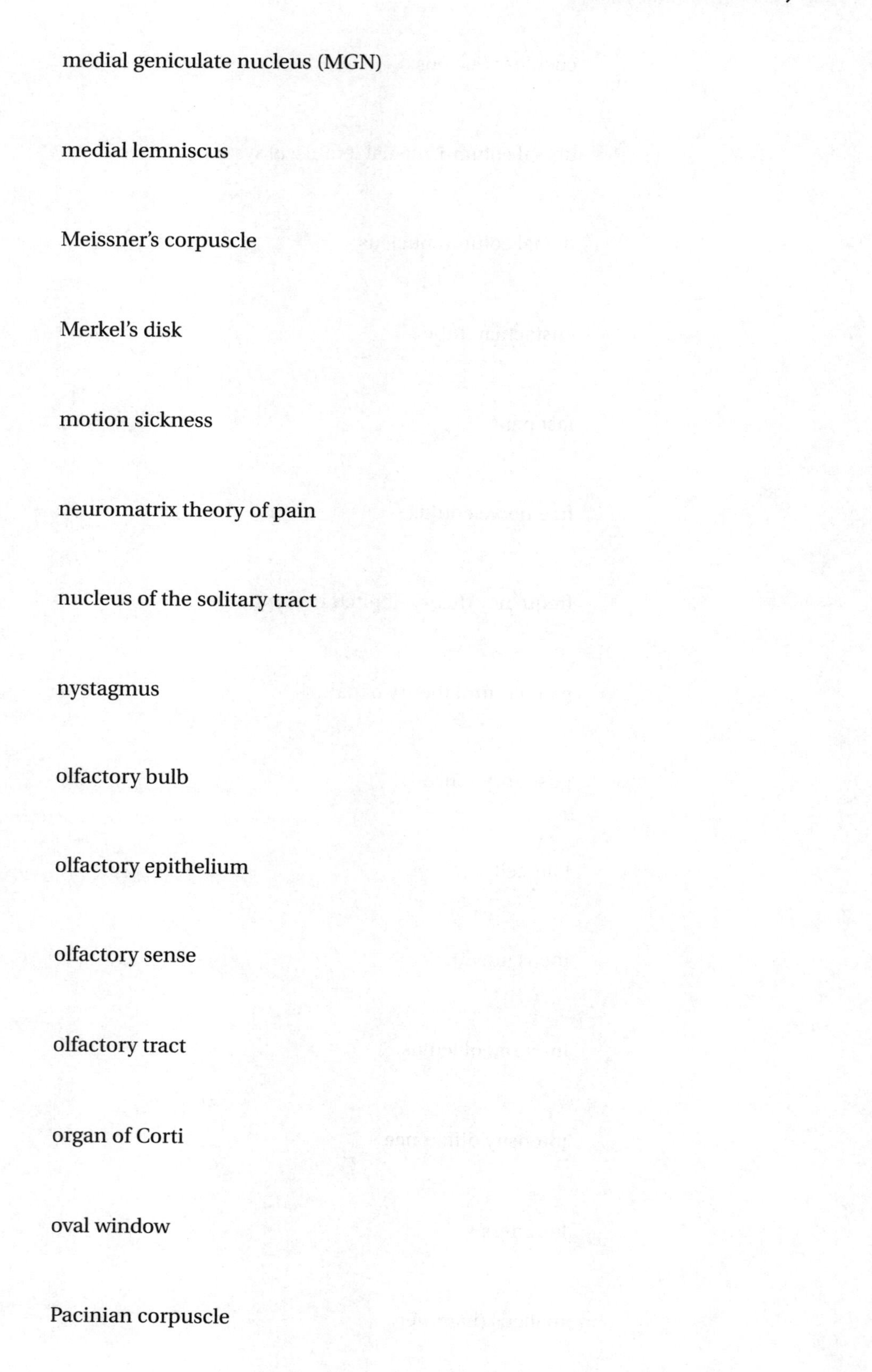

medial geniculate nucleus (MGN)

medial lemniscus

Meissner's corpuscle

Merkel's disk

motion sickness

neuromatrix theory of pain

nucleus of the solitary tract

nystagmus

olfactory bulb

olfactory epithelium

olfactory sense

olfactory tract

organ of Corti

oval window

Pacinian corpuscle

papilla

periaqueductal gray (PAG)

phantom limb pain

phase difference

pinna

pitch

place theory of pitch perception

posterior thalamic nucleus

primary auditory cortex (Heschl's gyrus)

primary gustatory cortex

primary olfactory cortex

primary somatosensory cortex

proprioception

remapping

round window

Ruffini's corpuscle

saccule

secondary auditory cortex

secondary somatosensory cortex

semicircular canal

slow pain

somatosense

sound

spinocerebellar system

spiral ganglion

stapes (stirrup)

superior olivary nucleus

taste bud

tectorial membrane

timbre

tonotopic distribution

tympanic membrane

utricle

ventral posterolateral thalamic nucleus

ventral posteromedial thalamic nucleus

vestibular ganglion

vestibular nerve

vestibular nucleus

vestibular sac

vestibular sense

volley principle

LABELING EXERCISES

1. The main structures of the ear are shown in the pictures below; for Figure (a), label the following structures:

   cochlea
   pinna
   tympanic membrane
   oval window
   vestibular system
   round window
   eustachian tube

   for Figure (b), label the following structures:

   oval window
   eustachian tube
   malleus
   stapes
   round window
   external auditory canal
   incus

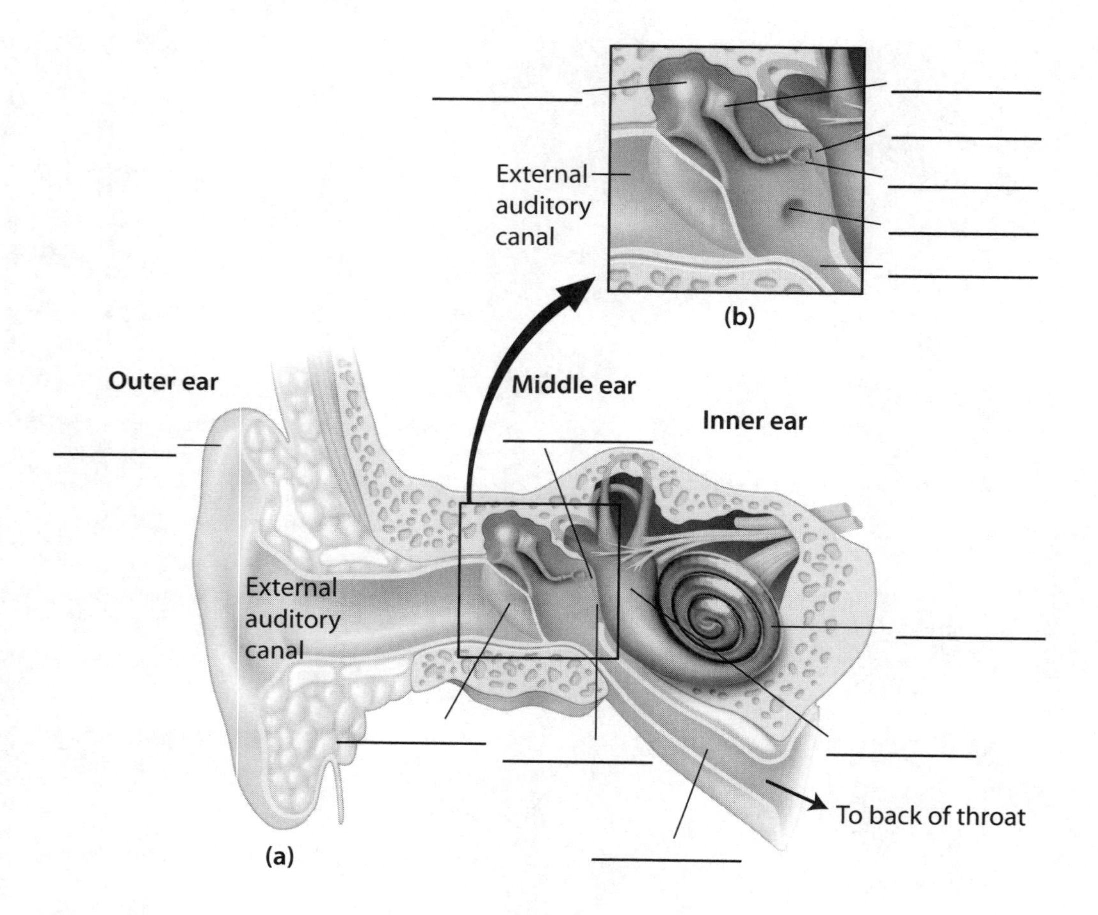

2. There are several cortical structures that receive somatosensory input. Label these structures in the figure below:

- occipital lobe
- temporal lobe
- prefrontal cortex
- posterior parietal cortex
- premotor cortex
- primary motor cortex (precentral gyrus)
- cerebellum
- supplementary motor area
- primary somatosensory cortex (postcentral gyrus)

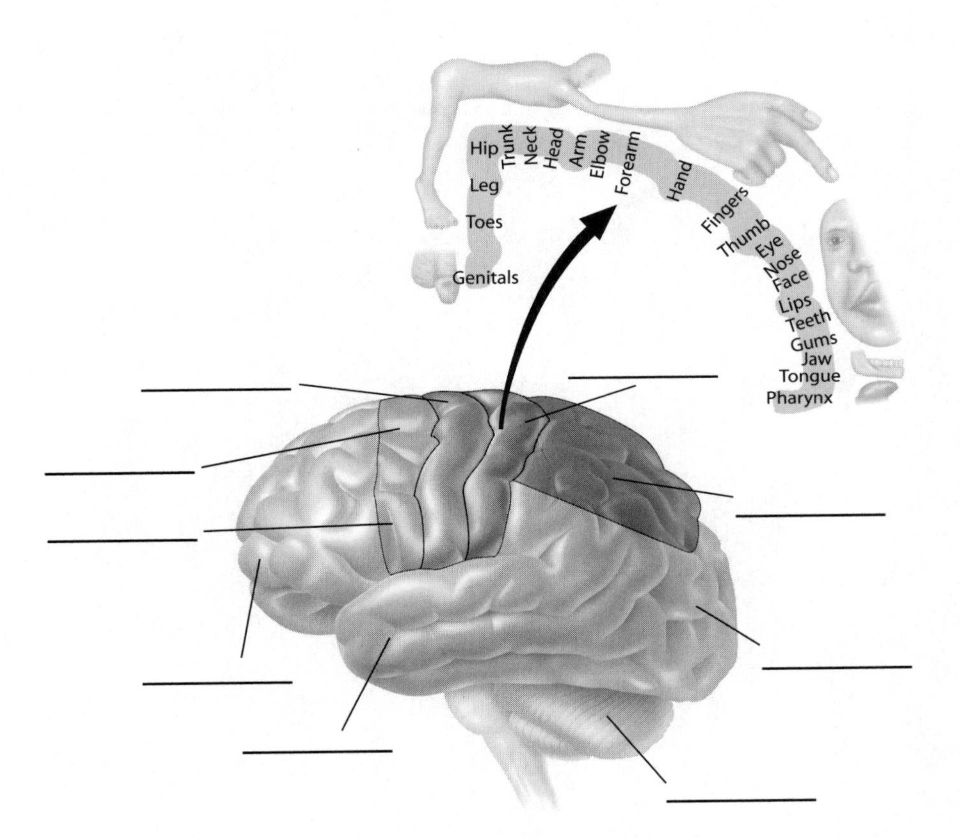

The Neurological Control of Movement

8

◆ CHAPTER ART LECTURE NOTEBOOK

The following is a selection of the important figures and tables introduced in Chapter 8. You can take notes during class in the space provided.

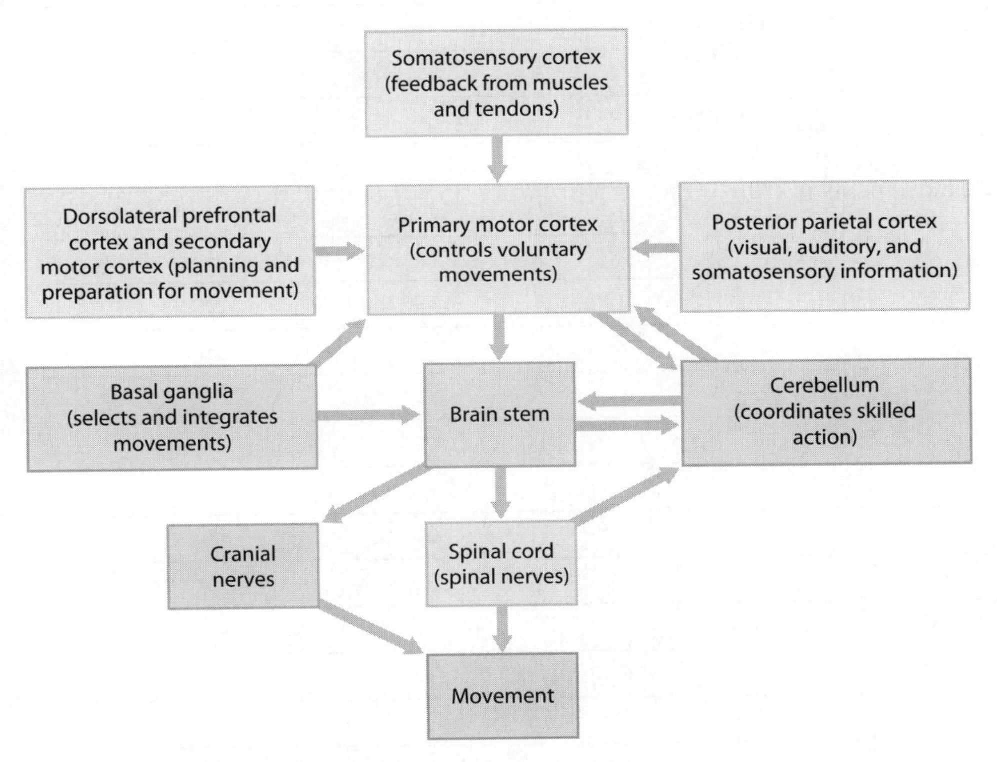

Figure 8.1 Key components in the control of movement, p. 269.

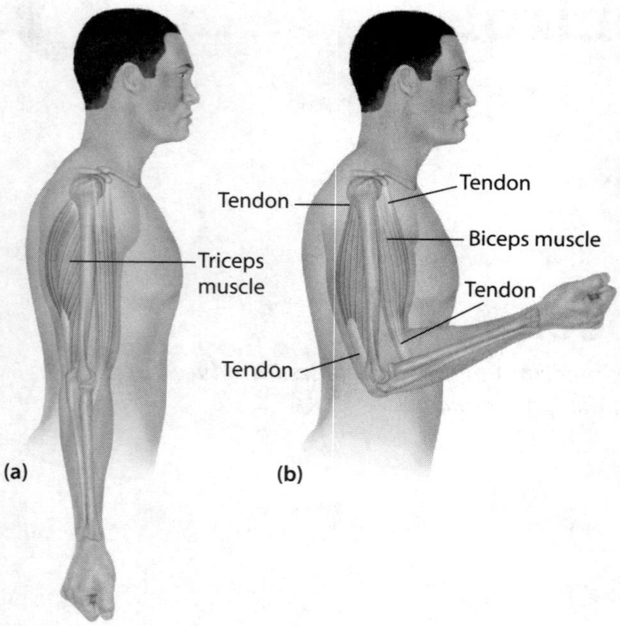

Figure 8.2 Opposing muscle movements, p. 270.

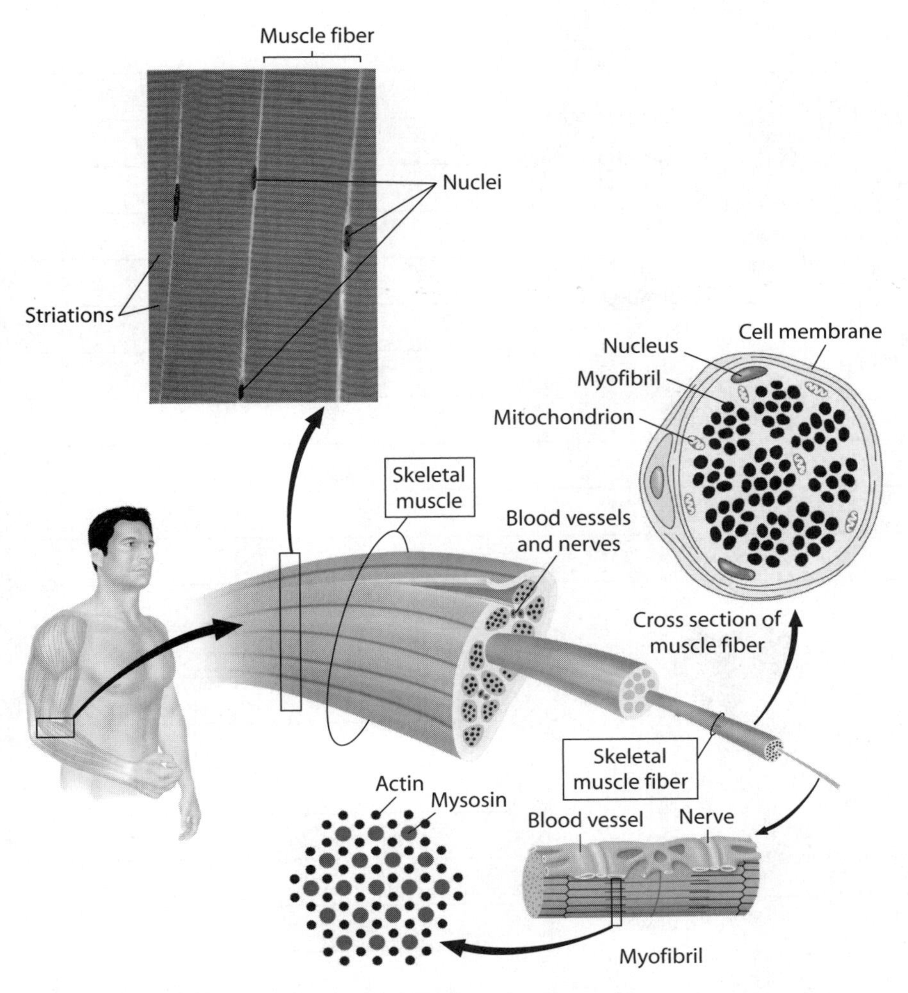

Figure 8.3 Major components of skeletal muscle, p. 271.

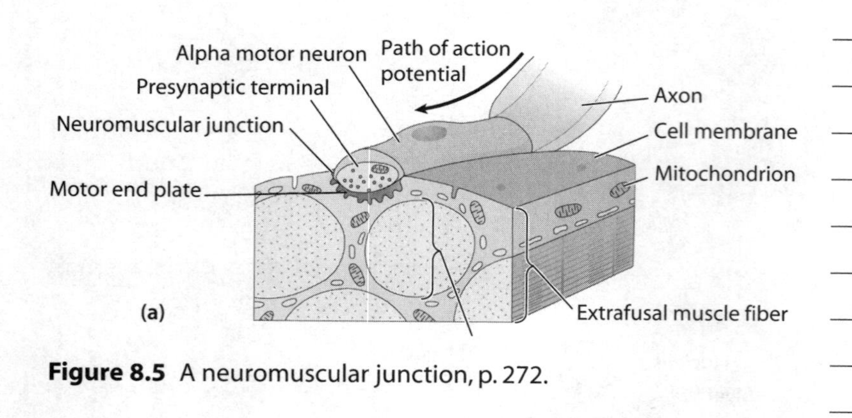

Figure 8.5 A neuromuscular junction, p. 272.

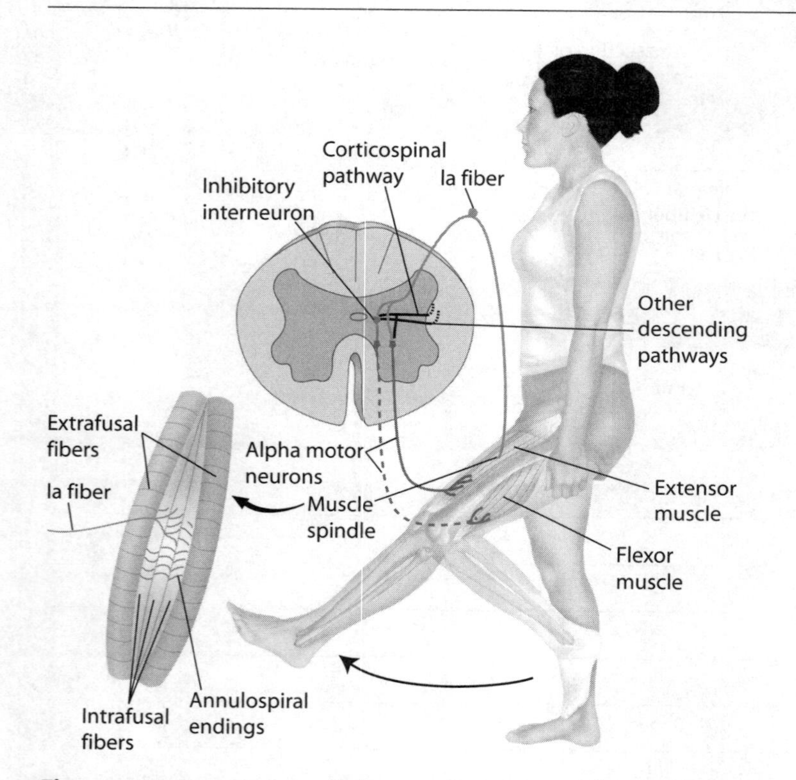

Figure 8.7 Components of the monosynaptic stretch reflex, p. 275.

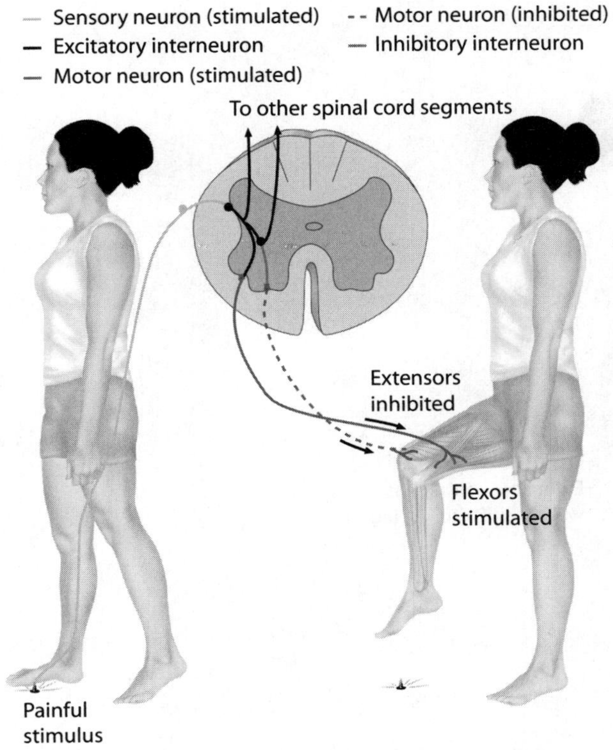

Figure 8.8 A polysynaptic reflex, p. 276.

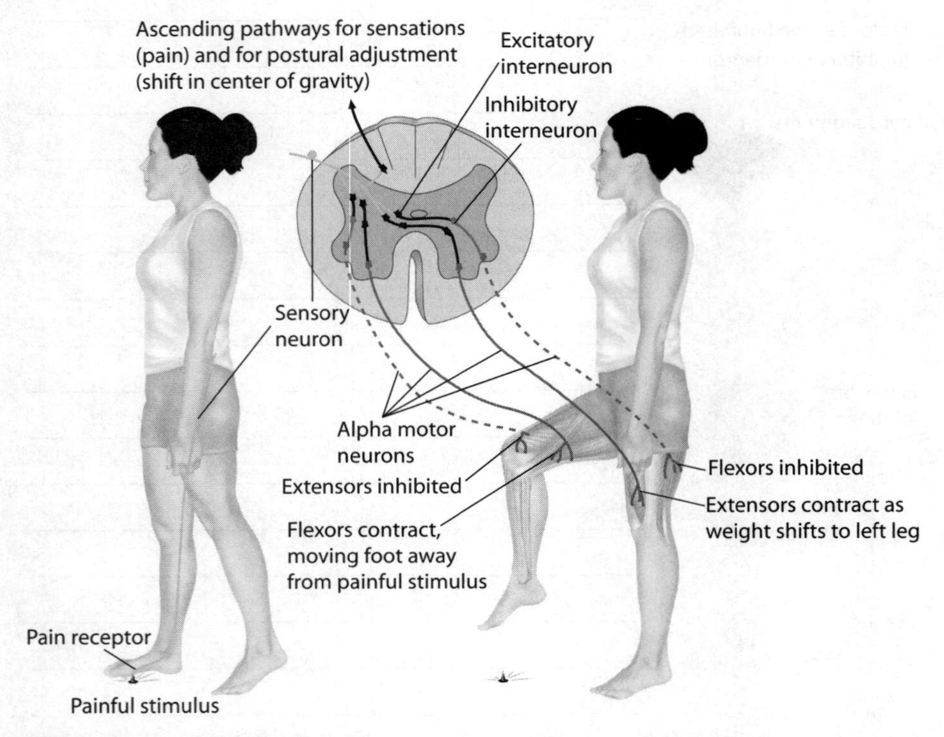

Figure 8.11 Neural control of opposing muscle pairs, p. 279.

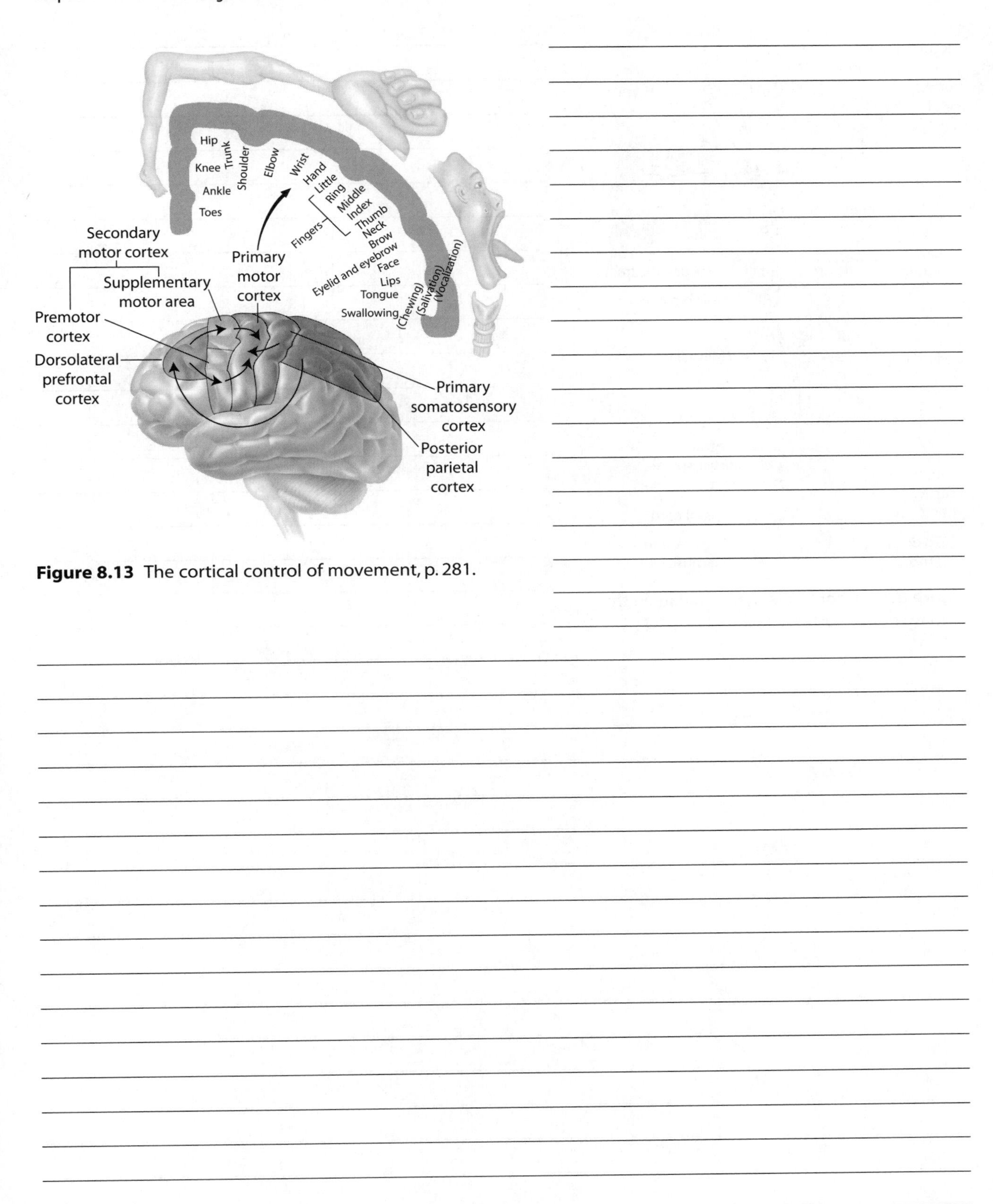

Figure 8.13 The cortical control of movement, p. 281.

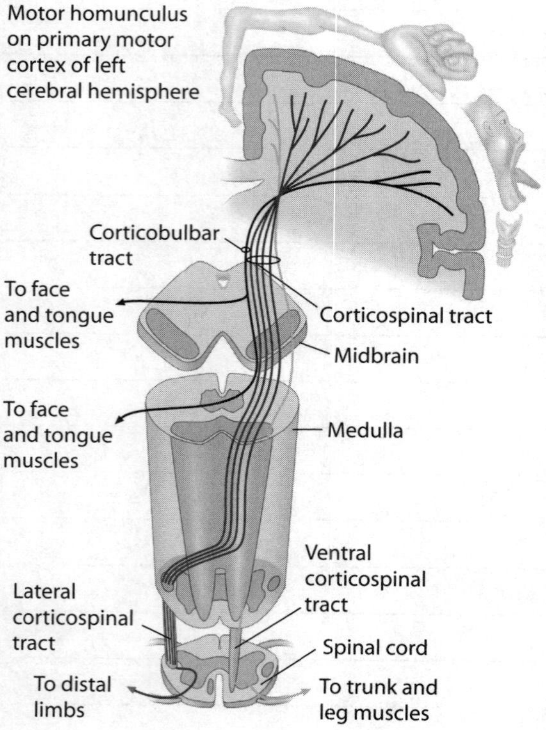

Figure 8.15 Fiber tracts that originate in the primary motor cortex, p. 288.

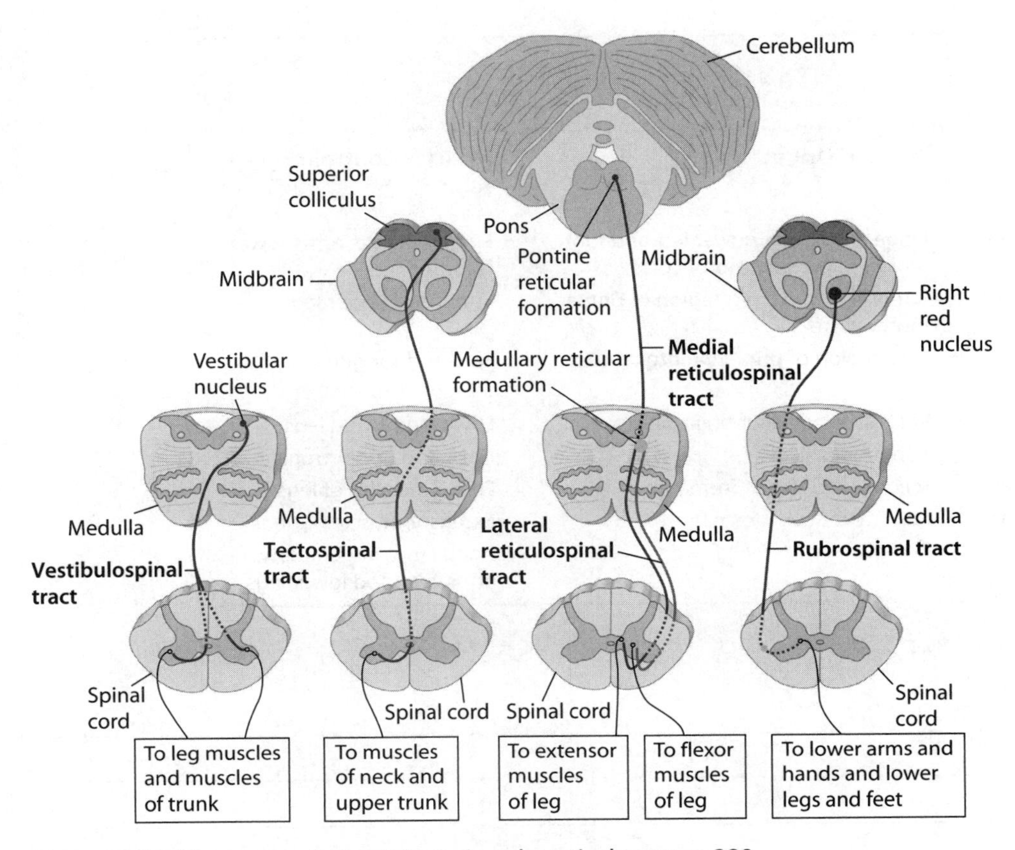

Figure 8.16 Fiber tracts that originate in subcortical areas, p. 289.

Table 8.1
Major Motor Pathways

Motor Tract	Point of Origin	Muscles Controlled
Corticospinal Tracts		
Lateral corticospinal tract	Finger, hand, arm, lower leg, and foot region of primary motor cortex	Fingers, hands, arms, lower legs, and feet
Ventral corticospinal tract	Trunk and upper leg region of primary motor cortex	Trunk and upper legs
Corticobulbar Tract	Face region of primary motor cortex	Face and tongue
Ventromedial Tracts		
Vestibulospinal tract	Vestibular nuclei of brain stem	Lower trunk and legs
Tectospinal tract	Superior colliculi	Neck and upper trunk
Lateral reticulospinal tract	Medullary reticular formation	Flexor muscles of legs
Medial reticulospinal tract	Pontine reticular formation	Extensor muscles of legs
Rubrospinal tract	Red nucleus	Hands (not fingers), lower arms, feet, and lower legs

Table 8.1 Major Motor Pathways, p. 290.

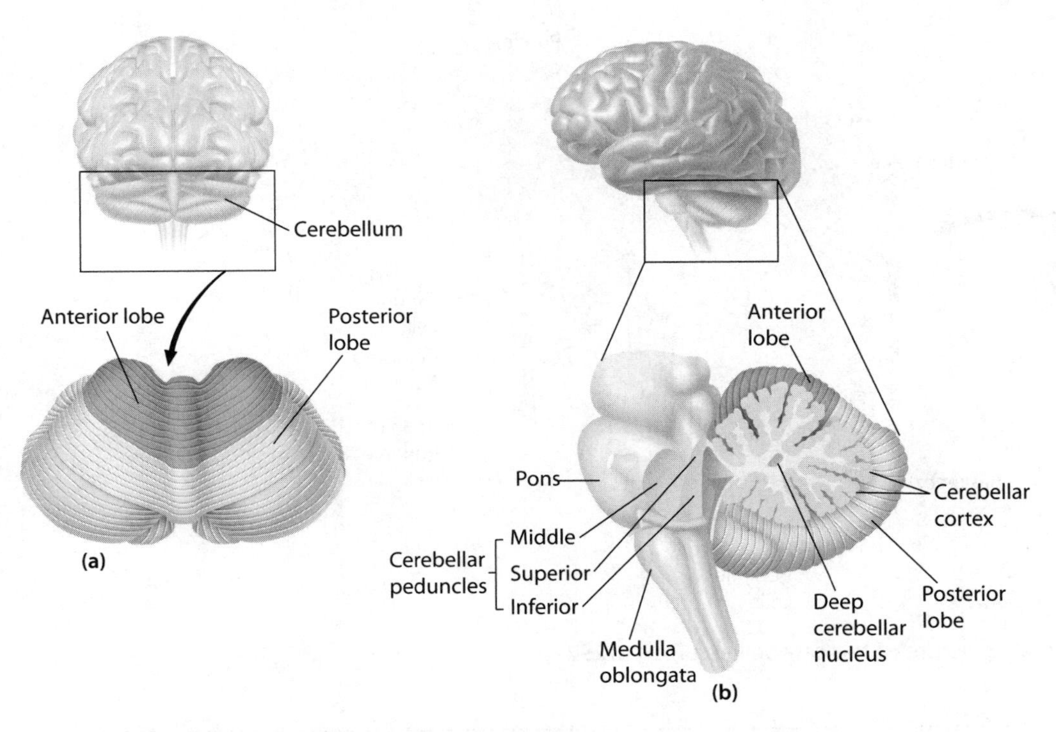

Figure 8.17 Key structures of the cerebellum, p. 291.

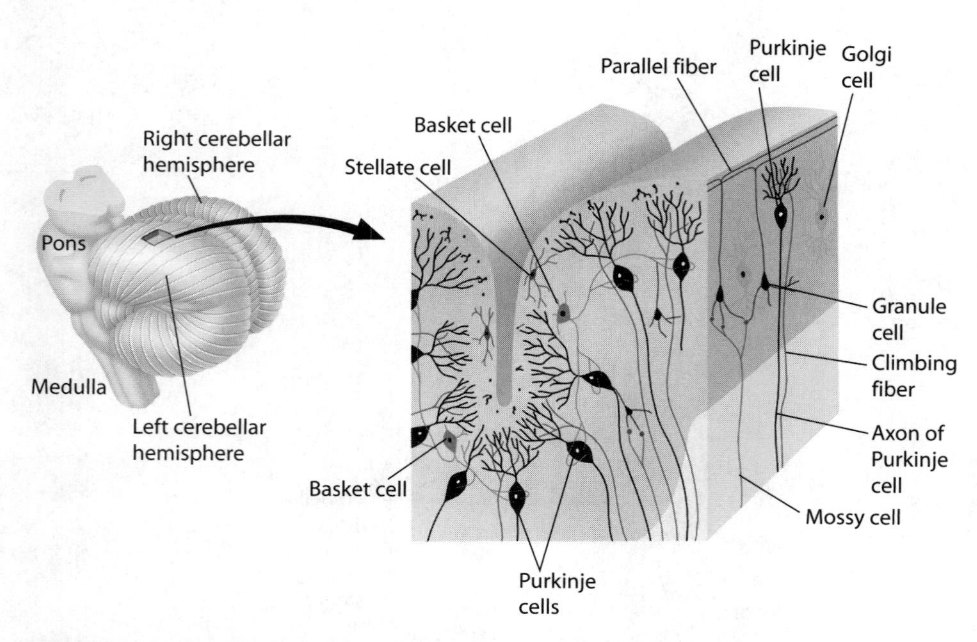

Figure 8.18 The cellular structure of the cerebellar cortex, p. 292.

CHAPTER SUMMARY

Movement refers to a change in the place or position of the body or any part of the body. In some cases, the spinal cord alone controls movement; in others, movement involves higher brain structures, including the cerebral cortex (dorsolateral prefrontal cortex, secondary motor cortex, primary motor cortex, posterior parietal cortex, and somatosensory cortex), the basal ganglia, and the cerebellum. There are three types of muscle tissue in the body: smooth muscles, cardiac muscles, and skeletal muscles. Skeletal muscles are attached to bones by tendons and bones move when skeletal muscles contract. A skeletal muscle contains many muscle fibers composed of myofibrils, which, in turn, consist of sarcomeres (myosin and actin proteins). There are three types of muscles (slow-twitch, fast-twitch, and intermediate-twitch muscles), each of which produce contractions of varying speed and duration.

Although the brain controls many movements, most reflexes are produced by the spinal cord without involvement of the brain. Such reflexes include: the patellar reflex (knee-jerk reflex); the monosynaptic stretch reflex; the polysynaptic reflex; and the withdrawal reflex. To prevent bones from breaking and muscles from being damaged, the Golgi tendon organs are activated when a muscle exerts too much force and acts to reduce the contraction of the extrafusal muscle fibers, decreasing the force the muscle exerts on the tendon and bone.

Several brain structures are involved in the control of movement. The dorsolateral prefrontal cortex and secondary motor cortex plan and prepare for voluntary movements. The primary motor cortex receives information from the primary somatosensory cortex about the current state of the motor system and plays a major role in initiating voluntary movement, including the precise movement of the hands and mouth. The primary motor cortex and somatosensory cortex are collectively referred to as the sensorimotor cortex. The posterior parietal cortex integrates input from the visual, auditory, and skin senses and relays it to the dorsolateral prefrontal cortex.

There are several fiber tracts in the motor pathway of these brain structures. The corticospinal tract controls the fingers, hands, arms, trunk, legs, and feet. The corticobulbar tract controls movements of the face and tongue. The vestibulospinal tract controls lower trunk and leg movements and plays a central role in posture. The tectospinal tract controls the upper trunk and neck and coordinates head and trunk movements. The lateral reticulospinal tract activates the flexor muscles of the legs, while the medial reticulospinal tract controls the extensor muscles of the legs. The rubrospinal tract controls movements of the hands (but not the fingers), lower arms, legs, and feet. The cerebellum also controls many body movements, in particular, rapid, coordinated responses or habits (i.e., ballistic movements). It also plays a central role in motor learning, which is accompanied by structural changes, including the establishment of motor circuits. Individuals with cerebellar damage can have the following: difficulty maintaining a stable posture; movements such as walking unsteady; slurred speech; uncoordinated eye movements; and difficulty focusing on an object.

The basal ganglia, made up of the caudate nucleus, putamen, and globus pallidus, is involved in integrating movement, controlling postural adjustments and muscle tone, and may be involved in selecting appropriate actions. Damage to the motor system can result in severe motor impairments such as that seen in Parkinson's disease and Huntington's disease. The motor impairments of Parkinson's disease include: muscle tremors; slowed movement (bradykinesia); impaired posture; increasing rigidity of the limbs; and festination. Huntington's disease is characterized by a slow, progressive deterioration of motor control, cognition, and emotion.

KEY TERMS

The following is a list of important terms introduced in Chapter 8. Give the definition of each term in the space provided.

actin

alpha motor neuron

amyotrophic lateral sclerosis (ALS)

annulospiral ending

apraxia

apraxia of speech

ballistic movement

basal ganglia

basket cell

bradykinesia

cerebral palsy

constructional apraxia

contralateral neglect

corpus striatum

corticobulbar tract

corticospinal tract

deep cerebellar nucleus

dorsolateral prefrontal cortex

extensor muscle

extrafusal muscle fiber

fast-twitch muscle

festination

flexor muscle

gamma motor neuron

Golgi tendon organ

Huntington's disease

Ia fiber

Ib fiber

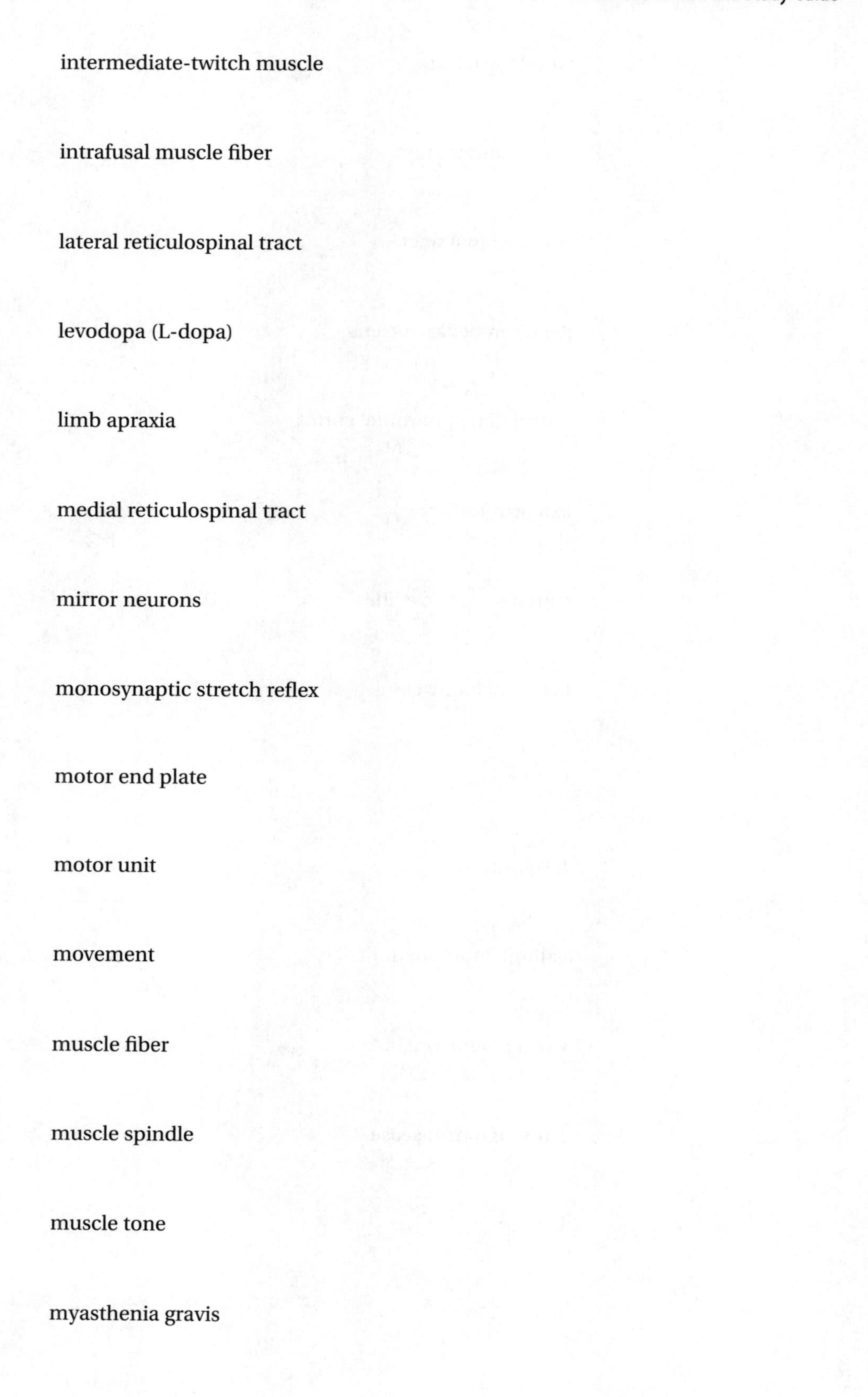

intermediate-twitch muscle

intrafusal muscle fiber

lateral reticulospinal tract

levodopa (L-dopa)

limb apraxia

medial reticulospinal tract

mirror neurons

monosynaptic stretch reflex

motor end plate

motor unit

movement

muscle fiber

muscle spindle

muscle tone

myasthenia gravis

myofibril

myofilament

myosin

neuromuscular junction

pallidotomy

Parkinson's disease

patellar reflex

polysynaptic reflex

posterior parietal cortex

precentral gyrus

premotor cortex

primary motor cortex

Purkinje cell

pyramidal cell

Renshaw cell

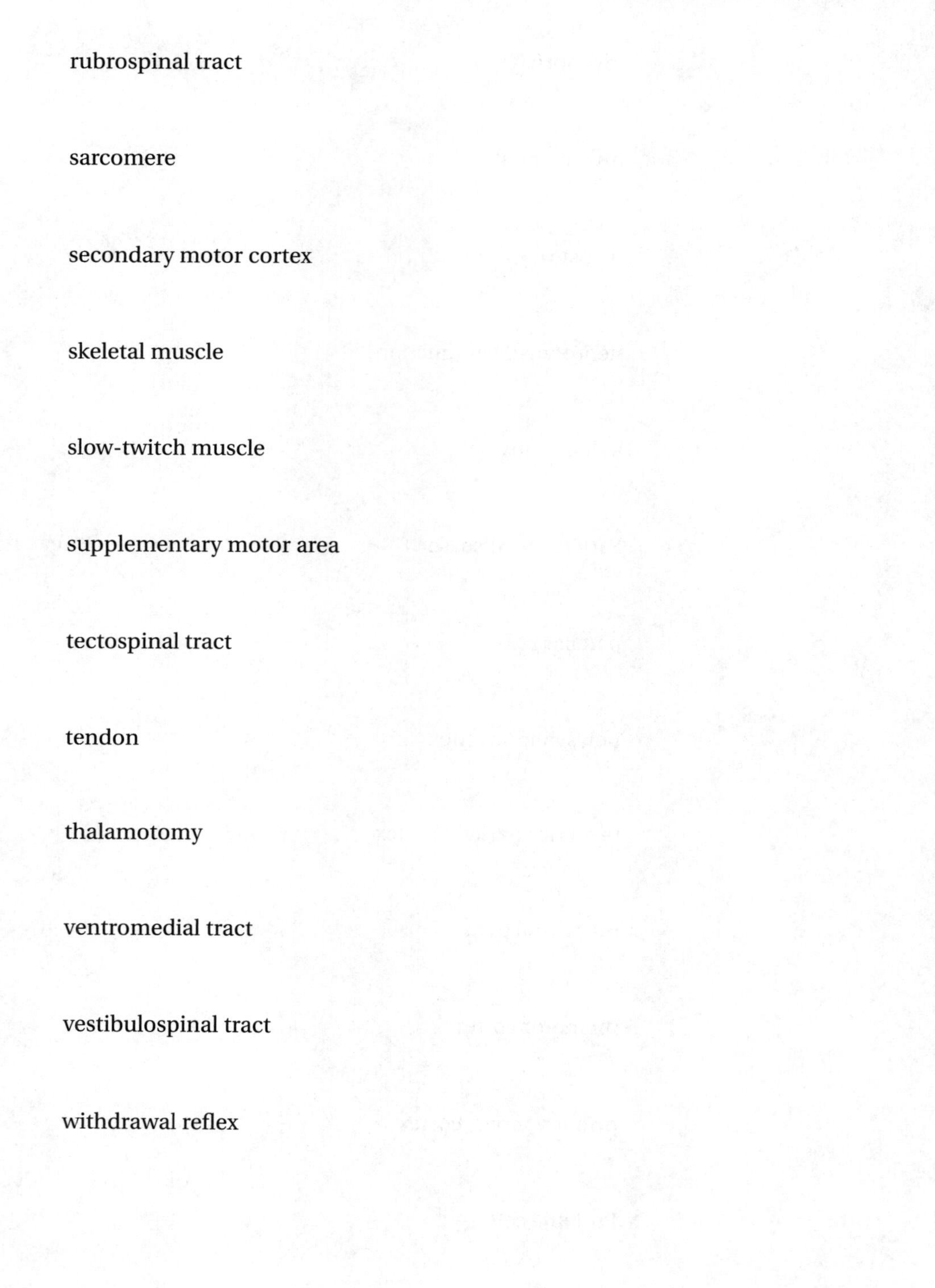

rubrospinal tract

sarcomere

secondary motor cortex

skeletal muscle

slow-twitch muscle

supplementary motor area

tectospinal tract

tendon

thalamotomy

ventromedial tract

vestibulospinal tract

withdrawal reflex

◆ LABELING EXERCISES

1. The cortical structures involved in the control of movement are shown in the figure below. Label the following areas:

posterior parietal cortex	supplementary motor area
primary motor cortex	dorsolateral prefrontal cortex
secondary motor cortex	premotor cortex
primary somatosensory cortex	

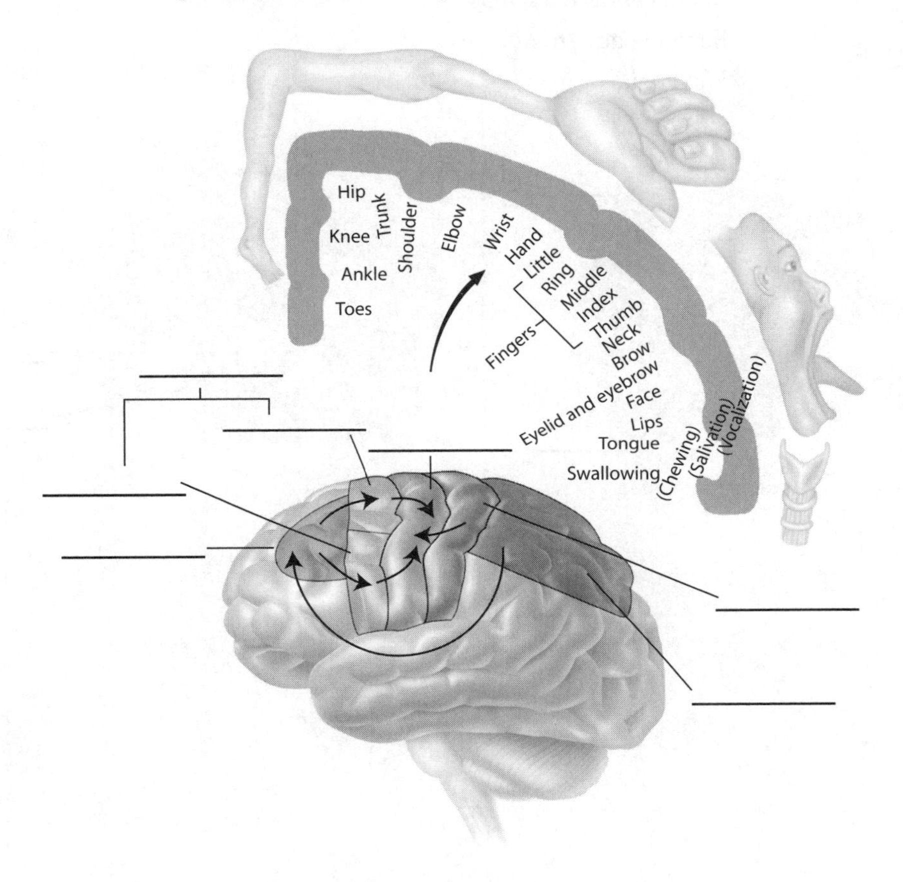

2. The structures of the basal ganglia are important in the control of movement. In both figures below, identify the following structures:

caudate nucleus

globulus pallidus *(place label once in each figure)*

putamen *(place label once in each figure)*

corpus callosum

thalamus

tail of caudate nucleus

head of caudate nucleus

amygdala

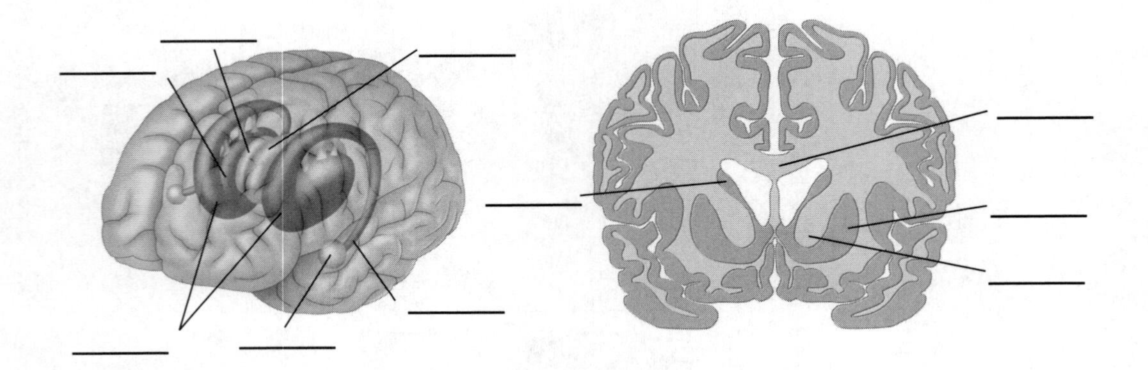

Wakefulness and Sleep

9

◆ CHAPTER ART LECTURE NOTEBOOK

The following is a selection of the important figures and tables introduced in Chapter 9. You can take notes during class in the space provided.

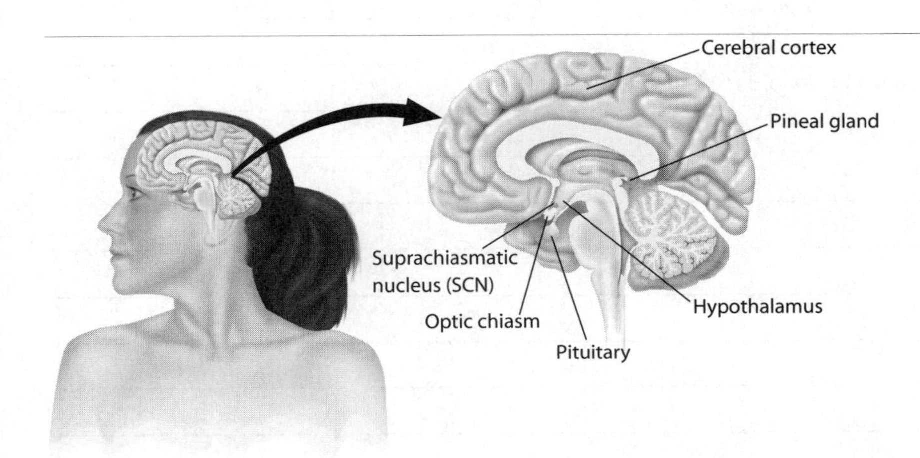

Figure 9.2 A sagittal view of the suprachiasmatic nucleus (SCN) and the pineal gland in the human brain, p. 309.

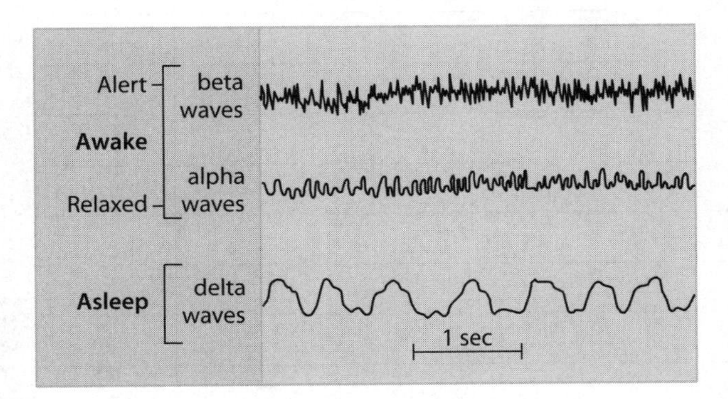

Figure 9.7 Three distinct EEG patterns, p. 316.

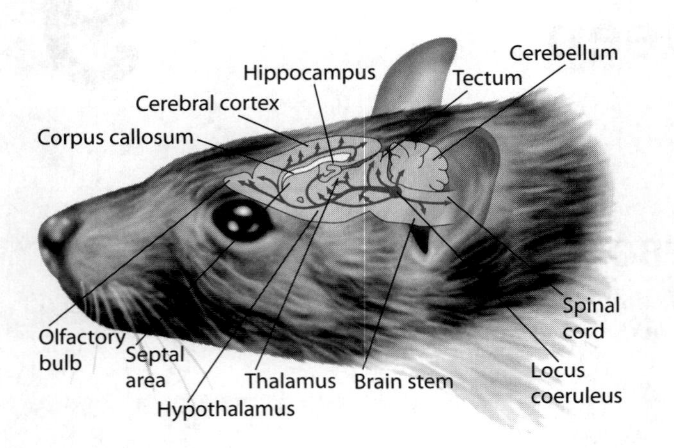

Figure 9.10 The locus coeruleus in a rat brain, p. 316.

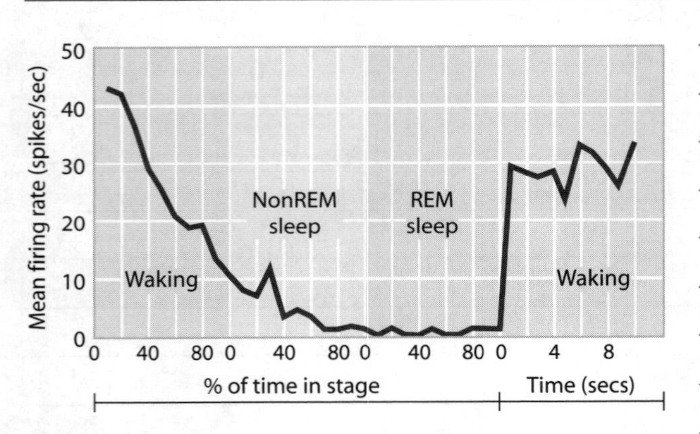

Figure 9.11 Locus coeruleus activity during wakefulness and sleep in a rat, p. 318.

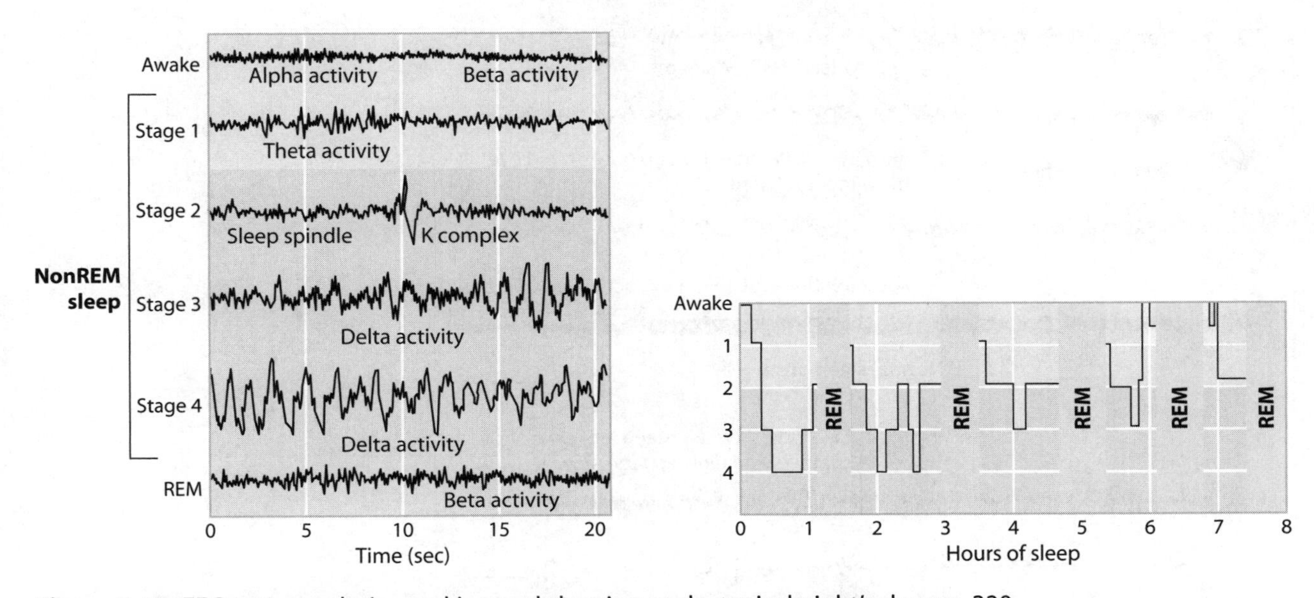

Figure 9.13 EEG patterns during waking and sleeping, and a typical night's sleep, p. 320.

Table 9.2
Hypotheses of the Function of Dreams

View	Central Idea
Freudian	Dreams represent acceptable release of sexual and aggressive instincts.
Cognitive	Dreams are a way to deal with life's problems, perhaps by previewing them. Also, dreams are involved in memory storage.
Activation-Synthesis	Dreams have no inherent meaning and result from mental interpretation of neural activity during sleep.

Table 9.2 Hypotheses of the Function of Dreams, p. 328.

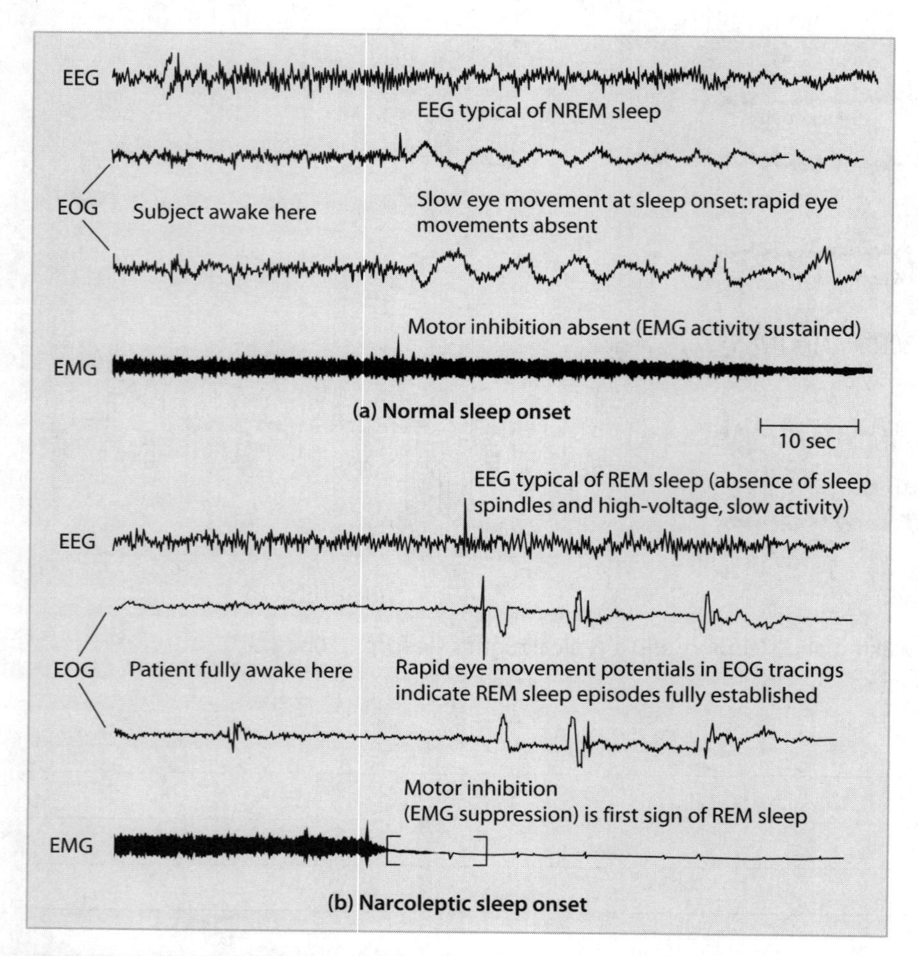

Figure 9.21 Narcolepsy and sleep onset, p. 334.

CHAPTER SUMMARY

Biological rhythms cause us to sleep and awaken at certain times. The circadian rhythm regulates biological and behavioral changes during a 24 hour circadian cycle. The circadian cycle is controlled by the suprachiasmatic nucleus (SCN), which, without external light cues, sets a circadian cycle of 25 (or more) hours. The SCN can be reset by using light therapy. Different levels of arousal are characterized by different EEG patterns. When we are awake and active, our brain wave EEG shows beta activity (rapid, desynchronized patterns of change). When we are relaxed, we display alpha activity (brain waves are larger and more synchronized).

During sleep, two distinct phases are experienced: nonREM (NREM) and rapid eye movement (REM) sleep. NREM sleep is characterized by high-amplitude, slow-wave, synchronized EEG patterns and includes four stages: stage 1 (characterized by theta activity); stage 2 (characterized by theta activity, sleep spindles, and K complexes); stage 3 (characterized by the addition of delta activity); and stage 4 (characterized by predominantly delta activity). REM sleep is characterized by low-amplitude, fast-wave EEG activity, with rapid lateral eye movements and loss of muscle tone. Because the EEG activity resembles that of the waking state, REM sleep is also referred to as paradoxical sleep.

There are three views regarding the function of sleep. The restorative view suggests that sleep acts to restore the biological reserves depleted during the day. Another view is that sleep is important for brain plasticity and, in adults, for learning and memory. The evolutionary view suggests that sleep enhances the survival of a species by keeping animals inactive, and therefore conserving energy, during the hours when food is scarce and there is more danger from predators.

NREM and REM sleep are each controlled by different mechanisms. NREM sleep is maintained by the raphé nuclei. The basal forebrain region, which includes the preoptic area, has also been shown to induce NREM sleep. REM sleep is initiated by the activation of the caudal reticular formation, whose inhibition is removed by a decrease in locus coeruleus activity. Activity in the locus coeruleus is associated with an absence of REM sleep (REM sleep occurs when the locus coeruleus is not active).

REM sleep is association with dreaming. Several hypotheses have been proposed to explain why we dream. The Freudian theory suggests that dreams represent an acceptable release of sexual and aggressive instincts. The cognitive perspective suggests that dreams represent a means of solving problems we may be facing in our lives. This view also suggests that dreams may help store certain memories and discard others. In contrast to these hypotheses, the activation-synthesis theory proposes that dreams have no inherent meaning and, instead, result from mental interpretations of the random neural activity that occurs during sleep.

Most sleep disorders can be categorized into two broad categories: insomnia and hypersomnia. Insomnia is characterized by a long-term inability to obtain adequate sleep. Sleep apnea is a type of insomnia in which sleep is repeatedly interrupted by the cessation of breathing. Hypersomnia is characterized by too much sleep and consists of two categories: NREM and REM sleep disorders. NREM sleep disorders include sleepwalking, night terrors, and bedwetting. REM sleep disorders include narcolepsy and REM behavior disorder.

KEY TERMS

The following is a list of important terms introduced in Chapter 9. Give the definition of each term in the space provided.

activation-synthesis theory

alpha activity

basal forebrain region

bedwetting

beta activity

cataplexy

caudal reticular formation

cerveau isolé preparation

circadian cycle

circadian rhythm

cognitive perspective

delta activity

diurnal animal

dream

drug-dependent insomnia

encéphale isolé preparation

free-running rhythm

hypersomnia

insomnia

jet lag

K complex

lark

light therapy

locus coeruleus

lucid dream

melatonin

microsleep

narcolepsy

night terror

nocturnal animal

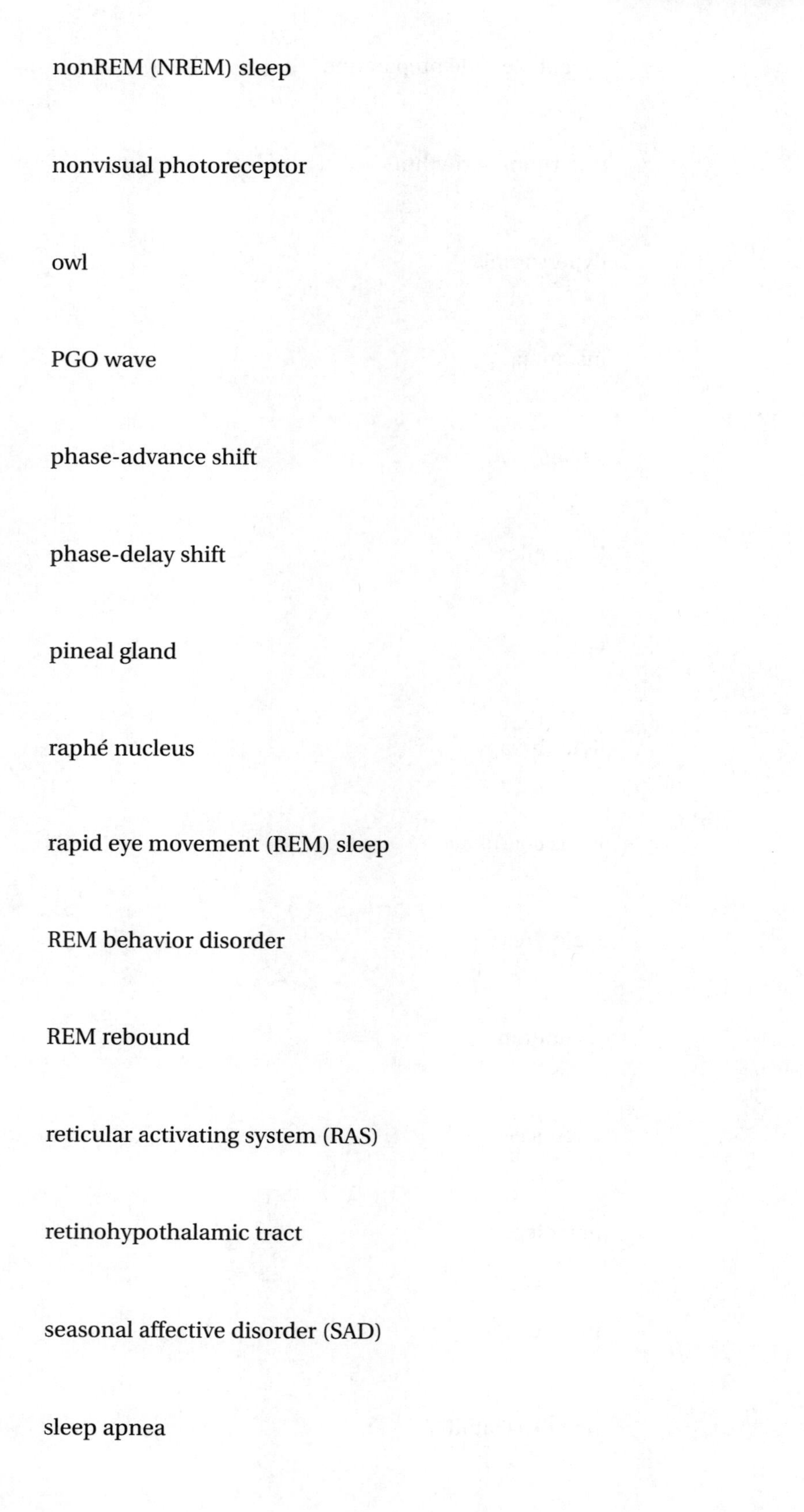

nonREM (NREM) sleep

nonvisual photoreceptor

owl

PGO wave

phase-advance shift

phase-delay shift

pineal gland

raphé nucleus

rapid eye movement (REM) sleep

REM behavior disorder

REM rebound

reticular activating system (RAS)

retinohypothalamic tract

seasonal affective disorder (SAD)

sleep apnea

sleep paralysis

sleep spindle

sleepwalking

slow-wave sleep (SWS)

stage 1 sleep

stage 2 sleep

stage 3 sleep

stage 4 sleep

suprachiasmatic nucleus (SCN)

theta activity

visual photoreceptor

zeitgeber

Labeling Exercises

1. The suprachiasmatic nucleus (SCN) and the pineal gland are important in the regulation of the sleep-wake cycle. Locate the following structures in the figure below:

pineal gland	cerebral cortex
suprachiasmatic nucleus (SCN)	hypothalamus
pituitary	optic chiasm

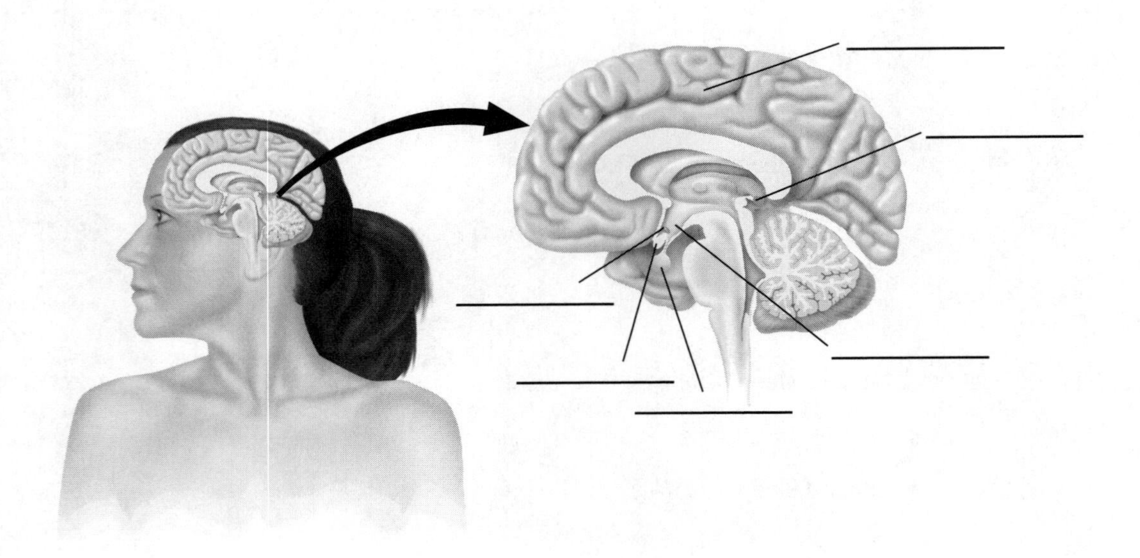

The Biology of Eating and Drinking

CHAPTER ART LECTURE NOTEBOOK

The following is a selection of the important figures and tables introduced in Chapter 10. You can take notes during class in the space provided.

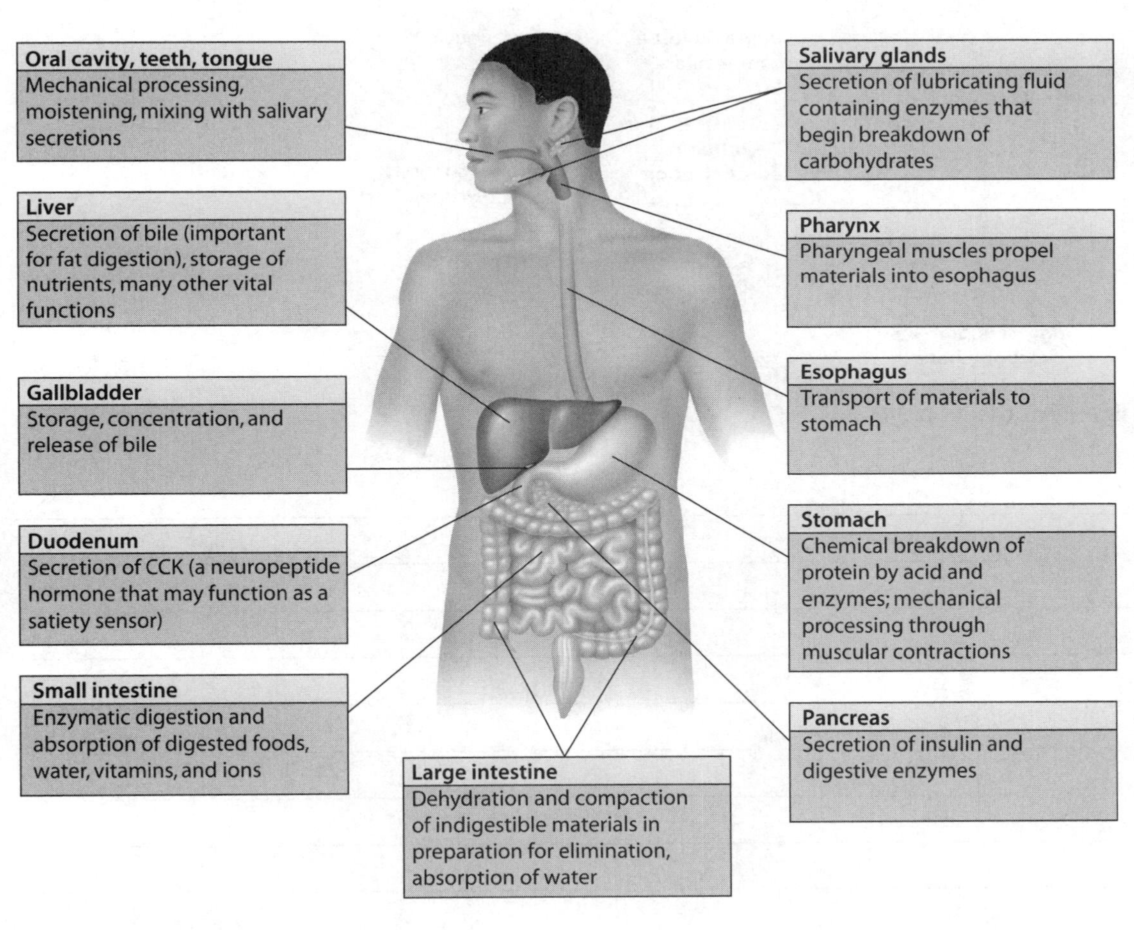

Figure 10.1 The digestive system, p. 343.

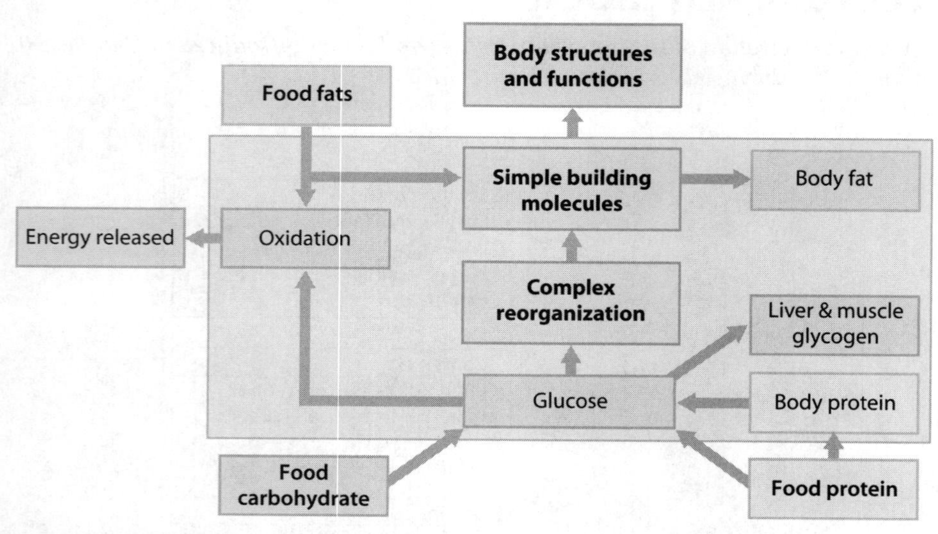

Figure 10.2 Energy nutrients, p. 343.

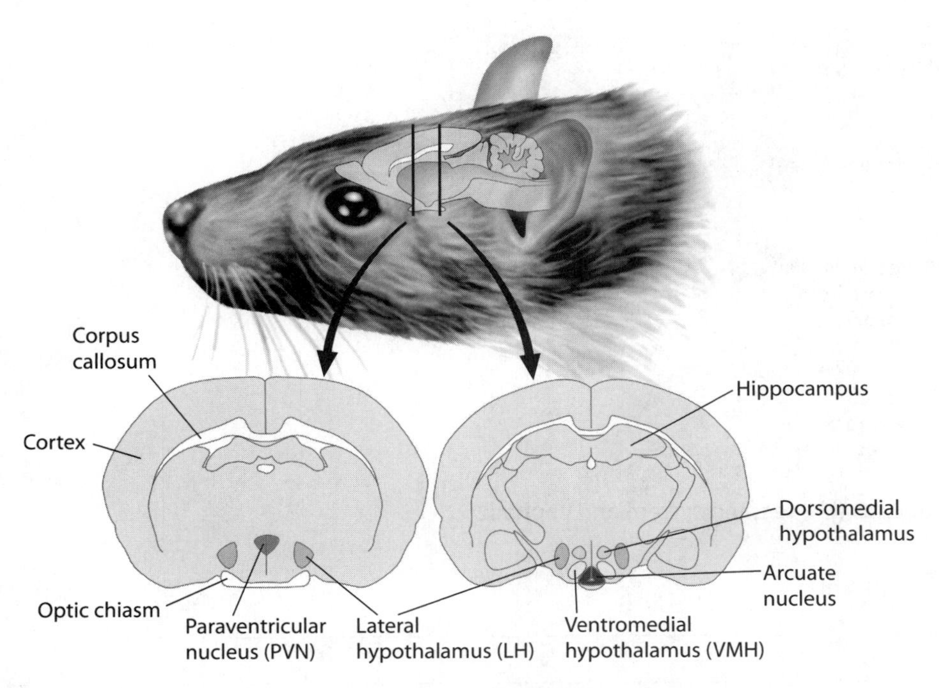

Figure 10.3 The hypothalamus and eating behavior, p. 344.

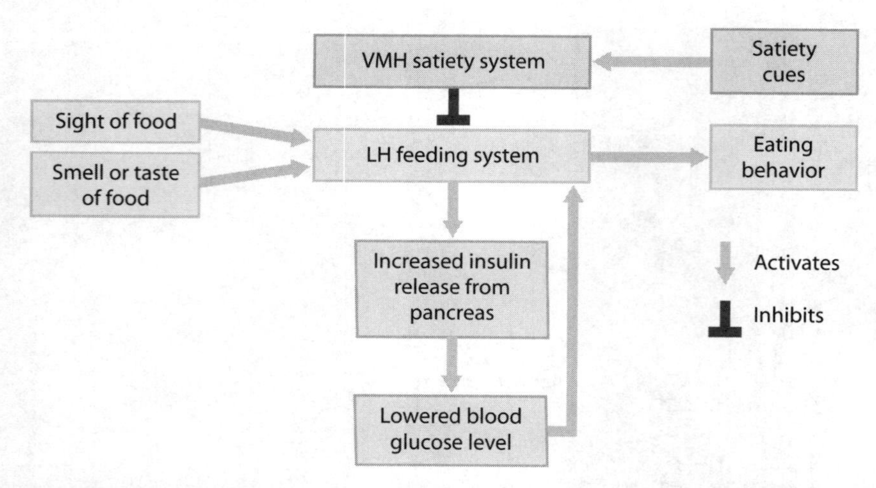

Figure 10.5 The lateral hypothalamus (LH) feeding system and cephalic reflexes, p. 347.

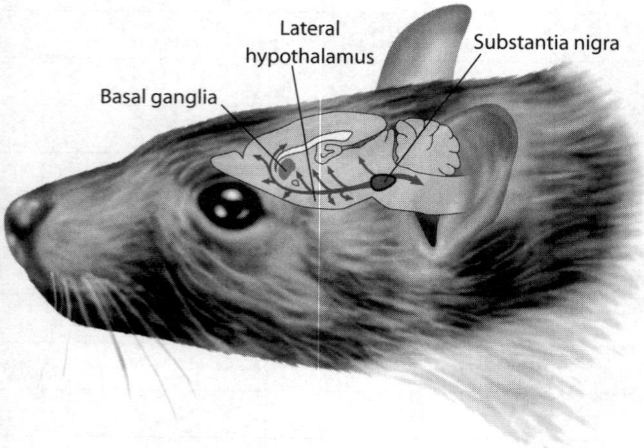

Figure 10.6 The nigrostriatal system of the rat brain, p. 349.

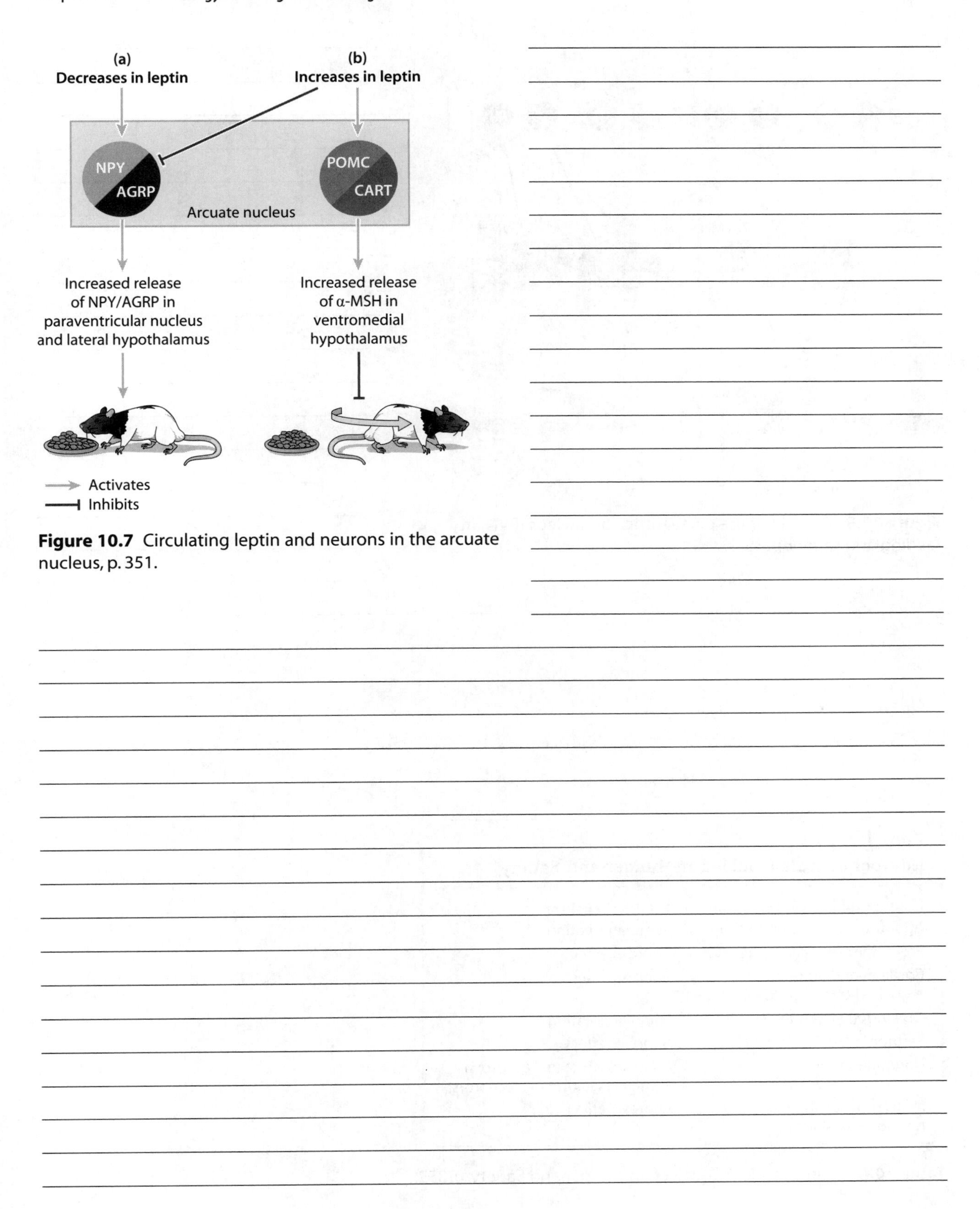

Figure 10.7 Circulating leptin and neurons in the arcuate nucleus, p. 351.

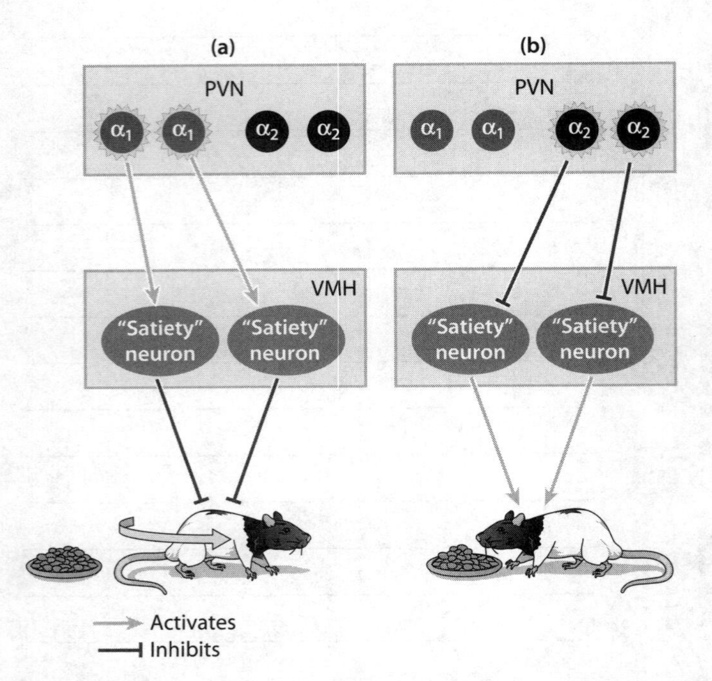

Figure 10.8 The role of the paraventricular nucleus (PVN) in feeding and satiety, p. 351.

Table 10.4

Neurochemicals Involved in Hunger and Satiety

Neuropeptide Y (NPY)	Stimulates eating
Agouti-related protein (AGRP)	Stimulates eating
Pro-opiomelanocortin (POMC)	Anorexic effect
Cocaine- and amphetamine-regulated transcript (CART)	Anorexic effect
Orexin-A (hypocretin-1)	Stimulates eating
Serotonin (5-HT)	Anorexic effect
Norepinephrine	Anorexic effect (α_1 receptors) Stimulates eating (α_2 receptors)
α-Melanocyte-stimulating hormone (α-MSH)	Anorexic effect

Table 10.4 Neurochemicals Involved in Hunger and Satiety, p. 352.

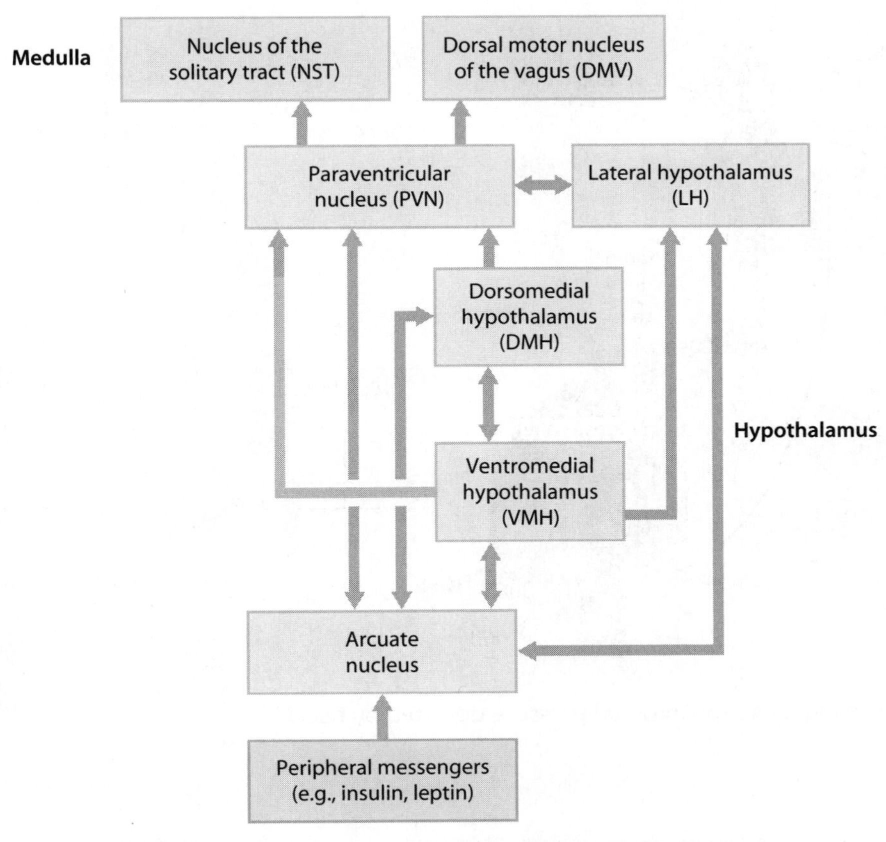

Figure 10.9 Hypothalamic nuclei involved in feeding and satiety, p. 353.

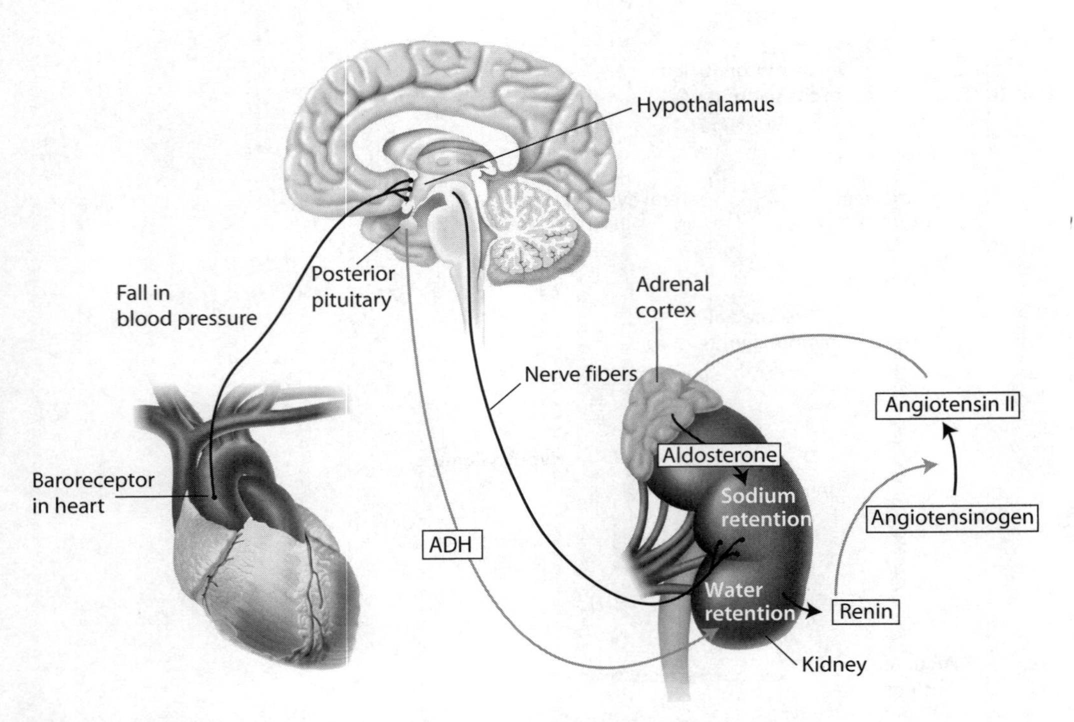

Figure 10.22 Hormonal changes initiated by a drop in blood pressure detected by heart baroreceptors, p. 377.

CHAPTER SUMMARY

The main function of eating is to regulate energy balance and maintain an optimal body weight. The operation of our biological functions requires energy from three types of nutritional substances: carbohydrates, fats, and proteins. Early research on the brain's control of hunger and satiety suggested that the lateral hypothalamus (LH) was involved in the initiation of eating, while the ventromedial hypothalamus (VMH) was involved in the inhibition of eating (satiety). Therefore, damage to the LH produces an animal that will not eat and damage to the VMH produces an animal that overeats. In addition to the LH and the VMH, the nigrostriatal pathway, which includes the substantia nigra, the lateral hypothalamus, and the basal ganglia, has been shown to be involved in hunger motivation. Research has also demonstrated that damage to the fiber tracts extending to the nucleus of the solitary tract and dorsal motor nucleus of the vagus from the paraventricular nucleus (PVN) can also cause the VMH-lesion syndrome.

Several neurotransmitters are involved in hunger and satiety, including norepinephrine, serotonin, and neuropeptide Y. Drug treatments for obesity that act on receptors for these neurotransmitters include drugs that reduce food intake (e.g., sibutramine), drugs that alter metabolism (e.g., olistat), and drugs that increase thermogenesis. Though the brain controls many aspects of eating, the mechanisms that initiate and suppress eating must rely on other biological systems for information regarding the nutritional condition of the body. Peripheral cues (i.e., oral sensations and stomach cues) are important in the control of hunger and satiety.

Metabolic cues, such as a deficiency in energy-rich substances, provide an explanation for the initiation of eating. The glucostatic theory suggests that the amount of sugar in the blood (blood glucose level) is involved in hunger, that is, hunger is caused by low blood glucose levels. Hormonal satiety cues also seem to be involved in hunger and satiety. The neuropeptide hormone cholecystokinin (CCK) may serve as a satiety sensor, monitoring food intake and inhibiting eating when a sufficient amount of food has been consumed. The gastrointestinal peptide ghrelin, however, appears to have an appetite-stimulating effect by stimulating neurons in the arcuate nucleus. Environmental cues, such as the sight and smell of food, also have an influence on eating behavior. This can be illustrated through classical conditioning by looking at conditioned hunger, conditioned satiety, and conditioned taste aversion.

There are two main theories as to how body weight is regulated over the long term. The lipostatic theory accounts for weight regulation with a mechanism based on fat deposits. The hormone leptin appears to provide feedback to the brain about the level of stored fat; low levels of leptin lead to an increase in hunger and food intake. The set-point theory proposes that animals maintain a constant body weight by having a critical level of stored fat. If the stored fat falls below the set point, the hunger system induces eating until the set point is reestablished. If the stored fat rises above the set point, the paraventricular system inhibits eating until the set point is reached. Incidences of eating disorders have become more prevalent, in part, as a result of society's obsession with thinness.

There are three major eating disorders: anorexia nervosa, bulimia nervosa, and binge eating disorder. Anorexia, most common in adolescent girls and young women, is characterized by self-starvation and a distorted body image. These individuals lose an average of 35% of their body weight, though they still feel and believe they look fat. Physiological effects of anorexia include loss of menstrual cycles, cardiac arrhythmias, and extremely low blood pressure. Bulimia is characterized by recurrent episodes of binge eating followed by purging (self-induced vomiting, use of laxatives, excessive exercise, and dieting). Physiological effects of bulimia can include tooth enamel erosion, chronic inflammation of the esophagus, cardiac arrhythmias, and cardiac arrest. Because people with bulimia tend to have a normal or slightly elevated weight, it is easier to hide than anorexia. Binge eating disorder is characterized by recurrent episodes of binge eating without the use of purging or other weight-loss measures.

The human body is made up of about 70% water. Eating salty foods increases the concentration of salt in extracellular fluid, increasing osmotic pressure and causing water to move out of the cells. This cellular dehydration produces osmotic thirst. Loss of extracellular fluid (through sweating, diarrhea, or bleeding) causes hypovolemic thirst, lowering blood pressure and leading to increased levels of angiotensin and aldosterone. Both of these types of thirst stimulate the release of ADH from the pituitary gland, which acts on the kidneys to conserve water and causes drinking behavior.

◆ KEY TERMS

The following is a list of important terms introduced in Chapter 10. Give the definition of each term in the space provided.

adipsia

aldosterone

allostasis

allostatic load

angiotensin

anorexia nervosa

antidiuretic hormone (ADH)

aphagia

arcuate nucleus

binge eating disorder

bulimia nervosa

cephalic reflex

cholecystokinin (CCK)

conditioned hunger

conditioned satiety

critical set point

diabetes mellitus

dorsal motor nucleus of the vagus

fen-phen

ghrelin

glucagon

glucoprivation

glucoreceptor

glucostatic theory

homeostasis

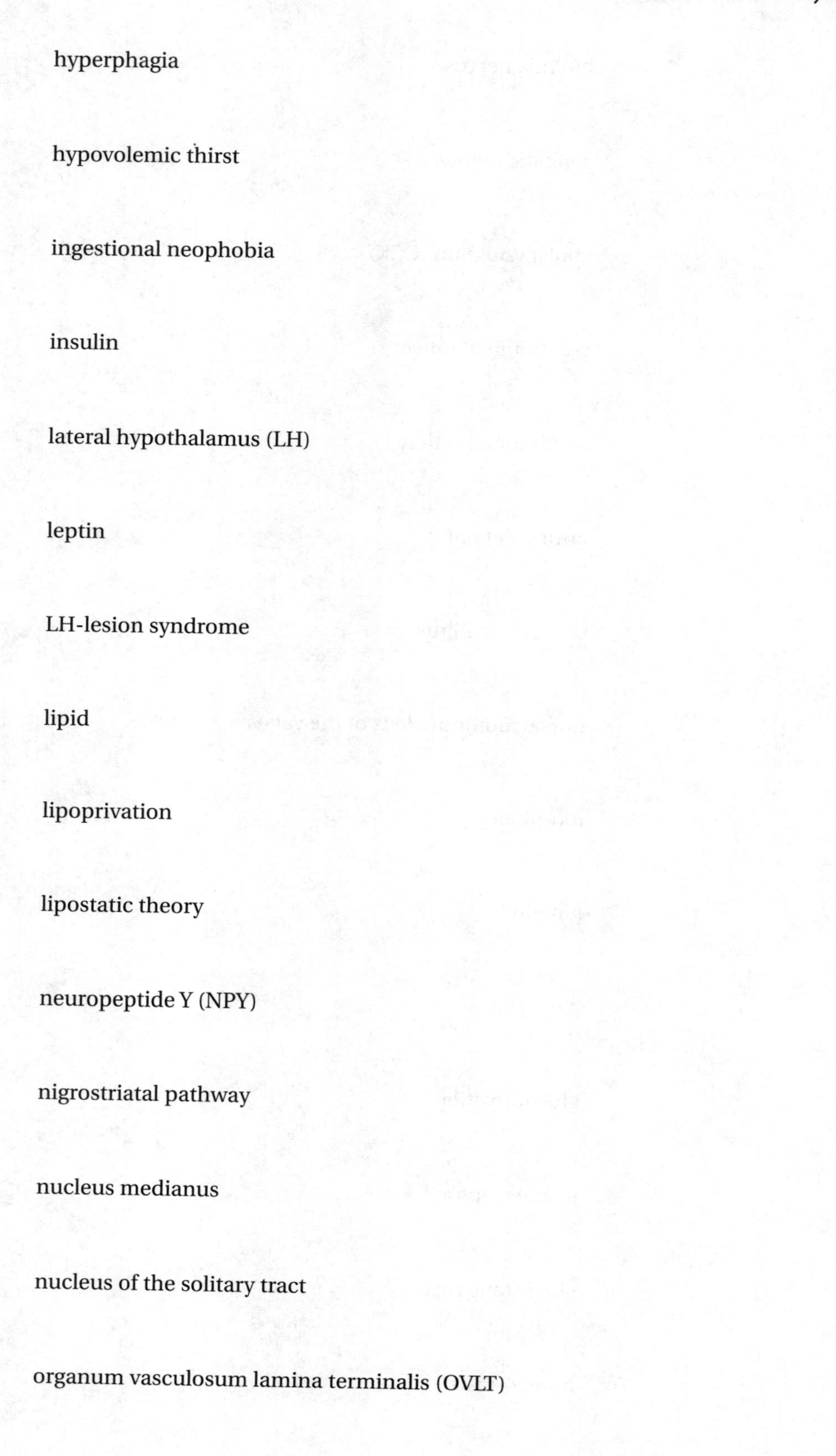

hyperphagia

hypovolemic thirst

ingestional neophobia

insulin

lateral hypothalamus (LH)

leptin

LH-lesion syndrome

lipid

lipoprivation

lipostatic theory

neuropeptide Y (NPY)

nigrostriatal pathway

nucleus medianus

nucleus of the solitary tract

organum vasculosum lamina terminalis (OVLT)

osmoreceptor

osmotic thirst

paraventricular nucleus (PVN)

prandial drinking

preloading

primary drinking

satiety

secondary drinking

subfornical organ (SFO)

ventromedial hypothalamus (VMH)

VMH-lesion syndrome

VMH paradox

LABELING EXERCISES

1. The hypothalamus is important in the control of hunger and satiety. In the figure below, areas of the hypothalamus are illustrated, as well as surrounding brain structures. Identify these structures:

cortex	dorsomedial hypothalamus
hippocampus	ventromedial hypothalamus (VMH)
arcuate nucleus	corpus callosum
paraventricular nucleus (PVN)	optic chiasm
lateral hypothalamus *(place two times)*	

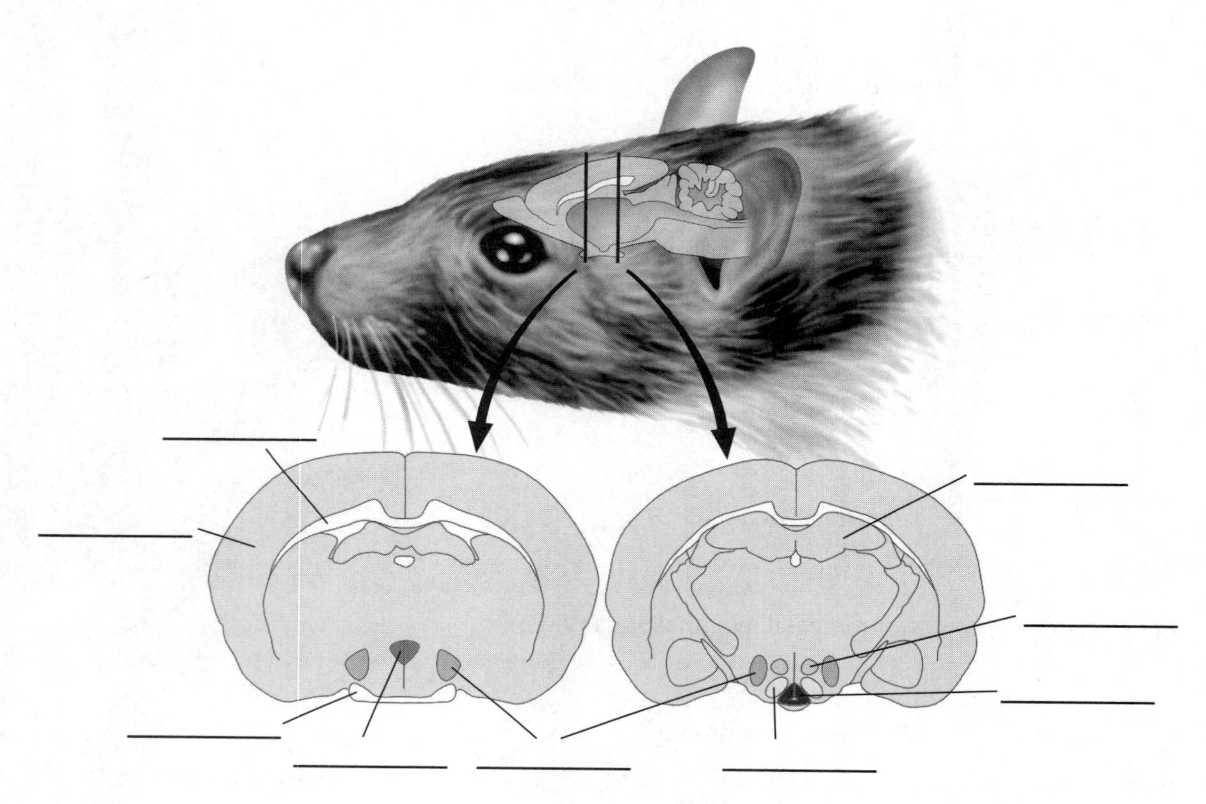

2. The figure below shows the location of osmoreceptors relative to other structures in the brain. Label the following structures:

subfornical organ (SFO)
organum vasculosum lamina terminalis (OVLT)
spinal cord
fourth ventricle
lateral ventricles
medulla oblongata
third ventricle
pons

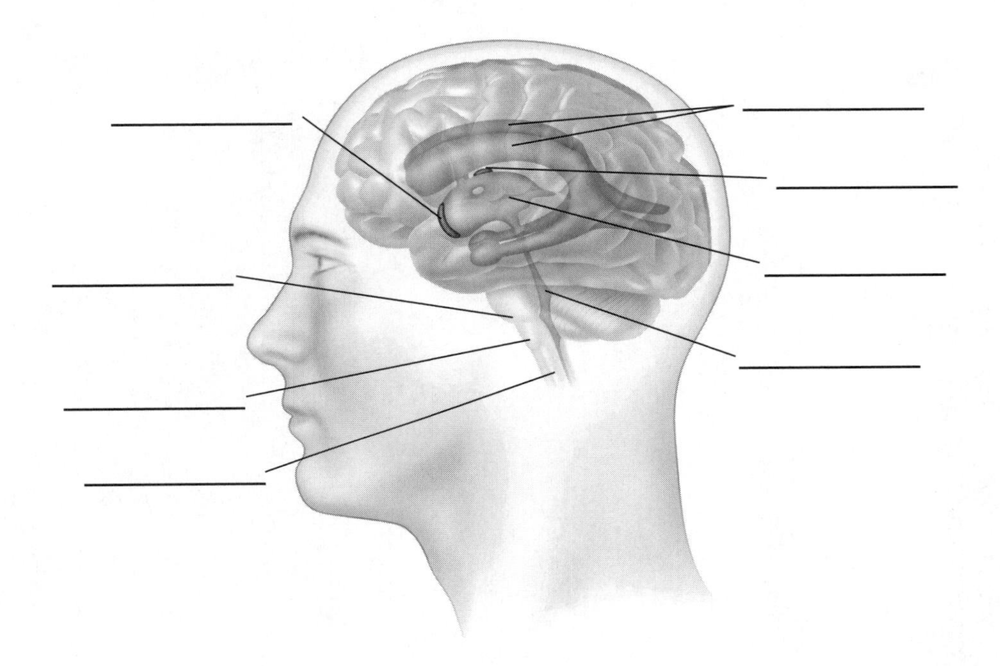

Sexual Development and Sexual Behavior

11

CHAPTER ART LECTURE NOTEBOOK

The following is a selection of the important figures introduced in Chapter 11. You can take notes during class in the space provided.

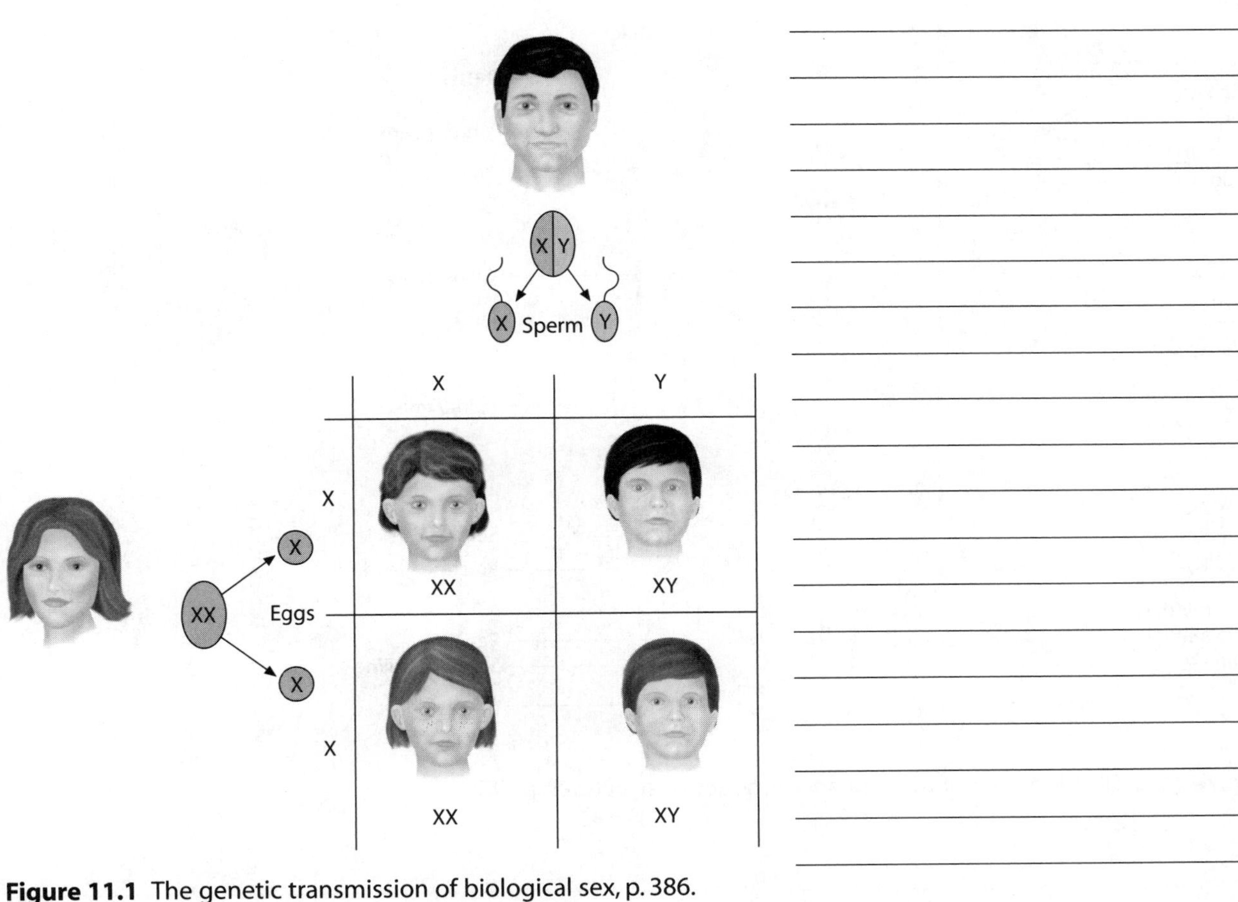

Figure 11.1 The genetic transmission of biological sex, p. 386.

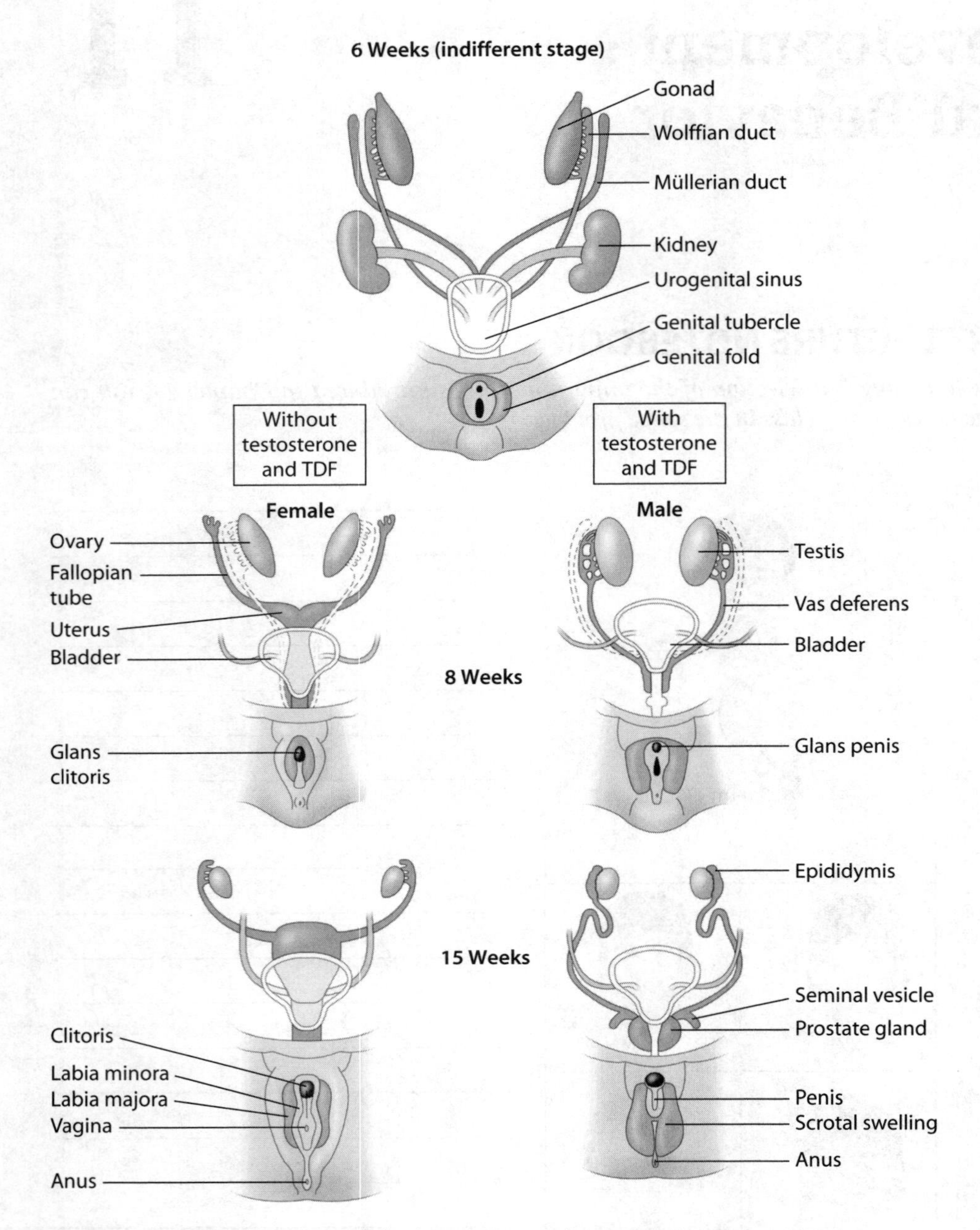

Figure 11.2 Development of the human reproductive structures, p. 387.

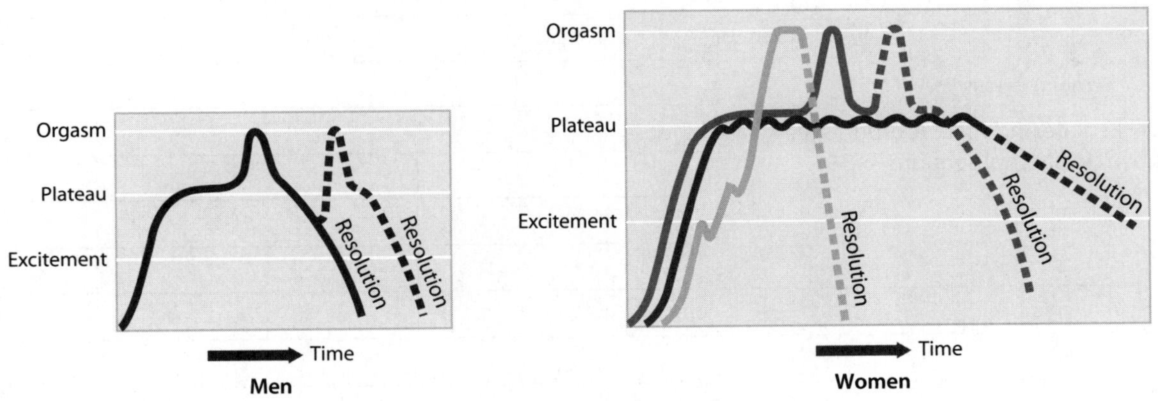

Figure 11.6 The four phases of the human sexual response, p. 395.

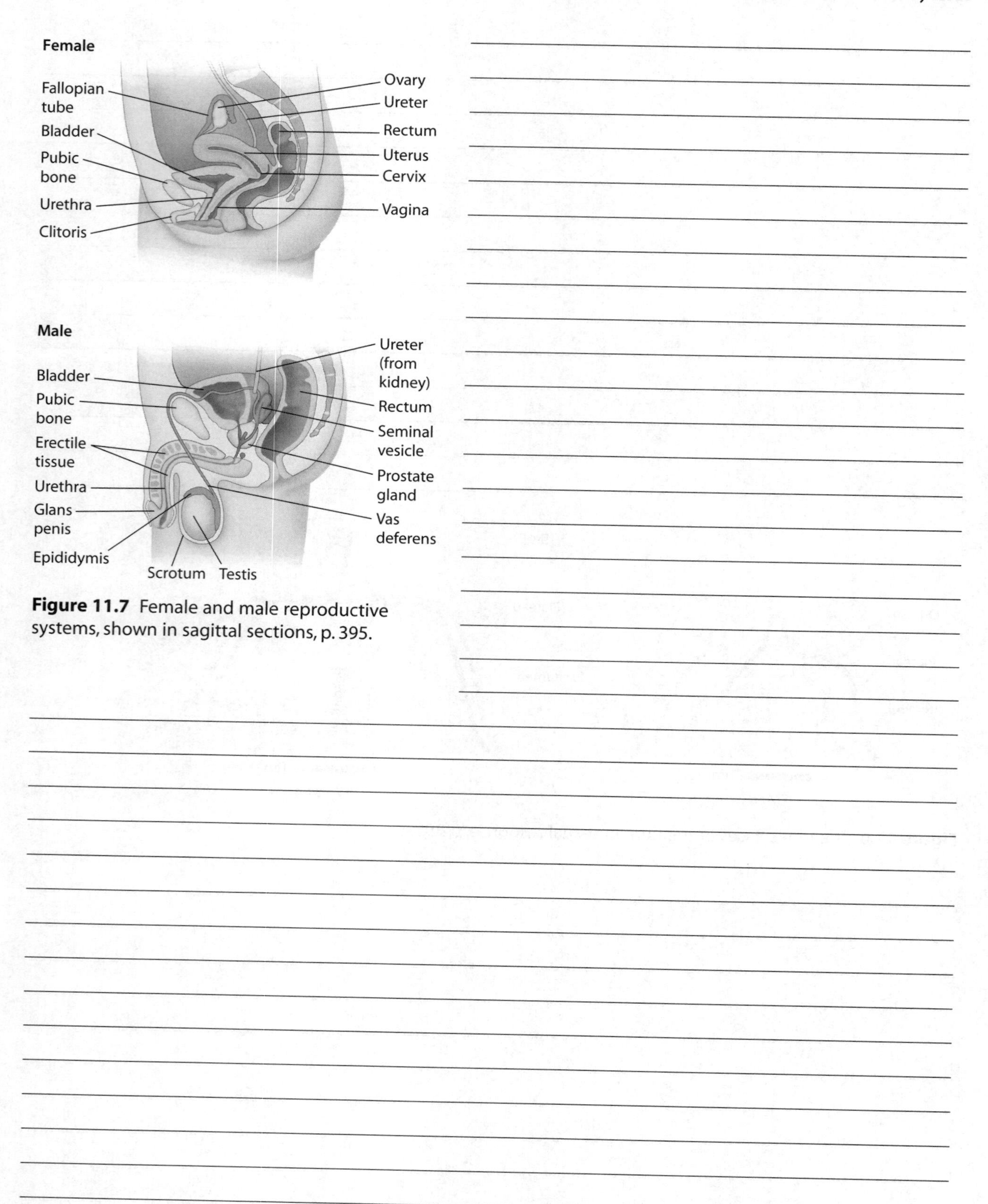

Figure 11.7 Female and male reproductive systems, shown in sagittal sections, p. 395.

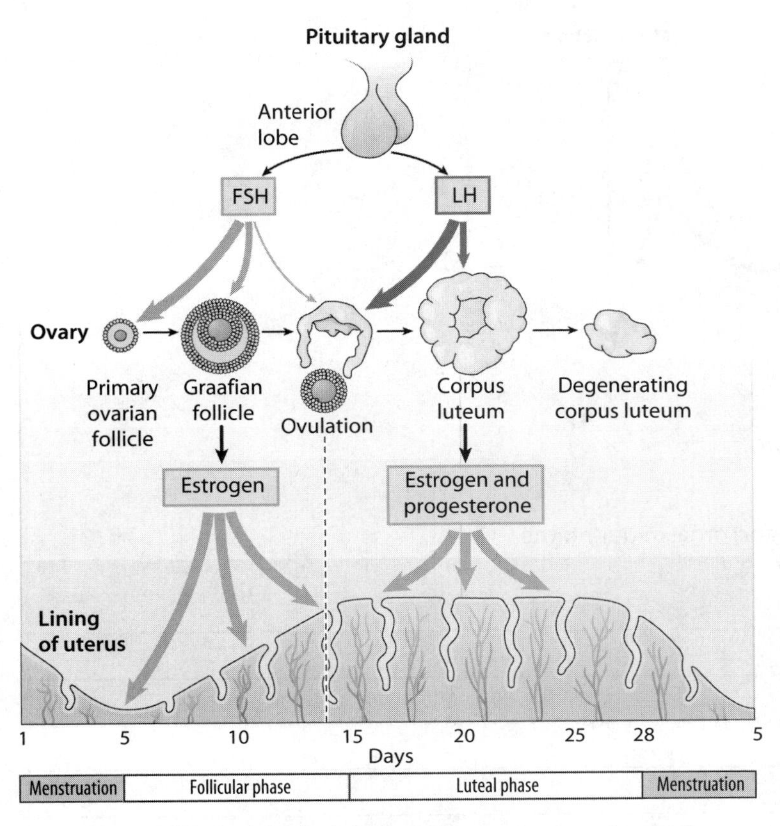

Figure 11.8 Changes in the pituitary hormones, ovaries, and uterine wall during the menstrual cycle, p. 397.

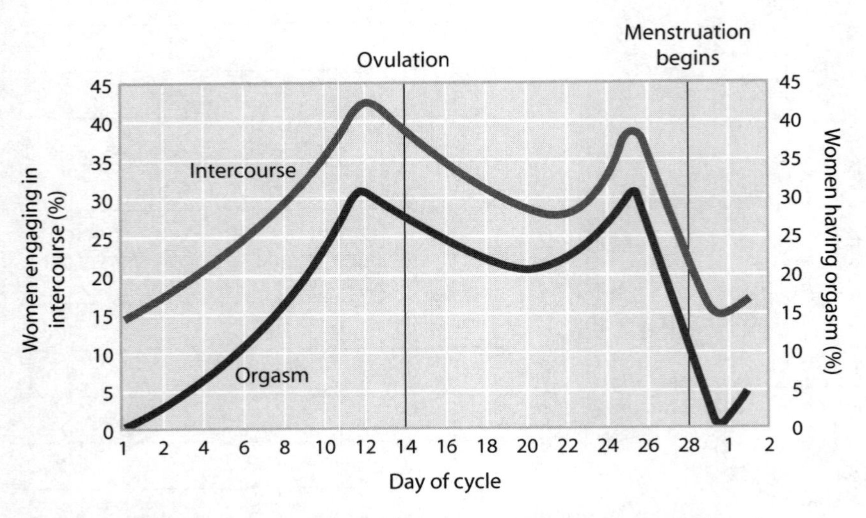

Figure 11.9 Frequency of sexual intercourse and orgasm during the menstrual cycle, p. 398.

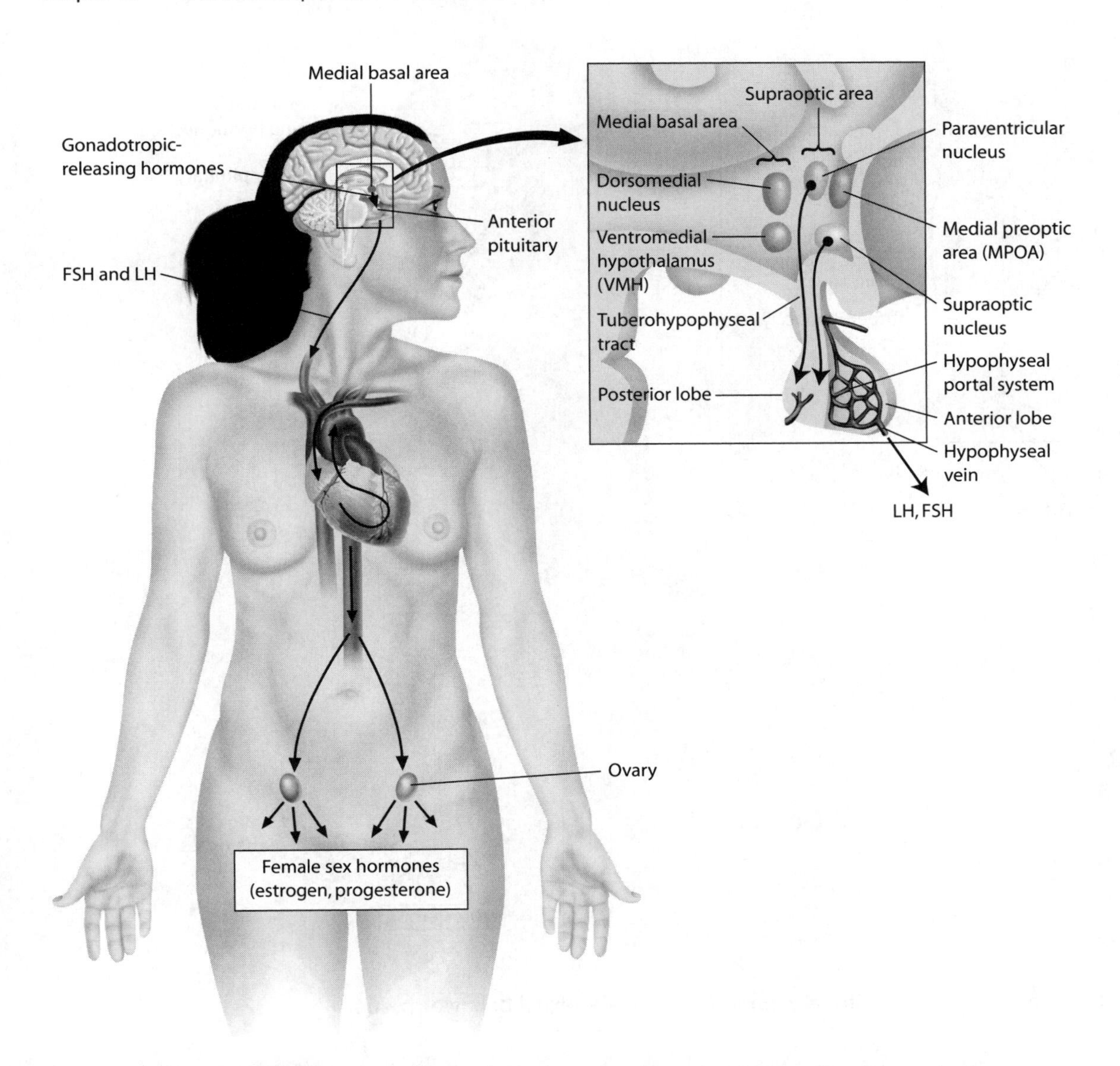

Figure 11.11 Hypothalamic and pituitary influences on female sexual behavior, p. 402.

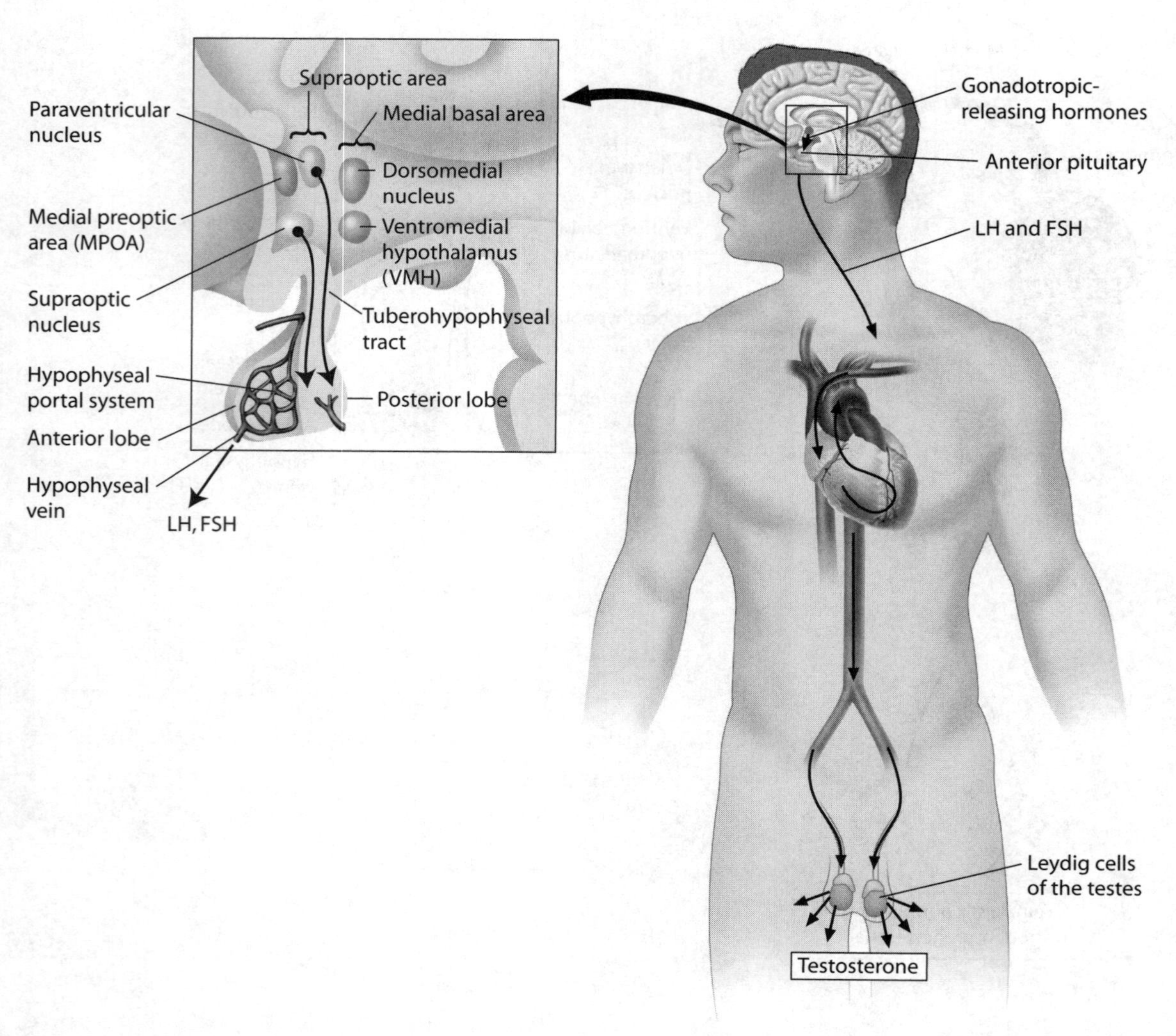

Figure 11.12 Hypothalamic and pituitary influences on male sexual behavior, p. 404.

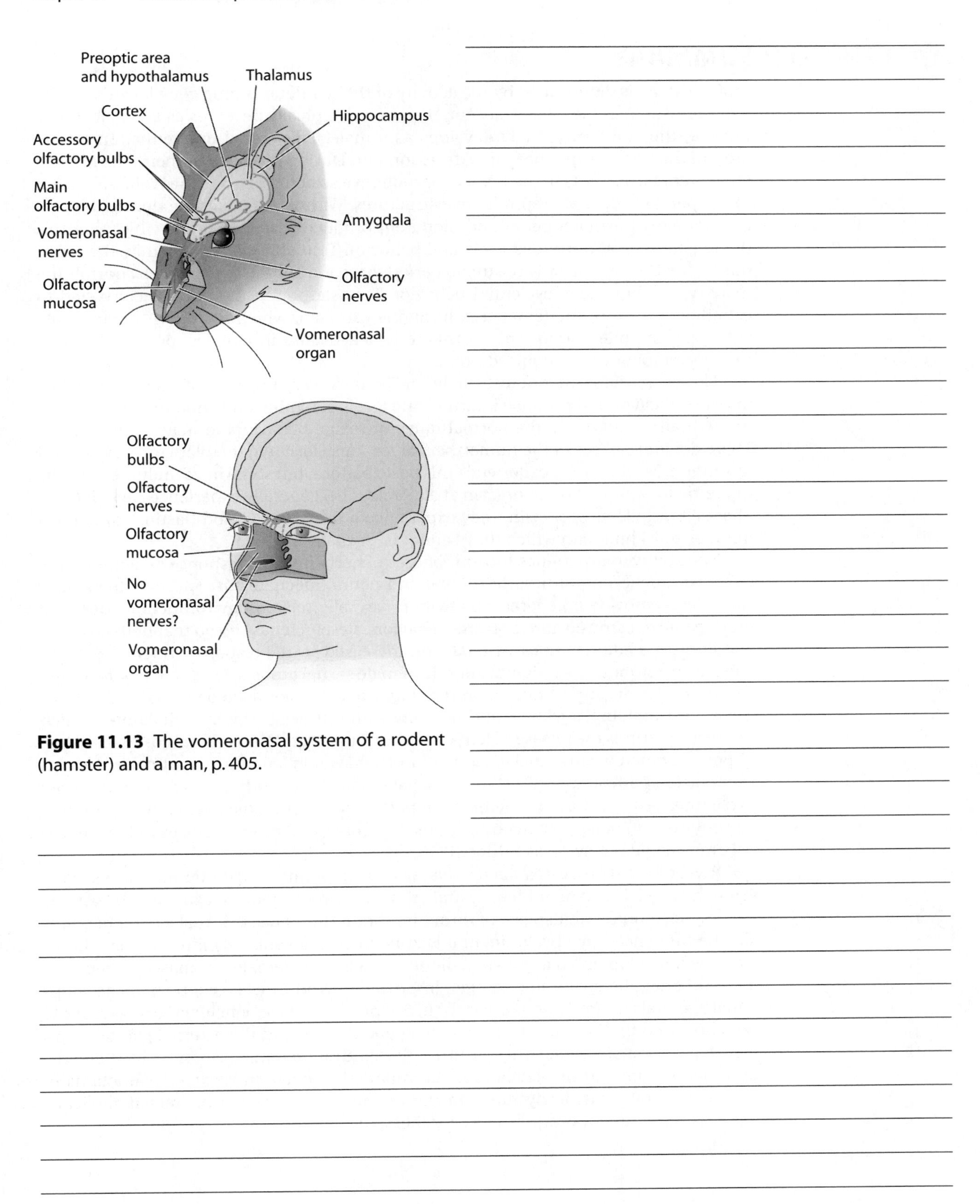

Figure 11.13 The vomeronasal system of a rodent (hamster) and a man, p. 405.

CHAPTER SUMMARY

Biological sex is determined by the activity of the sex-determining gene located on the Y chromosome. If the gene is absent, the embryo typically develops as a female; if it is present, the embryo typically develops as a male. This sexual differentiation occurs around the 8th week of embryonic development. During this development, the Müllerian system forms parts of the female reproductive structures, while the Wolffian system forms parts of the male reproductive structures. Without testosterone during the prenatal or early postnatal period, development produces a female brain, which controls the female-typical hormonal cycle and behavior. Testosterone produced by the testes during the prenatal or early postnatal period masculinizes the brain, which controls the male-typical hormonal cycle and behavior. Testosterone in the brain is converted to estradiol, a form of the female sex hormone estrogen, which is responsible for masculinizing the male brain. This hormone is deactivated in females, preventing them from developing a masculinized brain.

However, brains are not just "male" or "female." Varying levels of testosterone during the critical period produce intermediate levels of feminization and masculinization of the brain, resulting in the normal range of sexual behaviors in males and females. There are four phases of the human sexual response: excitement, plateau, orgasm, and resolution. Most females experience this basic pattern, but some have multiple orgasms (no refractory period) or no orgasm at all. Males also generally experience each of these phases, but following orgasm, they experience a refractory period (lasting from a few minutes to 24 hours) in which they cannot be sexually aroused.

The ability to experience the four phases of human sexual response depends on the effective functioning of both hormonal and neural mechanisms. These systems have two effects: provide a general sensitivity to sexually related environmental cues, and produce sexual arousal and motivate behaviors. Research has shown that both estrogen and androstenedione are associated with increased sexual response in females. Similarly, testosterone plays a significant role in male sexual arousal. Oxytocin has also been shown to play an important role in reproductive activities, such as sexual arousal, orgasm, nest building, suckling, and bonding with offspring. The hypothalamus (which indirectly controls the release of female sex hormones) and the cerebral cortex also have important functions in sexual receptivity and behavior in females. In particular, the ventromedial hypothalamus (VMH) and medial preoptic area (MPOA) seem to be involved in eliciting sexual behavior in females, in part by stimulating the mesolimbic reinforcement system. In males, the hypothalamus, amygdala, and cerebral cortex influence sexual arousal and behavior, as is the MPOA.

Psychological processes, such as classical conditioning and erotic stimuli, also govern sexual activity. Gender identity and sexual preference may be explained by genetic factors, hormonal imbalances, or structural brain differences. Sexual preference may also be influenced by developmental factors. In adrenogenital syndrome, the adrenal gland secretes too much androstenedione and a genetic female has masculinized genitals and often, behavior. In androgen insensitivity syndrome, a genetic male develops female genitals or ambiguous genitals. In 5-alpha-reductase deficiency, testosterone is not converted to dihydrotestosterone in a genetic male and the external genitals typically have a female appearance at birth. Sexual dysfunctions in men include erectile dysfunction, premature ejaculation, and retarded ejaculation; sexual dysfunctions in women include orgasmic dysfunction and vaginismus. These may be treated medically (e.g., Viagra) or therapeutically (e.g., sex therapy).

◆ KEY TERMS

The following is a list of important terms introduced in Chapter 11. Give the definition of each term in the space provided.

acquired sexual motive

adrenogenital syndrome

alpha-fetoprotein

androgen insensitivity syndrome (AIS)

androstenedione

castration

endometrium

erectile dysfunction

estradiol

estrogen

estrous cycle

5-alpha-reductase deficiency (5-ARD)

follicle-stimulating hormone (FSH)

gender

heat

Klinefelter syndrome

lordosis

luteinizing hormone (LH)

medial preoptic area (MPOA)

menstrual cycle

menstruation

Müllerian-inhibiting substance (MIS)

Müllerian system

myotonia

orgasm

orgasmic dysfunction

ovariectomy

oxytocin

pheromone

premature ejaculation

progesterone

retarded ejaculation

sex-determining gene

sex therapy

sexual dysfunction

testis-determining factor (TDF)

testosterone

Turner syndrome

vaginismus

vasocongestion

ventromedial hypothalamus (VMH)

vomeronasal organ

Wolffian system

◆ LABELING EXERCISES

1. The figures below show the male and female reproductive system; for the female, identify the following structures:

vagina	rectum
ovary	clitoris
bladder	cervix
urethra	ureter
fallopian tube	pubic bone
uterus	

for the male, identify the following structures:

scrotum	bladder
prostate gland	seminal vesicle
pubic bone	epididymis
glans penis	erectile tissue
testis	rectum
ureter	urethra
vas deferens	

Female

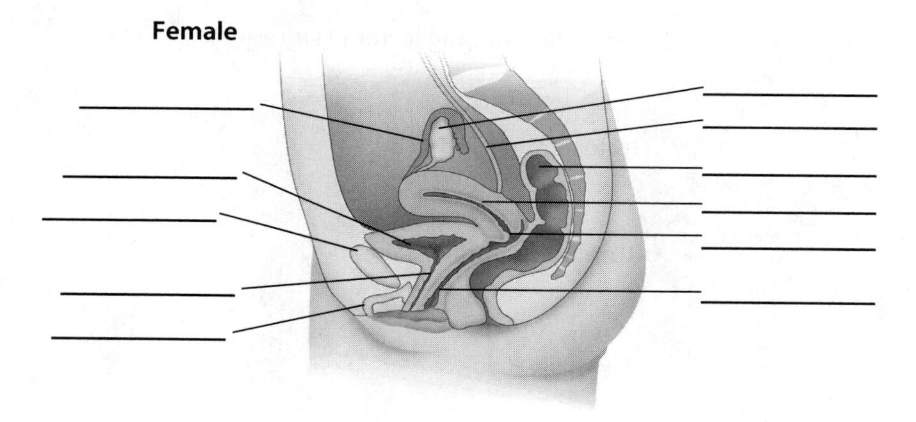

Male

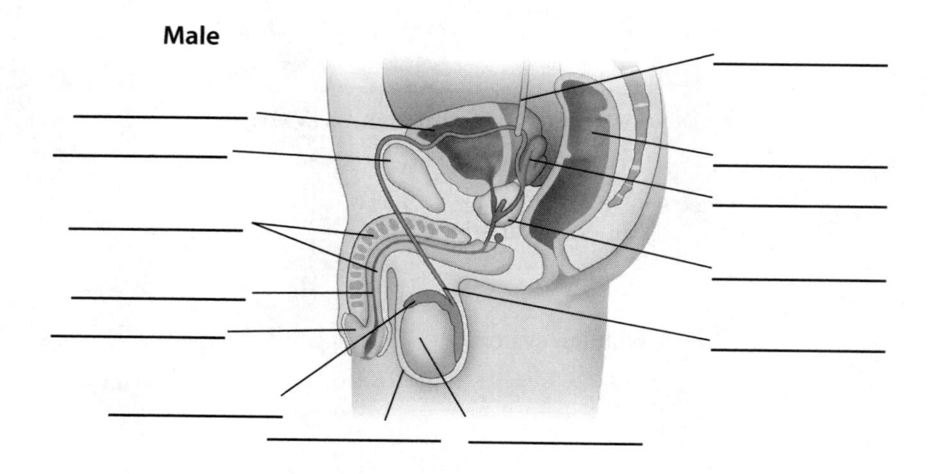

2. Female sexual behavior and hormonal release is greatly influenced by the hypothalamus and pituitary gland. In the figure below, identify the following structures:

posterior lobe	hypophyseal portal system
ventromedial hypothalamus (VMH)	medial preoptic area (MPOA)
supraoptic nucleus	ovary
tuberohypophyseal tract	gonadotropic releasing hormones
paraventricular nucleus	hypophyseal vein
anterior pituitary	anterior lobe
medial basal area *(place two times)*	supraoptic area
dorsomedial nucleus	

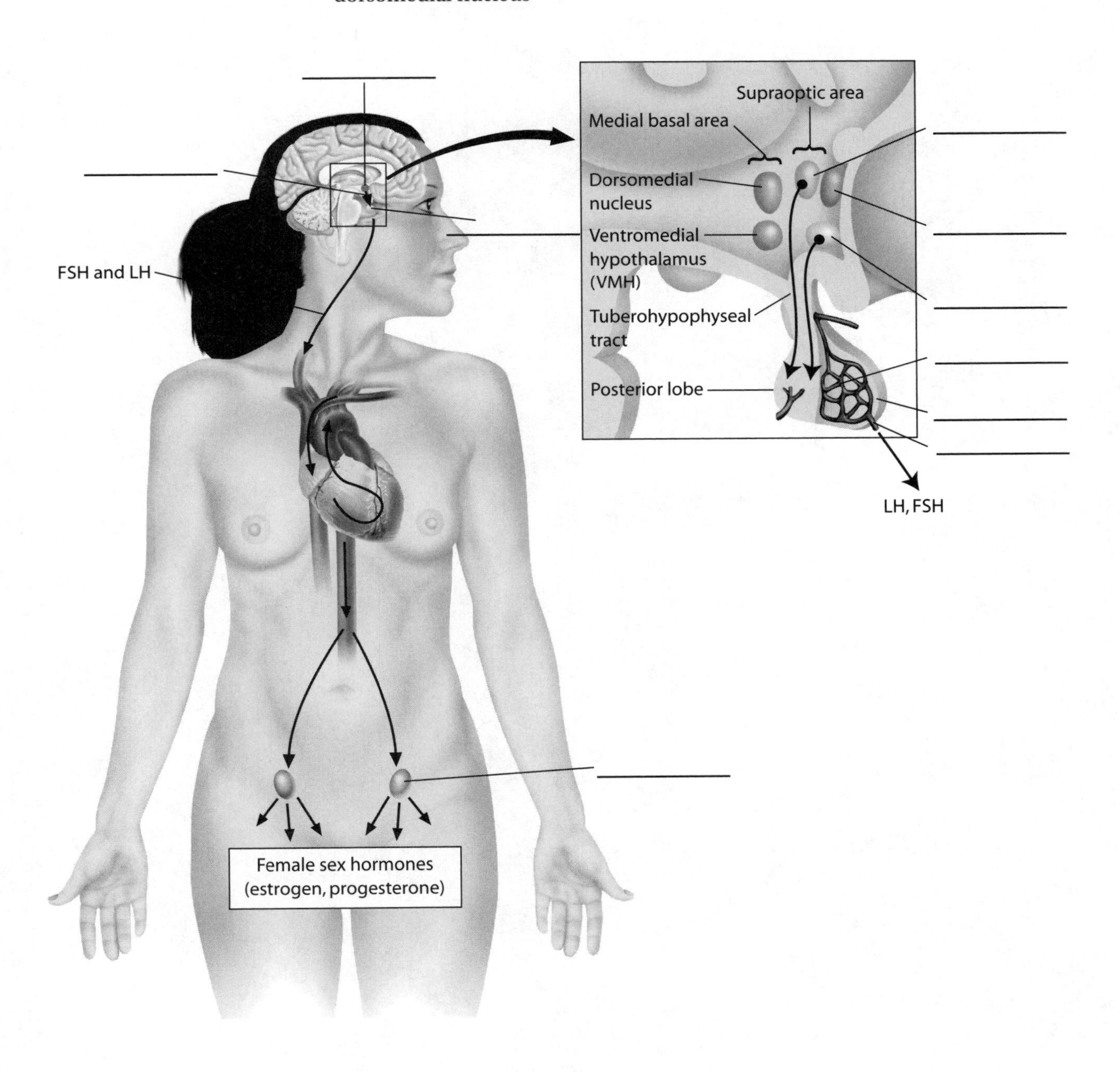

The Biology of Emotion and Stress

12

CHAPTER ART LECTURE NOTEBOOK

The following is a selection of the important figures and tables introduced in Chapter 12. You can take notes during class in the space provided.

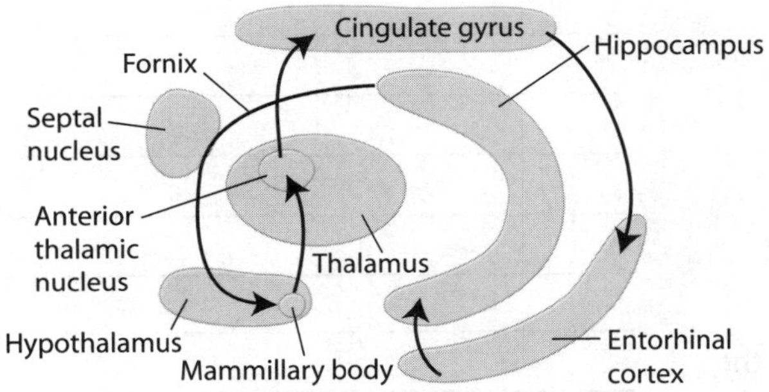

Cingulate gyrus
Hippocampus
Fornix
Septal nucleus
Anterior thalamic nucleus
Thalamus
Hypothalamus
Mammillary body
Entorhinal cortex

Figure 12.3 The Papez circuit, part of the limbic system, p. 425.

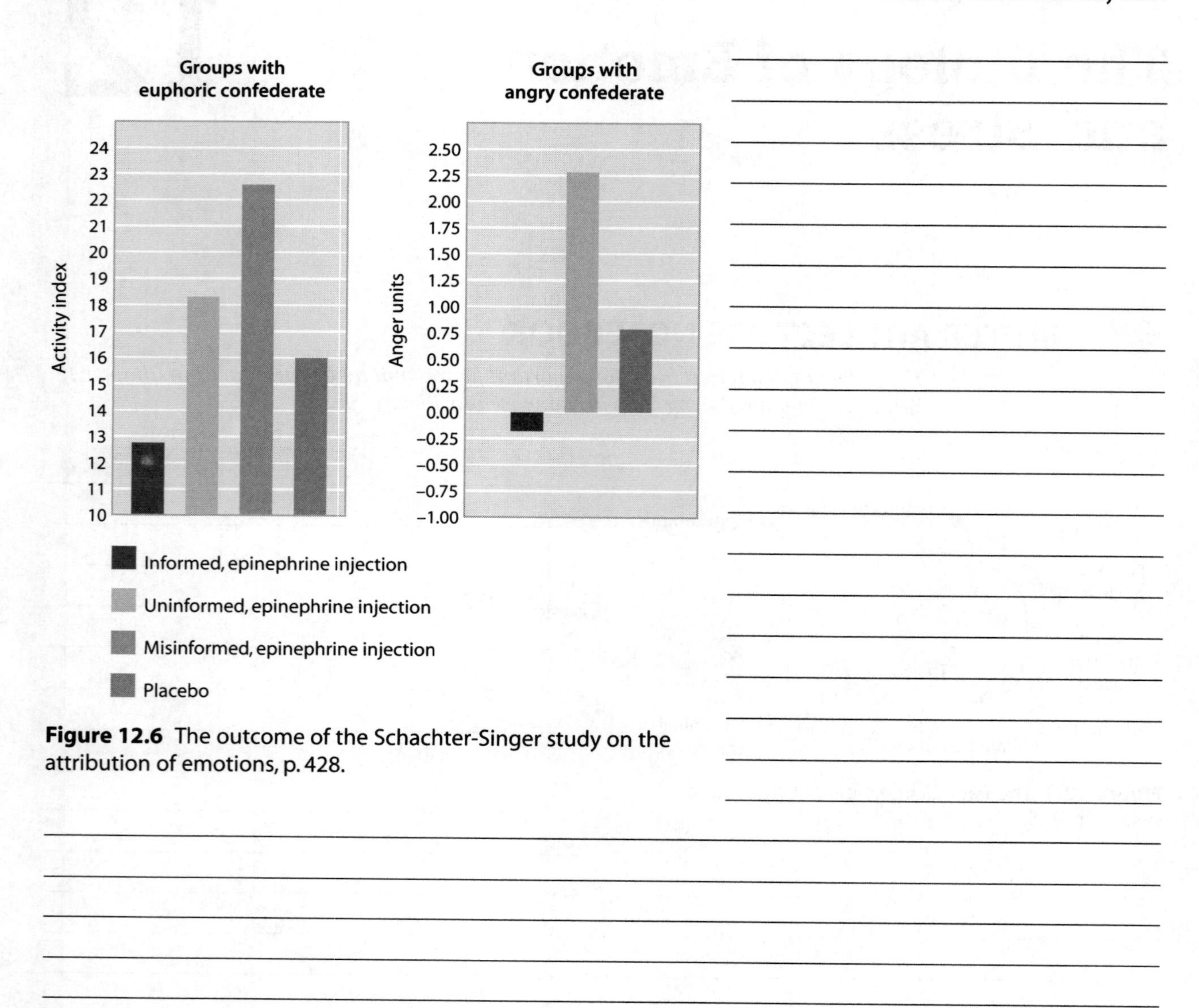

Figure 12.6 The outcome of the Schachter-Singer study on the attribution of emotions, p. 428.

Table 12.2
Eight Types of Aggression

Type	Description
Fear-induced	An animal cornered and unable to escape from danger becomes aggressive.
Instrumental	An animal emits an aggressive behavior to obtain a desired goal.
Intermale	A male threatens and then attacks a strange male of the same species.
Irritable	A frustrated or angry animal attacks another animal or object.
Maternal	A mother assaults a perceived threat to her young.
Predatory	An animal stalks, catches, and kills its natural prey.
Sex-related	A male becomes aggressive when encountering sex-related stimuli.
Territorial	An animal defends its territory against intrusion.

Table 12.2 Eight Types of Aggression, p. 431.

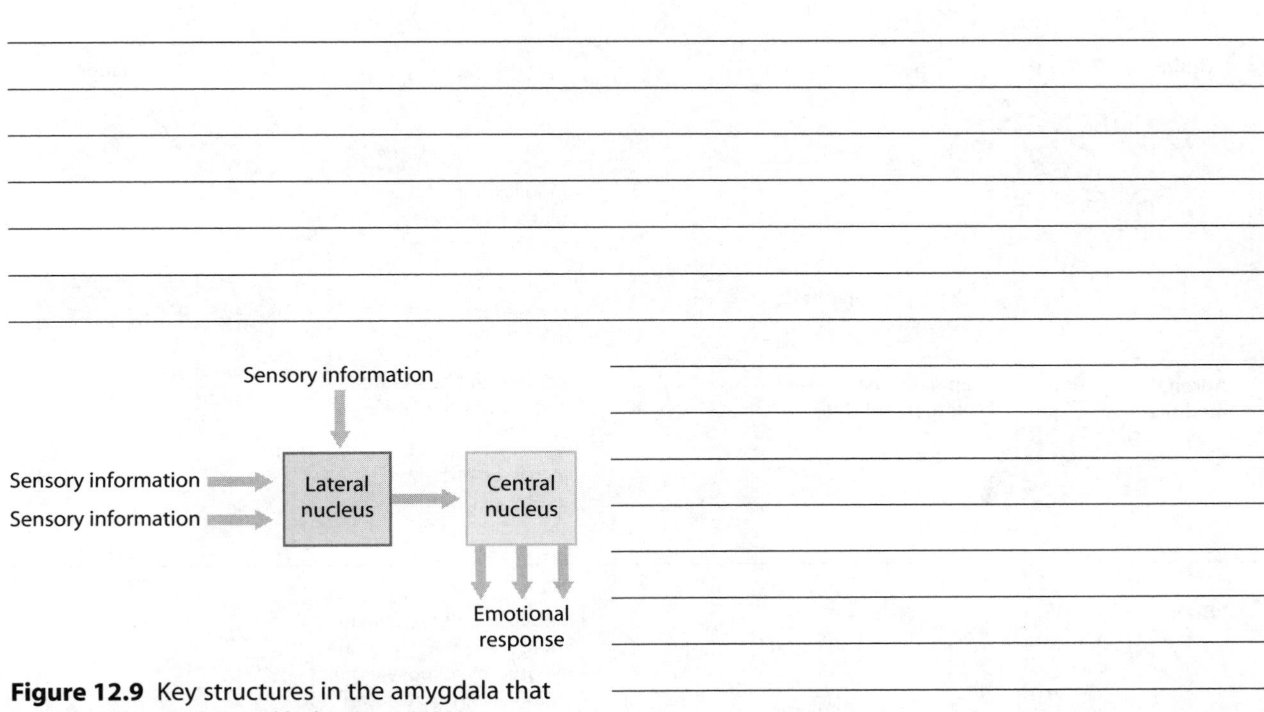

Figure 12.9 Key structures in the amygdala that are related to emotional behavior, p. 433.

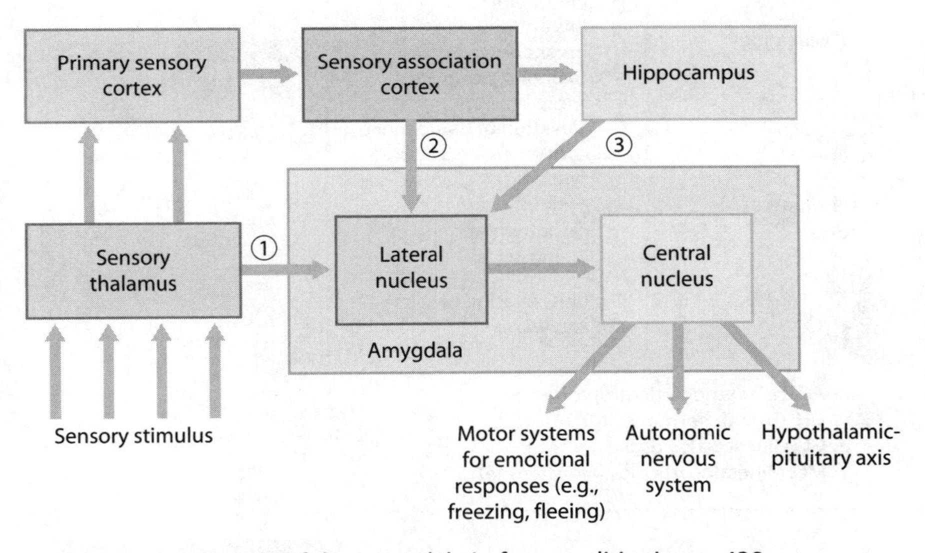

Figure 12.13 The role of the amygdala in fear conditioning, p. 439.

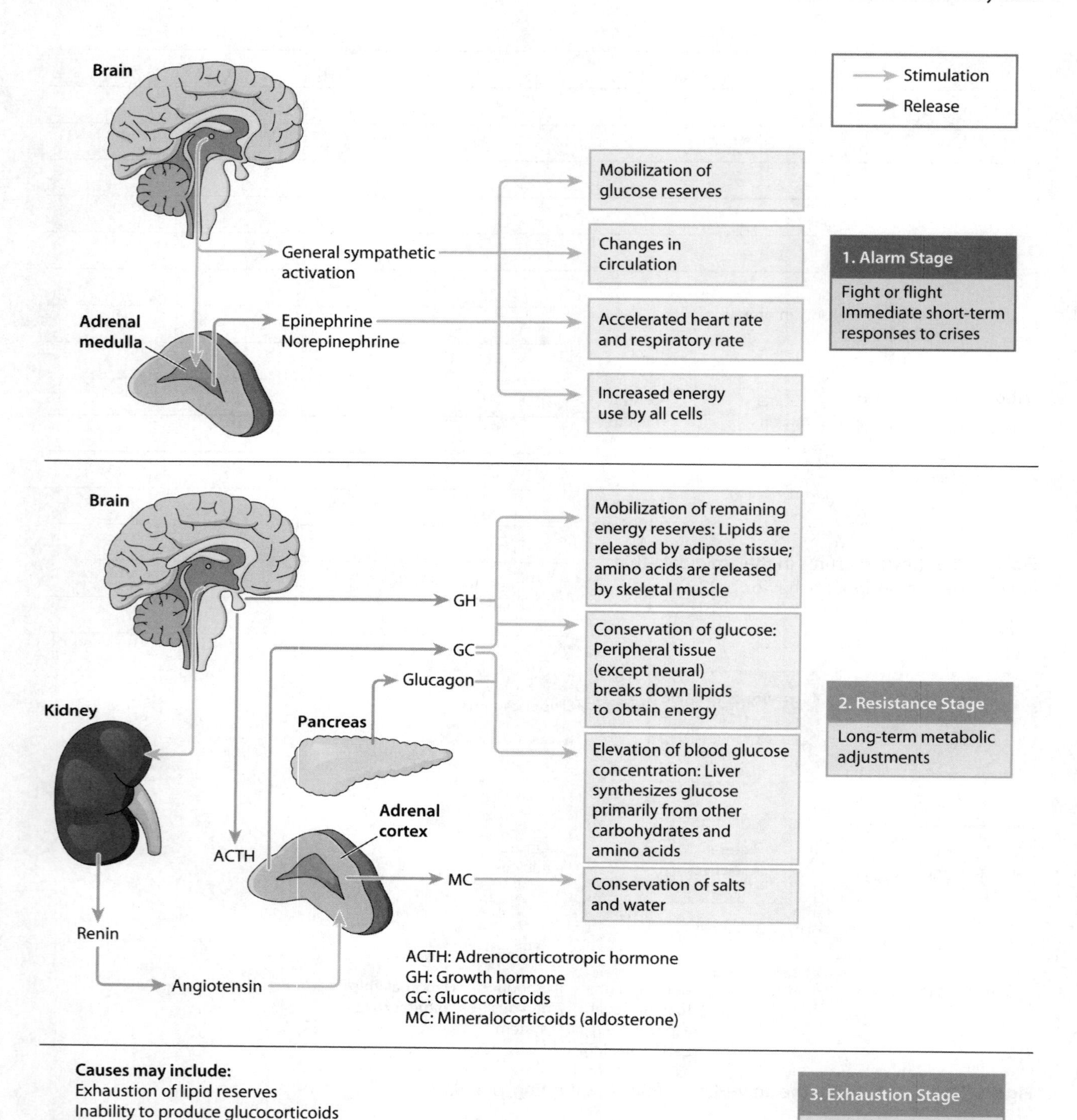

Figure 12.16 The general adaptation syndrome, p. 444.

CHAPTER SUMMARY

An emotion is a feeling that differs from the normal affective state of a person. Several models have been proposed to explain the nature of emotion. The James-Lange theory proposes that an event causes a distinctive physiological response and that interpretation of those internal physiological changes determines the experience of an emotion. That is, the expression of an emotion occurs before the experience of an emotion. The Cannon-Bard theory states that an emotion-causing event activates the thalamus, stimulating the cerebral cortex and internal organs, so that visceral changes and emotions occur simultaneously. That is, the expression and experience of an emotion occur at the same time. The Papez-MacLean model proposes that the limbic system, which includes the amygdala, hippocampus, cingulate gyrus, septum, hypothalamus and thalamus, influences the emotional reaction to an event. Schachter's cognitive model of emotion states that when unable to identify the cause of physiological arousal, a person attributes it to environmental conditions.

Aggression is a behavior motivated by the intent to harm a living being or an inanimate object. There are eight types of aggression: fear-induced, instrumental, intermale, irritable, maternal, predatory, sex-related, and territorial. Irritable aggression is an impulsive aggressive reaction elicited by anger and frustration that can range from mild to uncontrollable rage. Brain structures involved in irritable aggression include the temporal lobes, amygdala, and hypothalamus. Hormones associated with irritable aggression are testosterone, serotonin, estrogen, and progesterone. Fear-induced aggression occurs when an animal is cornered with no way to escape and involves intense autonomic arousal, defensive threat display, and attack. Neural structures involved in fear-induced aggression include the amygdala, lateral nucleus, central nucleus, hypothalamus, and the septum.

A stressor is an event that either strains or overwhelms the ability of a person to adjust to the environment. Stressors can be physiological or psychological, positive or negative. Pressure, conflict, and frustration are three types of stressor. When exposed to a stressor, we exhibit a pattern of internal biological changes. This stress response is called the general adaptation syndrome (GAS), which has three stages: the alarm stage (characterized by intense sympathetic nervous system arousal); the resistance stage (characterized by the mobilization of physiological resources to cope with a prolonged stressor); and the exhaustion stage (characterized by a depletion of resources, failure of the body's defense systems, and eventually death). Chronic, long-term exposure to stress can lead to diseases of adaptation (e.g., essential hypertension, ulcers, and colitis) and adversely affect learning and memory. However, eustress (positive stress) can have beneficial effects, such as enhancing competitive edge and performance. The pattern of behavior a person exhibits can determine the effects stress will have on that person. A type A person has a stronger biological reaction to stressors than a type B person and are, therefore, more susceptible to coronary disease. People high in hardiness are also better able to cope with stressors and, in particular, experience less emotional stress.

KEY TERMS

The following is a list of important terms introduced in Chapter 12. Give the definition of each term in the space provided.

aggression

alarm stage

amygdalectomy

Cannon-Bard theory of emotion

cognitive appraisal

diseases of adaptation

emotion

exhaustion stage

fear-induced aggression

general adaptation syndrome (GAS)

hardiness

irritable aggression

James-Lange theory of emotion

kindling

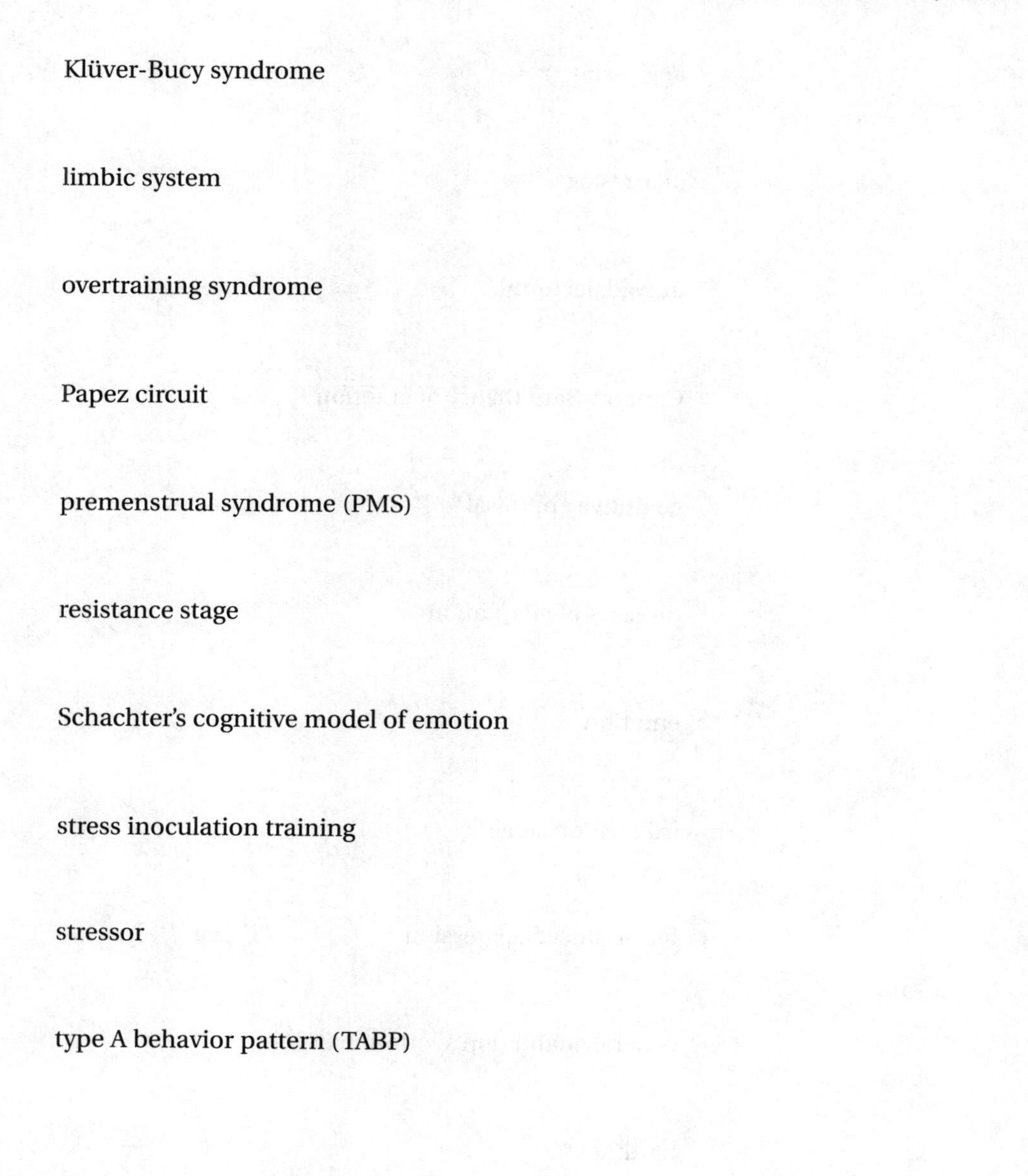

Klüver-Bucy syndrome

limbic system

overtraining syndrome

Papez circuit

premenstrual syndrome (PMS)

resistance stage

Schachter's cognitive model of emotion

stress inoculation training

stressor

type A behavior pattern (TABP)

◆ LABELING EXERCISES

1. The diagram below illustrates the James-Lange theory of emotion. In the boxes provided, describe the sequence of events that occurs when an emotion is experienced according to this theory.

2. The diagram below illustrates the Cannon-Bard theory of emotion. In the boxes provided, describe the sequence of events that occurs when an emotion is experienced according to this theory.

3. The diagram below illustrates Schachter's cognitive model of emotion. In the boxes provided, describe the sequence of events that occurs when an emotion is experienced according to this theory.

Language and Lateralization 13

◆ CHAPTER ART LECTURE NOTEBOOK

The following is a selection of the important figures and tables introduced in Chapter 13. You can take notes during class in the space provided.

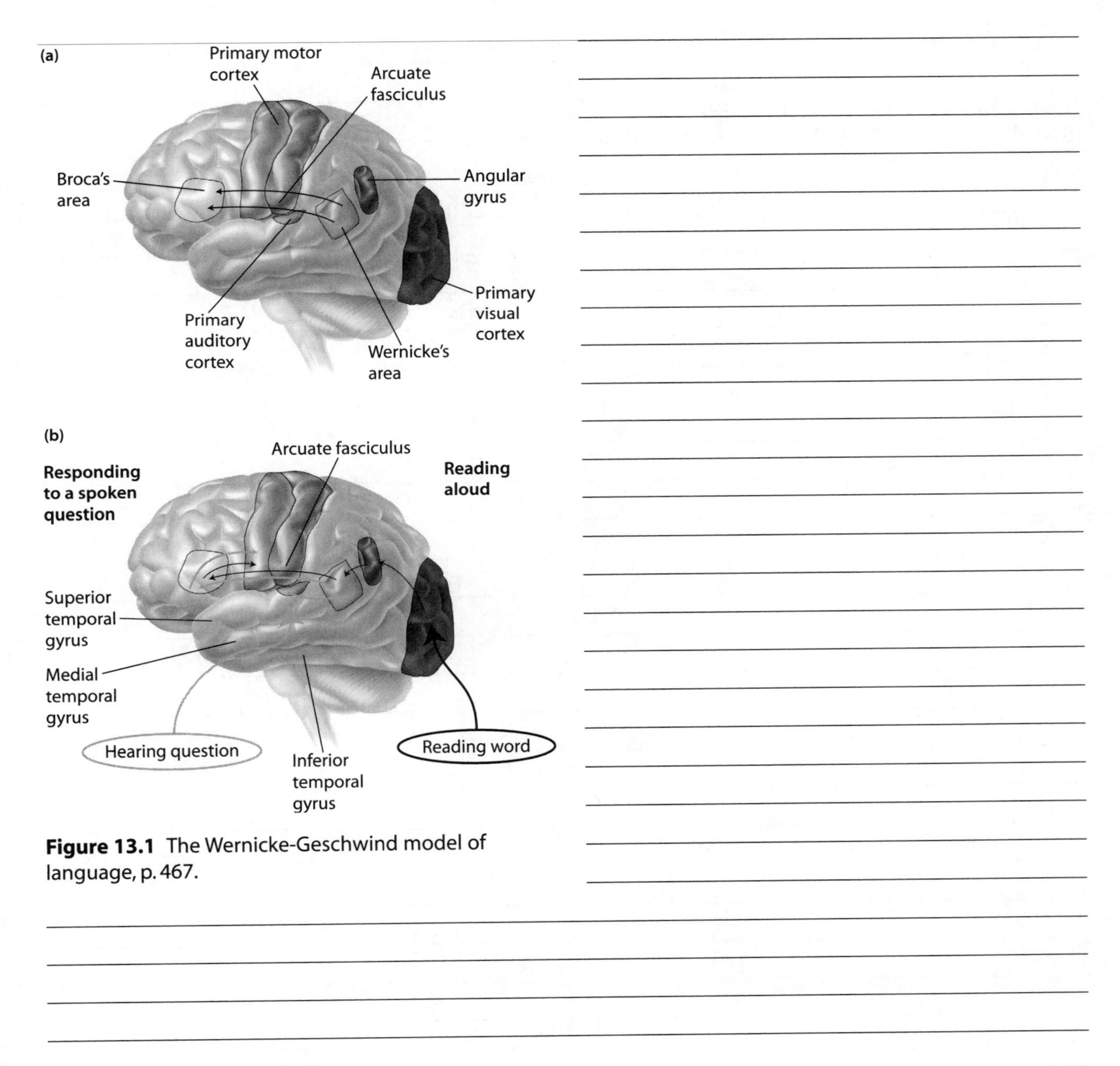

Figure 13.1 The Wernicke-Geschwind model of language, p. 467.

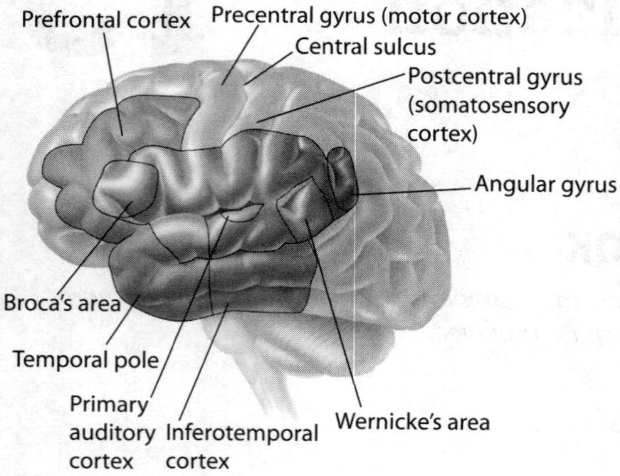

Figure 13.2 Systems controlling language perception and production, p. 468.

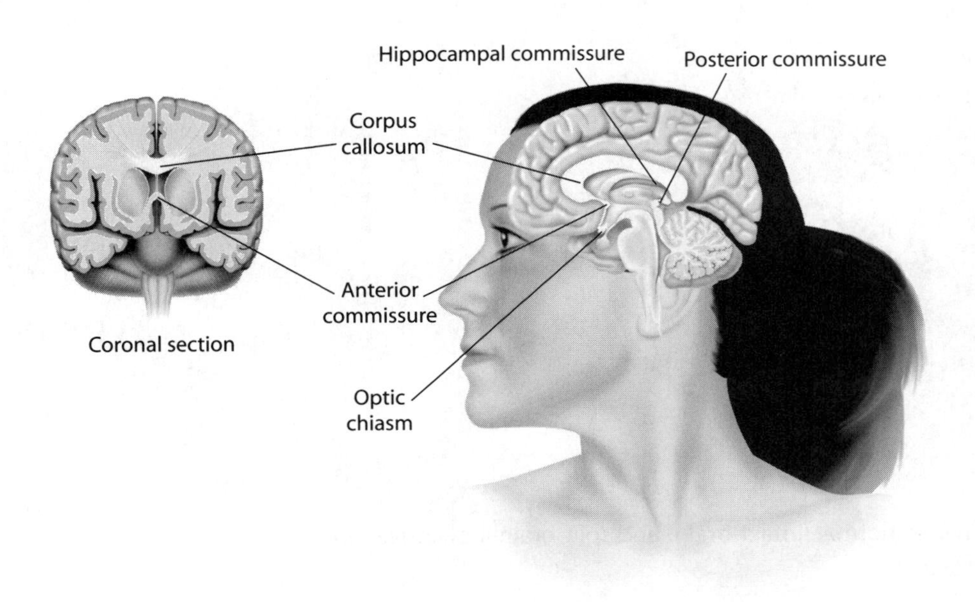

Figure 13.3 The cerebral commissures, p. 469.

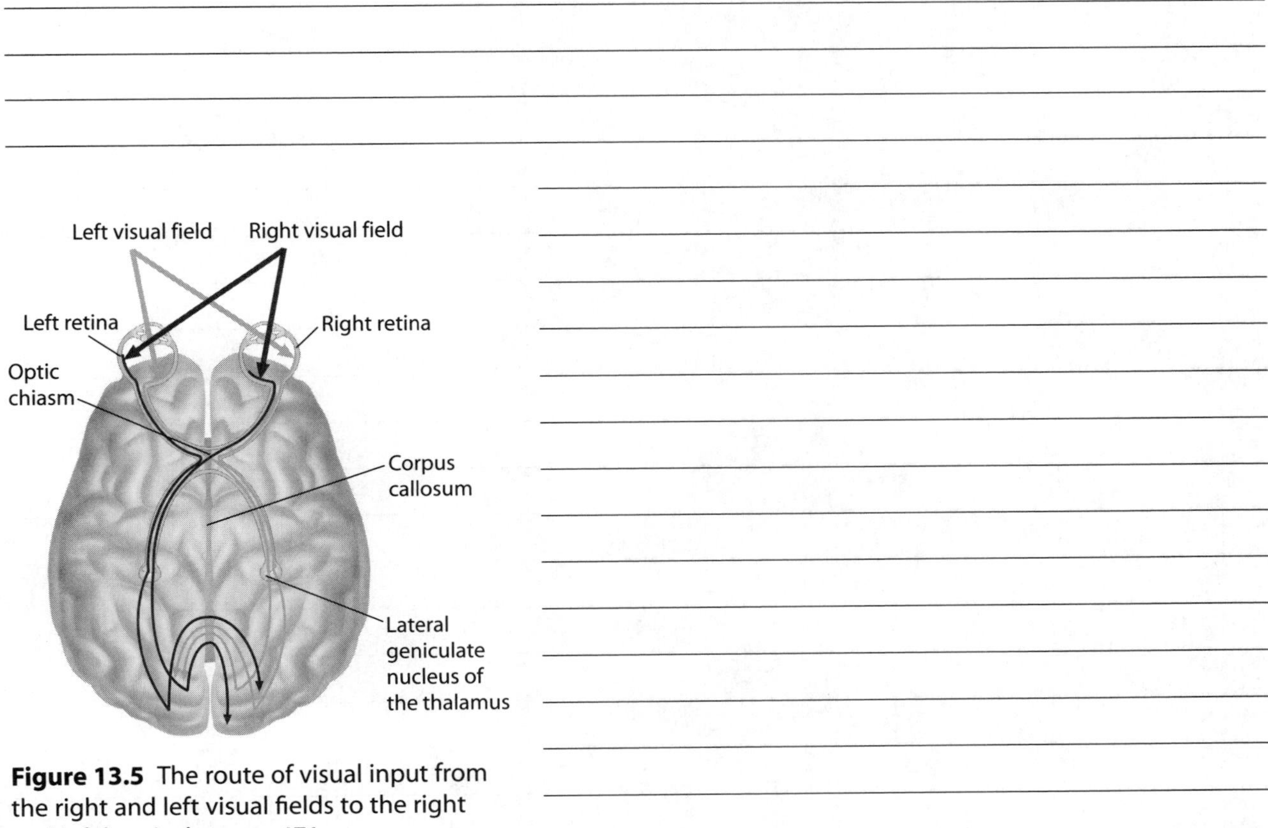

Figure 13.5 The route of visual input from the right and left visual fields to the right and left hemispheres, p. 471.

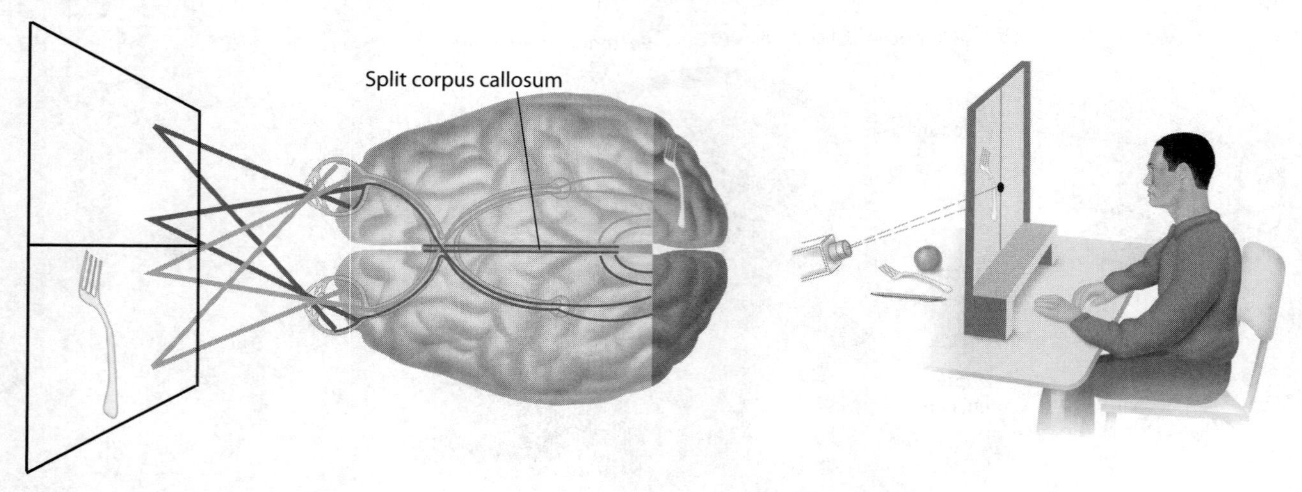

Figure 13.6 The difference between normal (intact-brain) and split-brain individuals, p. 472.

Table 13.1

Lateralization of Function of the Left and Right Hemispheres

Function	Left Hemisphere	Right Hemisphere
Visual system	Letters, words	Complex geometric patterns Faces
Auditory system	Language-related sounds	Nonlanguage environmental sounds Music
Somatosensory system	?	Tactile recognition of complex patterns Braille
Movement	Complex voluntary movement	Movements in spatial patterns
Memory	Verbal memory	Nonverbal memory
Language	Speaking Reading Writing Arithmetic	Emotional intonation Prosody?
Spatial processes		Geometry Sense of direction Mental rotation of shapes

Note: Functions of the respective hemispheres that are predominantly mediated by one hemisphere in right-handed people.
Source: Adapted from Kolb, B., & Whishaw, I. Q. (2003). *Fundamentals of human neuropsychology* (5th ed.). New York: Worth.

Table 13.1 Lateralization of Function of the Left and Right Hemispheres, p. 477.

Table 13.2
Sites of Lesion and Characteristics of Nonfluent and Fluent Aphasias

Disorder	Site of Lesion	Spontaneous Speech	Speech Comprehension	Repetition	Naming
Broca's aphasia	Left frontal cortex rostral to base of motor cortex	Nonfluent	Relatively intact	Poor	Poor
Global aphasia	Anterior and posterior language areas	Nonfluent	Poor	Poor	Poor
Transcortical motor aphasia	Areas of premotor cortex anterior and superior to Broca's area	Nonfluent	Relatively intact	Intact	Poor
Wernicke's aphasia	Posterior part of superior and middle left temporal gyrus and left temporoparietal cortex	Fluent	Poor	Poor	Poor
Conduction aphasia	Left temporoparietal region, above and below posterior Sylvian fissure	Fluent	Relatively intact	Poor	Intact
Anomic aphasia	Left temporo-occipital junction	Fluent	Relatively intact	Intact	Poor
Transcortical sensory aphasia	Areas surrounding and including Wernicke's area	Fluent	Poor	Intact	Poor

Table 13.2 Sites of Lesion and Characteristics of Nonfluent and Fluent Aphasias, p. 485.

Table 13.3
Sites of Lesion and Characteristics of Nonaphasic Communicative Disorders

Disorder	Site of Lesion	Characteristics
Apraxia of speech	Third frontal convolution anterior to primary motor cortex (Broca's area)	Inability to voluntarily sequence speech production
Auditory-verbal agnosia	Connections from primary auditory cortex and secondary auditory cortex	Inability to identify spoken words as meaningful
Alexia/dyslexia	Connections from primary visual cortex to angular gyrus	An inability to read/ difficulty in reading
Agraphia/ dysgraphia	Inferior parietal lobe and superior temporal lobe	An inability to write/ difficulty in writing

Table 13.3 Sites of Lesion and Characteristics of Nonaphasic Communicative Disorders, p. 490.

CHAPTER SUMMARY

Language is a system of words, word meanings, and the rules for combining words into phrases and sentences. A language has three functions: the communication of ideas, the facilitation of thought and the recording of experiences and ideas in written or other form, that helps us to retain knowledge of past events and to overcome the limitations of our memory system. Spoken language consists of four main structural units: phonemes, morphemes, phrases, and sentences. Phonology and syntax prescribe the rules in which these structural units can be combined, while semantics determines the meaning of language.

An instinctive view of human language acquisition was proposed by Chomsky, who suggested that children are born with a language-generating mechanism called the language acquisition device (LAD) that allows children to readily grasp the syntax relevant to their native language. According to the Wernicke-Geschwind model of language production, Wernicke's area is responsible for comprehending spoken language and sends a neural representation of the verbal response through the arcuate fasciculus to Broca's area, which is responsible for the production (expression) of the verbal response.

Hemispheric lateralization is the differentiation of functions between the two hemispheres of the brain. Much of the evidence for such lateralization has come from Sperry's split-brain research, in which a person's corpus callosum had been cut as a treatment for epilepsy and, therefore, the two hemispheres could not communicate. Such research has demonstrated that, in most people, the left hemisphere processes the phonetic, syntactic, and semantic aspects of language, whereas the right hemisphere interprets the intonational, emotional, and nonliteral aspects of language (e.g., metaphors and humor) and controls visual-spatial functions. While the purpose of lateralization is not completely known, it may have evolved to allow parallel processing of information and to provide a mechanism for hemispheric sharing of that information. For language, it may be more efficient to process the different aspects separately and then combine them through the cerebral commissures. Despite this lateralization, the brain illustrates some plasticity in that damage to left hemisphere language areas sometimes leads to right hemisphere language abilities that would not otherwise have developed.

Communication disorders are impairments in speech, hearing, and/or language. An aphasia is an acquired language impairment caused by damage to the areas of the brain that control language functioning. The aphasias can be characterized as nonfluent (difficulty producing fluent, well-articulated, and self-initiated speech) and fluent (inability to understand the language of others and the production of less meaningful speech than normal). The three types of nonfluent aphasia are: Broca's aphasia, global aphasia, and transcortical motor aphasia. The four types of fluent aphasia are: Wernicke's aphasia, conduction aphasia, anomic aphasia, and transcortical sensory aphasia. Other communicative disorders include apraxia of speech, auditory-verbal agnosia, alexia, agraphia, dyslexia, and dysgraphia. Communicative disorders can be caused by many things, including strokes, head trauma, infectious disease, tumor, exposure to toxic substances, and metabolic disorders.

Because the different types of communicative disorders can be difficult to distinguish from one another and diagnose, treatment should be based on particular symptoms and behaviors rather than specific diagnosis. Studies of treatment effectiveness have shown that recovery of language abilities is enhanced when treatment is begun in the first months after damage. Such recovery appears to be mediated by the activation of right hemisphere areas corresponding to damaged left hemisphere areas and by increased activation of undamaged left hemisphere language areas.

◆ KEY TERMS

The following is a list of important terms introduced in Chapter 13. Give the definition of each term in the space provided.

agrammatical speech

agraphia

alexia

angular gyrus

anomia

anomic aphasia

aphasia

apraxia of speech

arcuate fasciculus

auditory verbal agnosia

Broca's aphasia

commissurotomy

conduction aphasia

dysgraphia

dyslexia

echolalia

fluent aphasia

global aphasia

hemispheric lateralization

language

language acquisition device (LAD)

morpheme

neologistic jargon

nonfluent aphasia

paragrammatical speech

paraphasia

phoneme

phonology

phrase

pure alexia

semantics

sentence

split-brain preparation

syntax

temporoparietal cortex

transcortical motor aphasia

transcortical sensory aphasia

visual-verbal agnosia

Wernicke-Geschwind model

Wernicke's aphasia

Williams syndrome

◆ LABELING EXERCISES

1. There are many systems that control language perception and production in the brain. Label the following areas in this figure:

   prefrontal cortex

   angular gyrus

   temporal pole

   postcentral gyrus (somatosensory cortex)

   Wernicke's area

   precentral gyrus (motor cortex)

   primary auditory cortex

   Broca's area

   central sulcus

   inferotemporal cortex

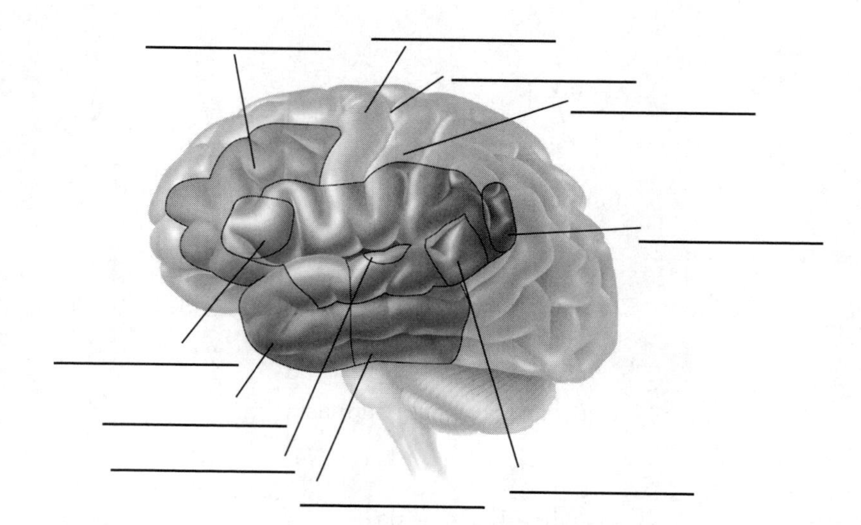

2. Both hemispheres of the brain communicate through the structures shown in this figure. Label the following structures:

optic chiasm
hippocampal commissure
corpus callosum
posterior commissure
anterior commissure.

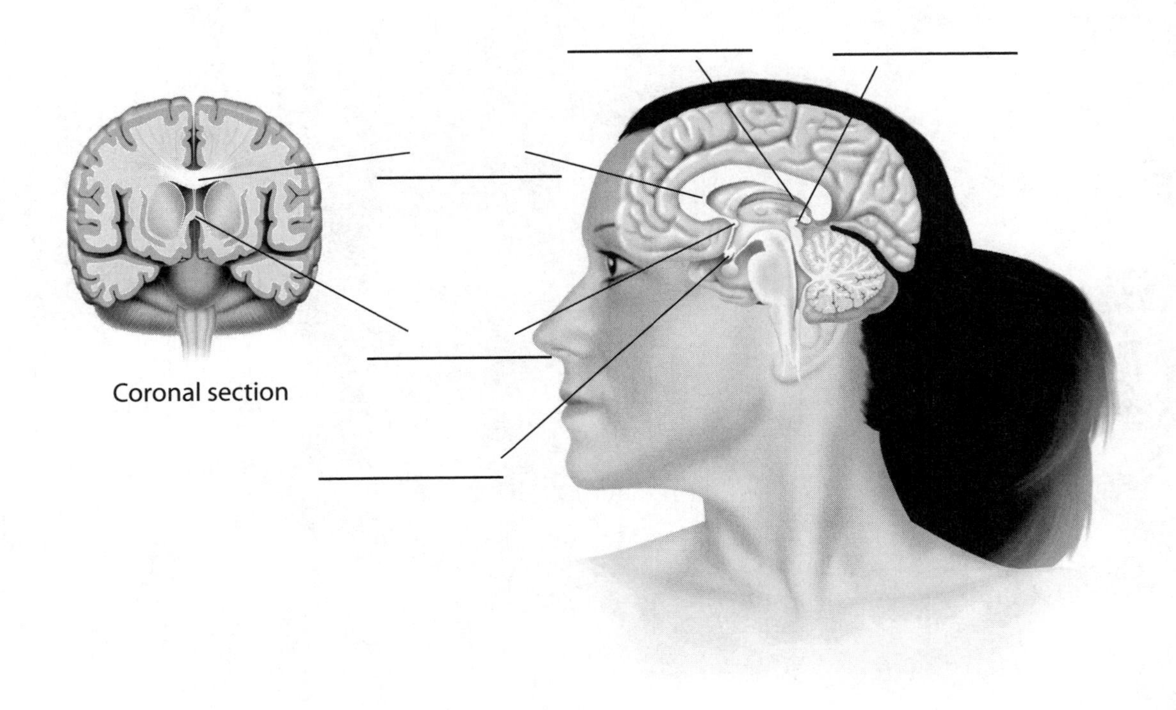

The Biology of Learning and Memory

14

◆ CHAPTER ART LECTURE NOTEBOOK

The following is a selection of the important figures and tables introduced in Chapter 14. You can take notes during class in the space provided.

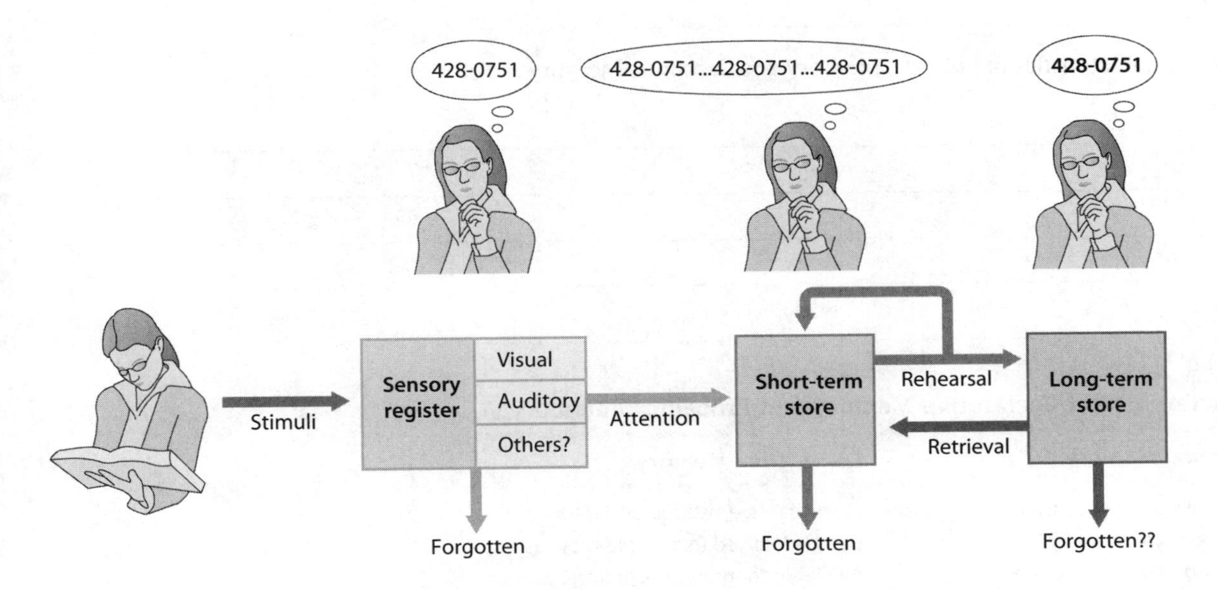

Figure 14.3 The Atkinson-Shiffrin three-stage model of memory storage, p. 505.

Table 14.1
Characteristics of Episodic Memory and Semantic Memory

Episodic Memory	Semantic Memory
Stores events	Stores ideas or concepts
Organized temporally	Organized conceptually
Based on personal belief	Based on social agreement
Reported as remembrance	Reported as knowledge
Access is deliberate	Access is automatic
Affect relatively important	Affect relatively unimportant
Very susceptible to amnesia	Relatively unsusceptible to amnesia
Stored late in childhood	Stored early in childhood

Source: Adapted from Tulving, E. (1983). *Elements of episodic memory.* Oxford: Clarendon Press/Oxford University Press.

Table 14.1 Characteristics of Episodic Memory and Semantic Memory, p. 508.

Table 14.2
Characteristics of Declarative Memory and Procedural Memory

Procedural Memory	Declarative Memory
Stores skills and procedures	Stores facts, episodes, and data
Is learned incrementally	Can be learned in a single trial
Contained within processing systems (e.g., sensory, motor)	Available to many processing systems
Information is modality specific	Information is modality general
Phylogenetically primitive	Phylogenetically late
Developmentally early	Developmentally late
Preserved in amnesia	Impaired in amnesia
Inaccessible to conscious recollection	Accessible to conscious recollection

Source: Adapted from Squire, L. R. (1984). The neuropsychology of memory. In P. Marler & H. Terrace (Eds.), *The biology of learning* (pp. 667–685). Berlin: Springer-Verlag.

Table 14.2 Characteristics of Declarative Memory and Procedural Memory, p. 509.

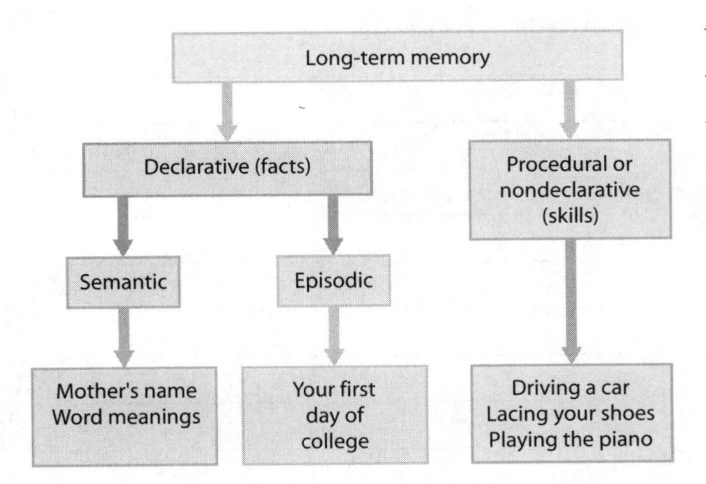

Figure 14.4 Types of long-term memory, p. 509.

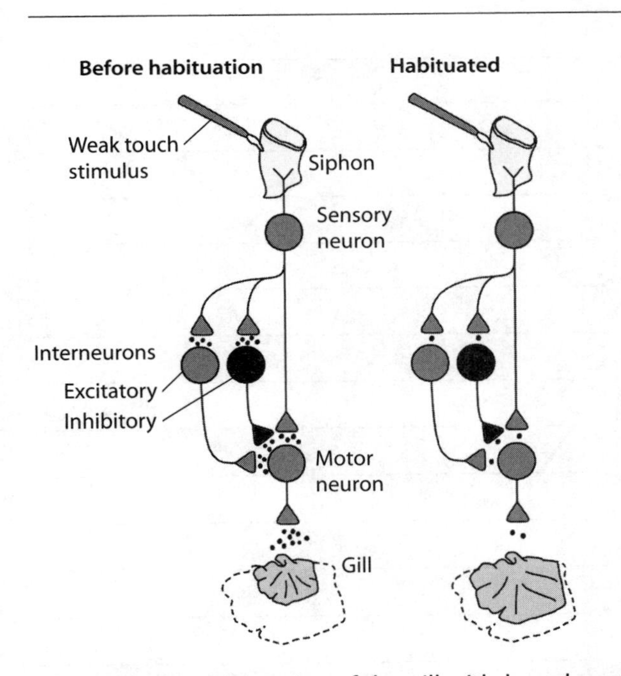

Figure 14.10 Habituation of the gill withdrawal response in Aplysia, p. 517.

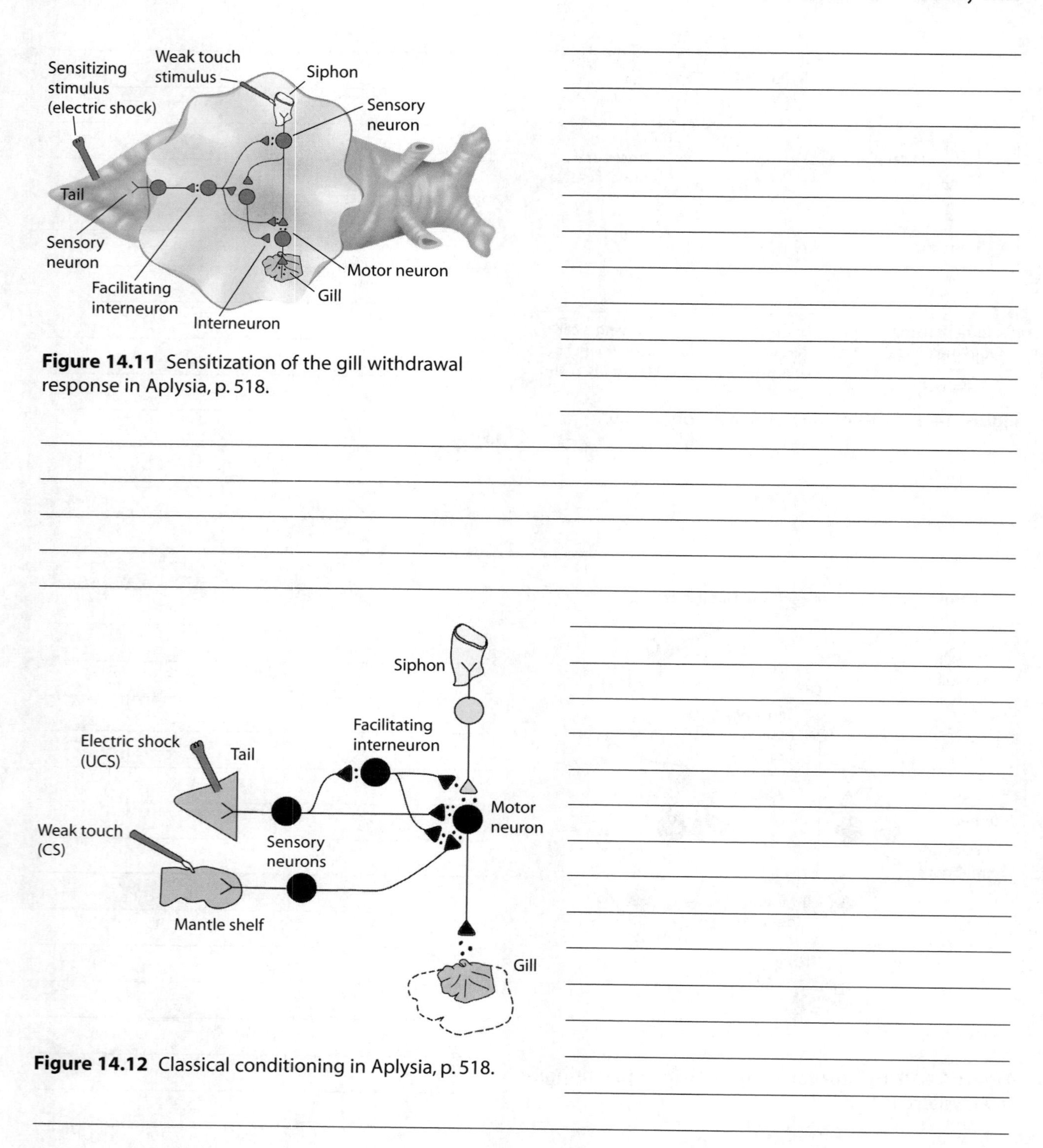

Figure 14.11 Sensitization of the gill withdrawal response in Aplysia, p. 518.

Figure 14.12 Classical conditioning in Aplysia, p. 518.

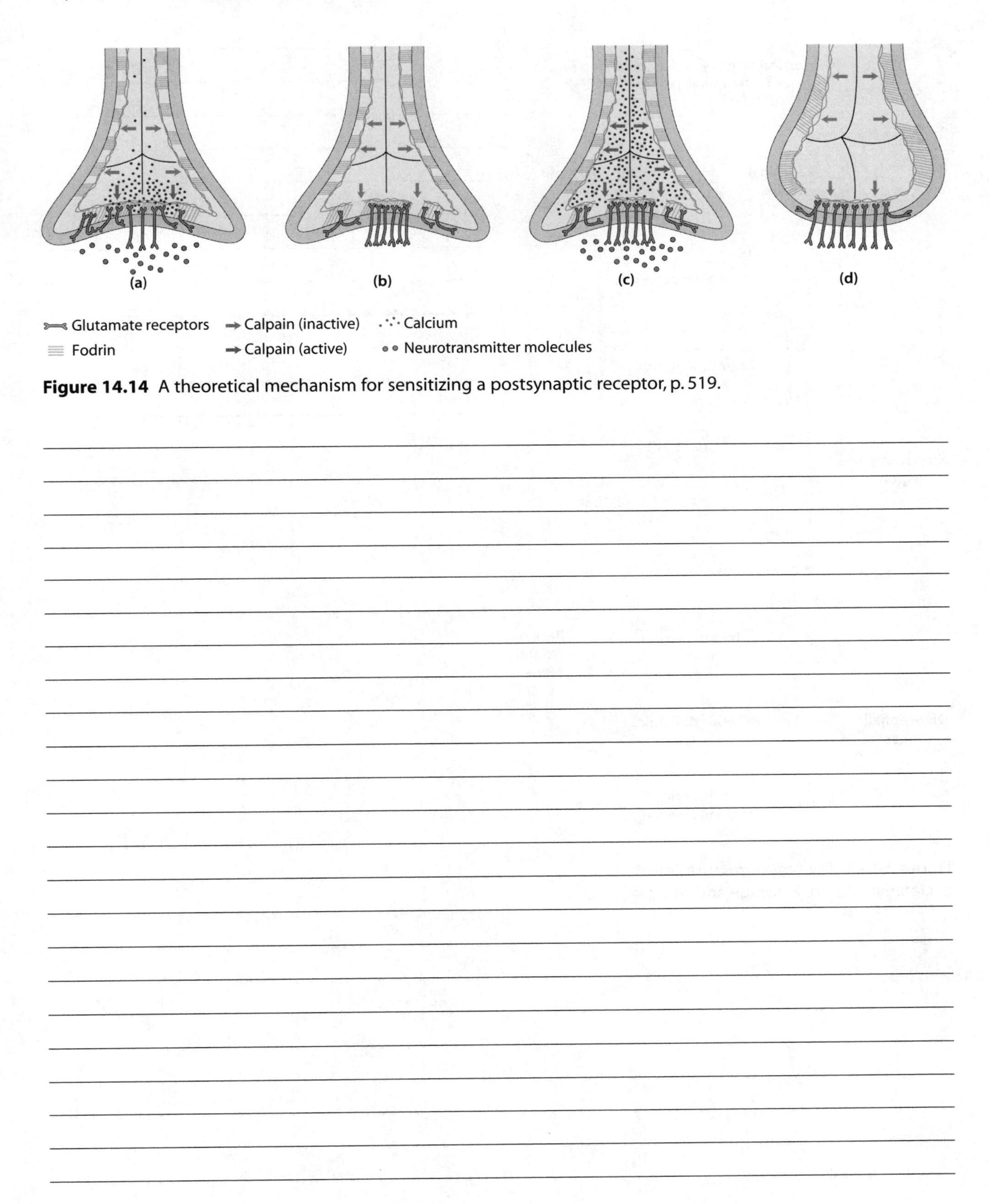

Figure 14.14 A theoretical mechanism for sensitizing a postsynaptic receptor, p. 519.

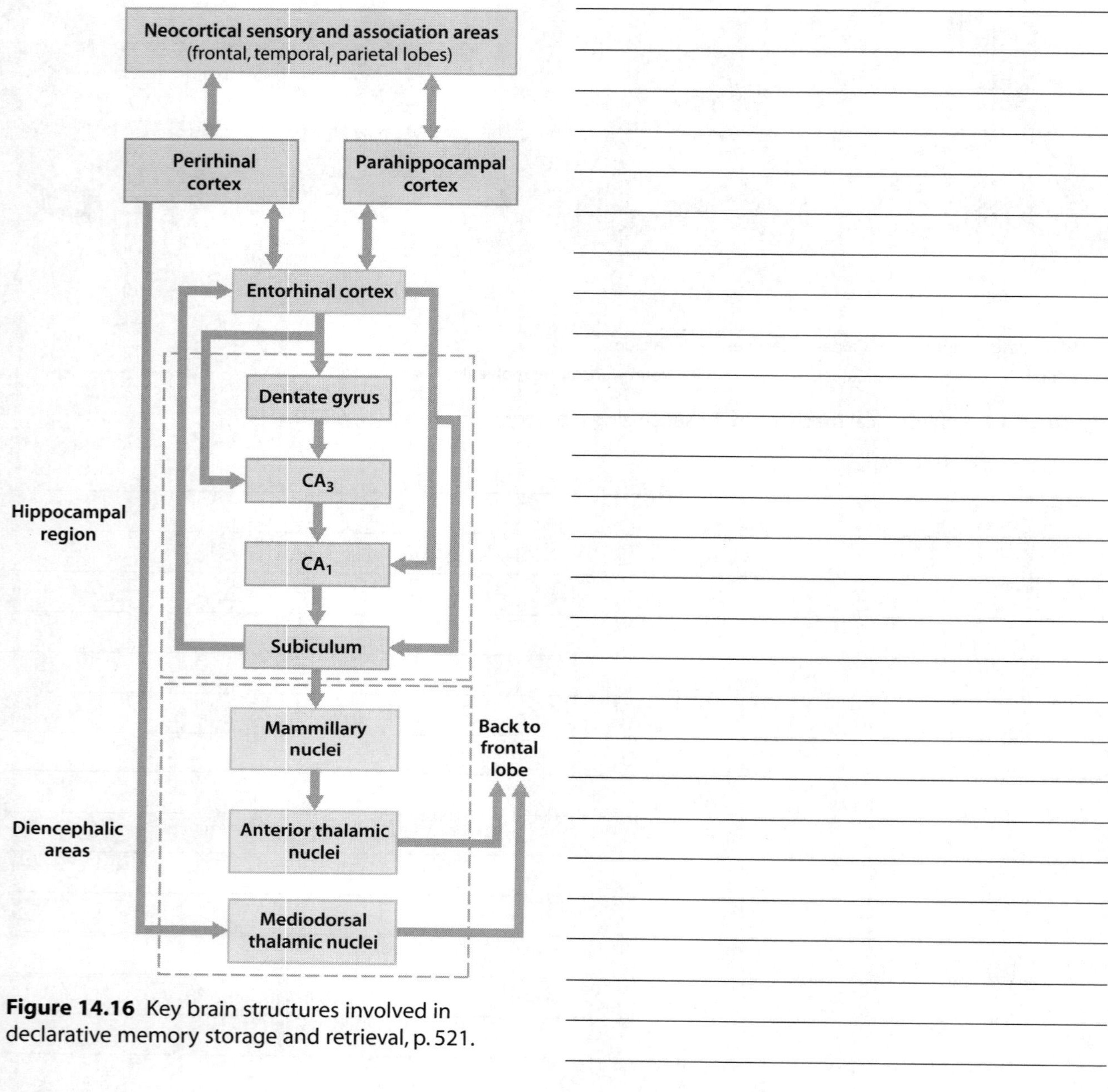

Figure 14.16 Key brain structures involved in declarative memory storage and retrieval, p. 521.

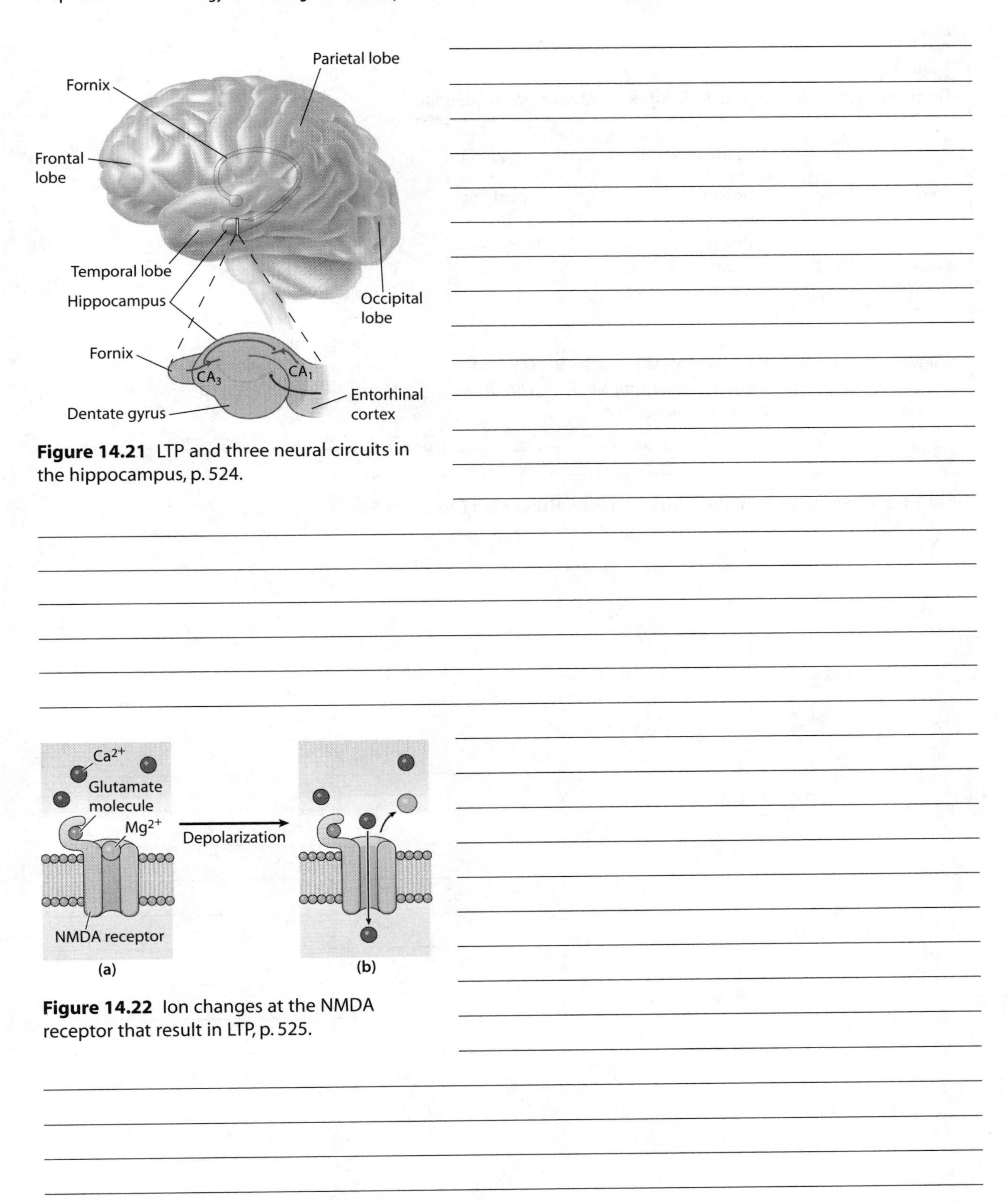

Figure 14.21 LTP and three neural circuits in the hippocampus, p. 524.

Figure 14.22 Ion changes at the NMDA receptor that result in LTP, p. 525.

Table 14.3
Characteristics of the Three Stages of Alzheimer's Disease

	Other Terms	Intelligence	Personality	Language
Stage I	Early Mild	Forgetful Disoriented Careless	Apathetic Anxious Irritable	Comprehension nearly normal Vague words in talk Naming may be impaired
Stage II	Middle	Recent events forgotten Math skills reduced	Restless	Comprehension reduced Paraphasias, jargon Naming becomes wordy Poor self-monitoring
Stage III	Late	Recent events fade fast Remote memory impaired Family not recognized	Unresponsive Withdrawn	Unresponsive Mute

Source: Adapted from Davis, G. A. (1993). *A survey of adult aphasia and related language disorders* (2nd ed.). Boston: Allyn & Bacon.

Table 14.3 Characteristics of the Three Stages of Alzheimer's Disease, p. 532.

◆ CHAPTER SUMMARY

Learning is a long-term change in behavior as a function of experience. Four types of learning are: habituation, sensitization, Pavlovian conditioning (or classical conditioning), and operant conditioning.

Memory refers to the capacity to retain and retrieve past experiences. A variety of models have been proposed to account for memory storage and retrieval. The Atkinson-Shiffrin model proposes that there are three stages of memory storage: sensory register (initial storage site), short-term store (rehearses and organizes experiences), and long-term store (site of permanent memory storage). Baddeley's rehearsal systems approach suggests that memories are transferred directly from the sensory register to long-term storage using a system called working memory. While short-term memory primarily maintains information for memorization, working memory maintains the information in order to perform complex cognitive tasks with or upon it. Lockhart and Craik's model proposes that memories differ only in the extent to which they have been processed, not in their storage level. The more completely a memory has been processed, the more likely a person is to remember it later.

There are several different types of memory: episodic (memory for information about temporally related events), semantic (memory for information about ideas or concepts organized conceptually), procedural (skill memory) and declarative (memory of facts). The workings of memory at the cellular level have long intrigued neuroscientists. Hebb proposed that our experiences activate neural circuits in the CNS that continues to reverberate in order to provide a temporary storage and record of the experience until it can be stored in permanent memory. This neural circuit was called a cell assembly.

The strength of a memory depends on the amount of time the initial experience is available. Research has supported this theory, demonstrating that specific neural circuits have the plasticity that allows them to be modified by experience. Researchers have also proposed that learning changes neural responsiveness. This cellular modification theory states that learning permanently enhances the functioning of existing neural circuits or establishes new neural connections. Research has shown that experience causes dendrite coating to break down, resulting in the establishment of new neural connections. Though this structural change appears to underlie the permanent storage of experiences, evidence indicates that memories are not stored in any specific location in the brain.

Research into the anatomy of learning and memory has implicated several brain structures. Information is first processed in the cortical sensory areas, then travels to the medial temporal lobe and the mediodorsal thalamus for further processing. In the medial temporal lobe, the hippocampus (which is connected to the frontal lobe) appears to be the key memory structure. Additionally, the caudate nucleus and putamen (in the basal ganglia) are important for procedural learning; and the amygdala modulates the memory of emotional experiences. The mediodorsal thalamus has also been associated with profound memory impairment, in particular Korsakoff's syndrome seen in chronic alcoholics.

Alzheimer's disease, a form of dementia, is a progressive impairment in mental functioning that includes deficits in language, memory, visual-spatial orientation, and judgment. There are three stages of Alzheimer's disease: stage I is characterized by mild forgetfulness and disorientation, stage II is characterized by greater forgetfulness of recent events and reduced comprehension of language, and stage III is characterized by severe memory loss, nonrecognition of family members, unresponsiveness, and total loss of language skills. Several neurological changes can be seen in people with Alzheimer's disease, including neurofibrillary tangles, senile plaques, and progressive degeneration of cholinergic and glutamatergic neurons in the hippocampus and neocortex. There is no cure for Alzheimer's disease, though current treatments aim at increasing neural ACh or reducing neuronal degeneration by limiting oxidative damage.

KEY TERMS

The following is a list of important terms introduced in Chapter 14. Give the definition of each term in the space provided.

Alzheimer's disease (AD)

amyloid beta protein

anterograde amnesia

Atkinson-Shiffrin model

cell assembly

cellular modification theory

conditioned response (CR)

conditioned stimulus (CS)

confabulation

contingency

declarative memory

dementia

episodic memory

habituation

interference

Korsakoff's syndrome

interpositus nucleus

learning

long-term depression (LTD)

long-term potentiation (LTP)

long-term store

medial temporal lobe

mediodorsal thalamus

memory

memory attribute

mossy fiber pathway

neurofibrillary tangle

neuroplasticity

NMDA receptor

operant conditioning

Pavlovian conditioning

perforant fiber pathway

procedural memory

punisher

rehearsal systems approach

reinforcer

retrograde amnesia

retrograde messenger

reverberatory activity

Schaffer collateral fiber pathway

semantic memory

senile plaque

sensitization

sensory register

short-term store

Skinner box

unconditioned response (UCR)

unconditioned stimulus (UCS)

working memory

◆ LABELING EXERCISES

1. In the diagram below give an example of each type of memory.

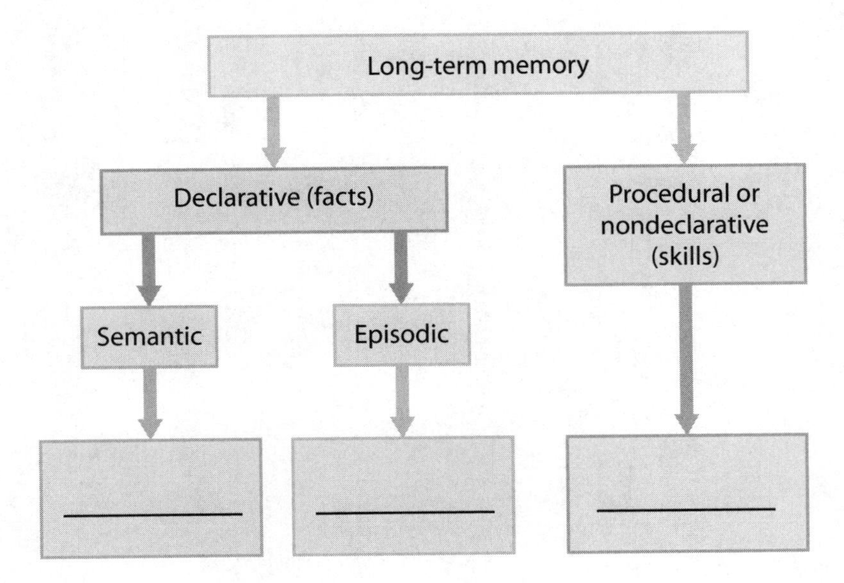

2. In the figure below label these parts

occipital lobe	fornix *(place two times)*
frontal lobe	hippocampus
parietal lobe	entorhinal cortex
temporal lobe	dentate gyrus

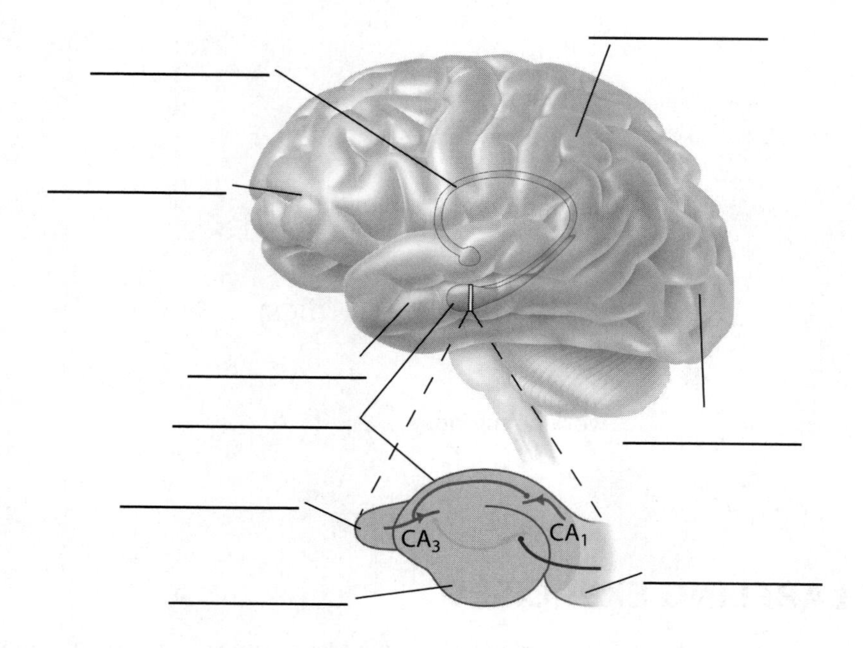

The Biological Basis of Affective Disorders and Schizophrenia

15

CHAPTER ART LECTURE NOTEBOOK

The following is a selection of the important figures introduced in Chapter 15. You can take notes during class in the space provided.

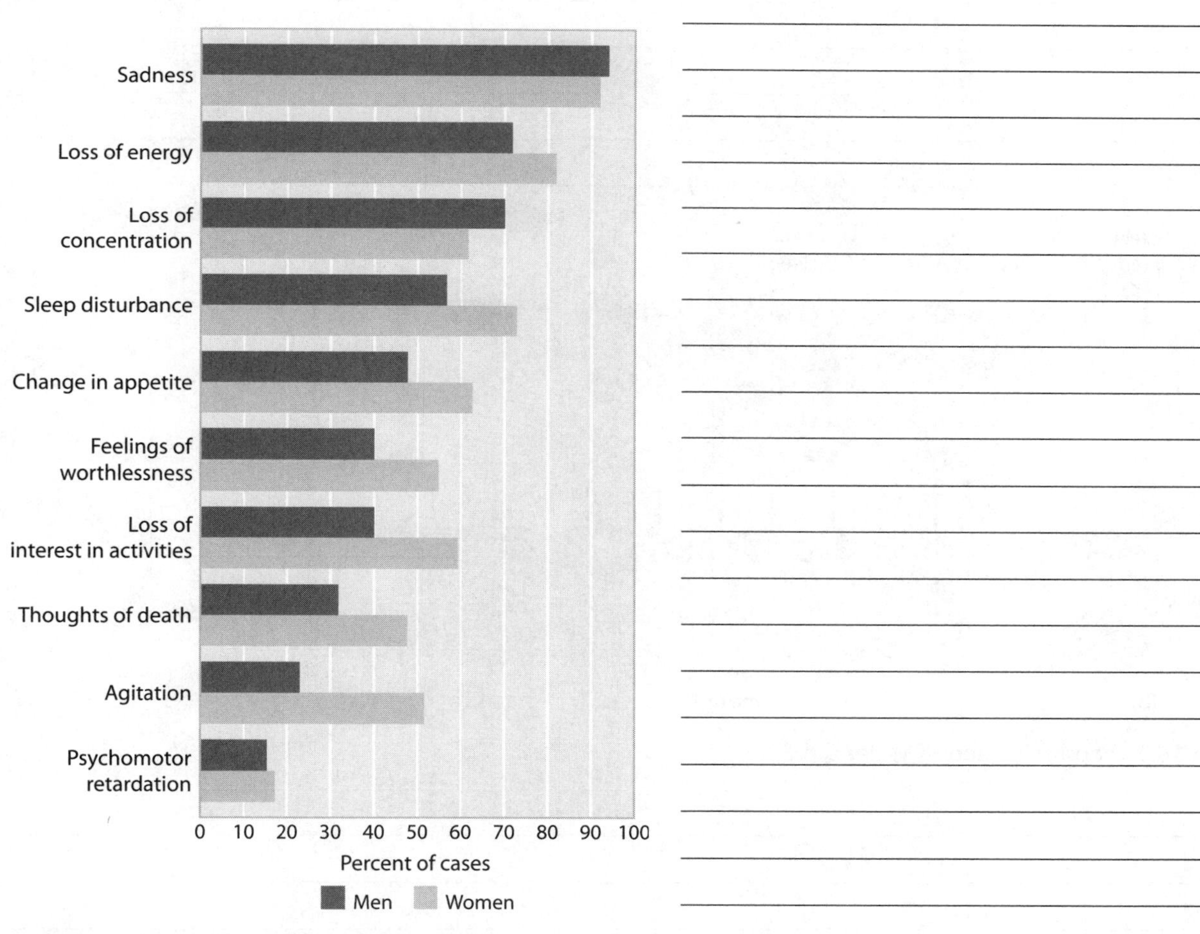

Figure 15.2 Percentage of men and women experiencing symptoms of major depression, p. 545.

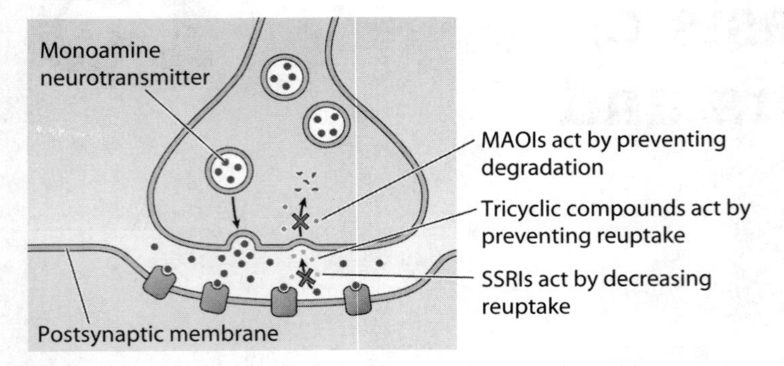

Figure 15.5 The synaptic effects of three types of antidepressant drugs, p. 551.

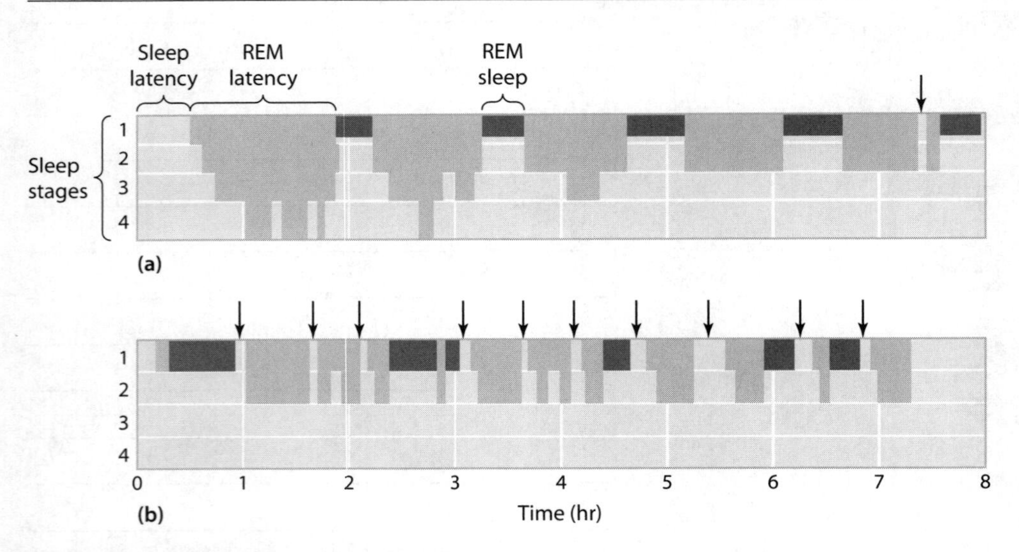

Figure 15.7 Depression and REM sleep, p. 558.

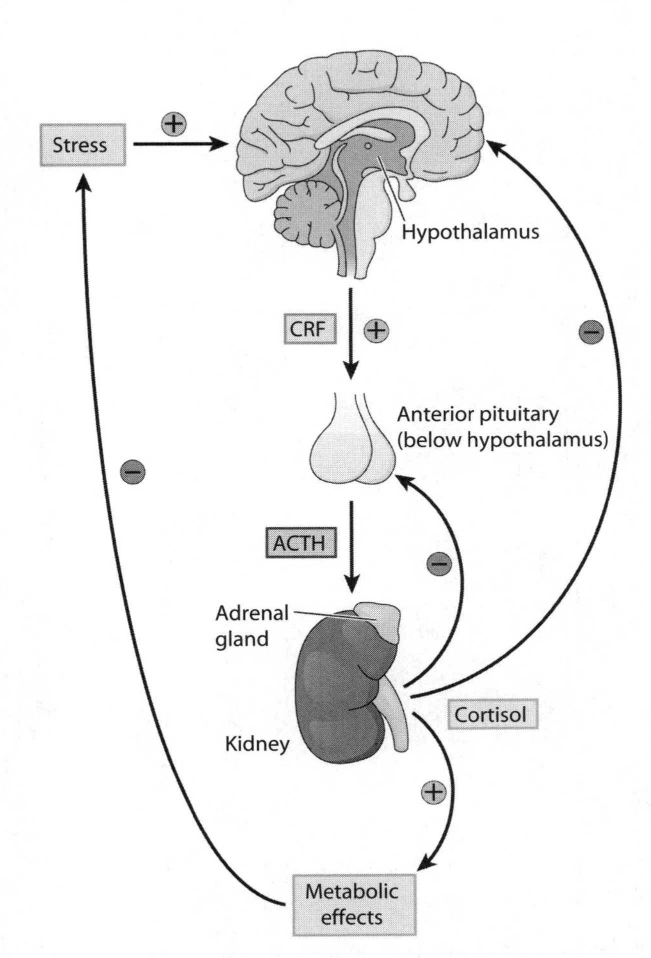

Figure 15.8 The hypothalamic-pituitary-adrenal axis, p. 559.

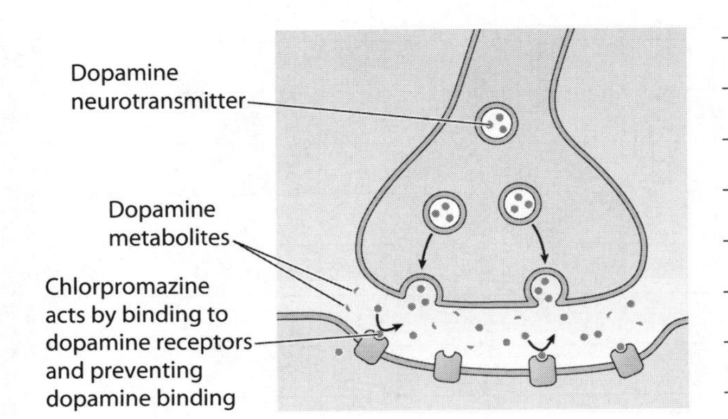

Figure 15.12 The synaptic effect of chlorpromazine, p. 565.

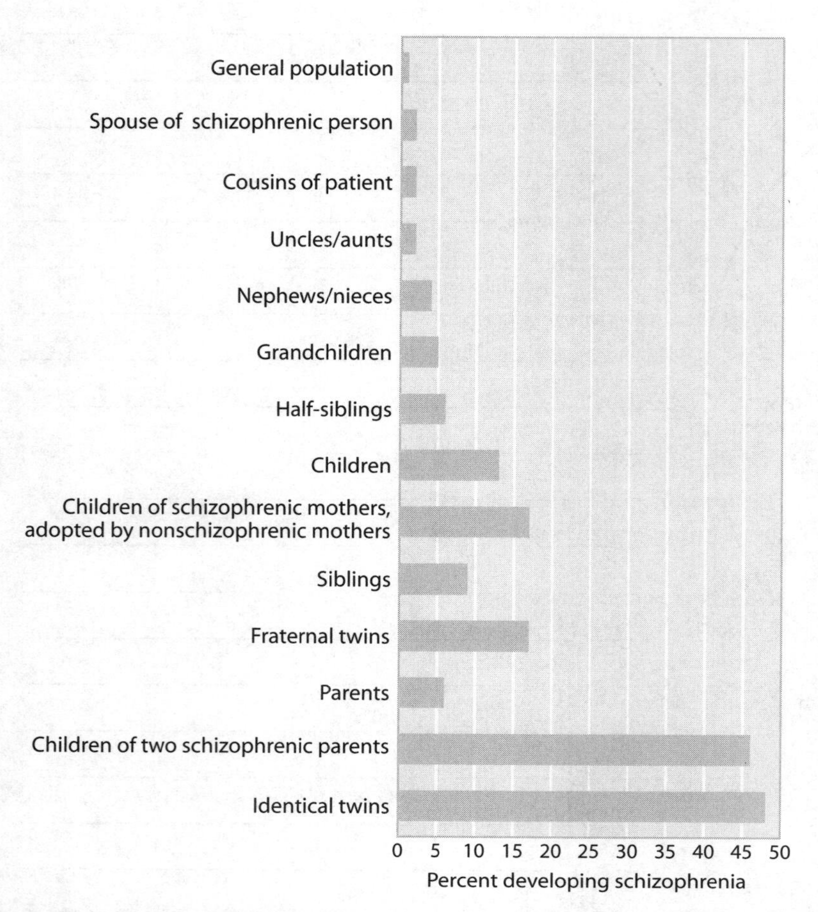

Figure 15.18 Family relationships and the risk of developing schizophrenia, p. 572.

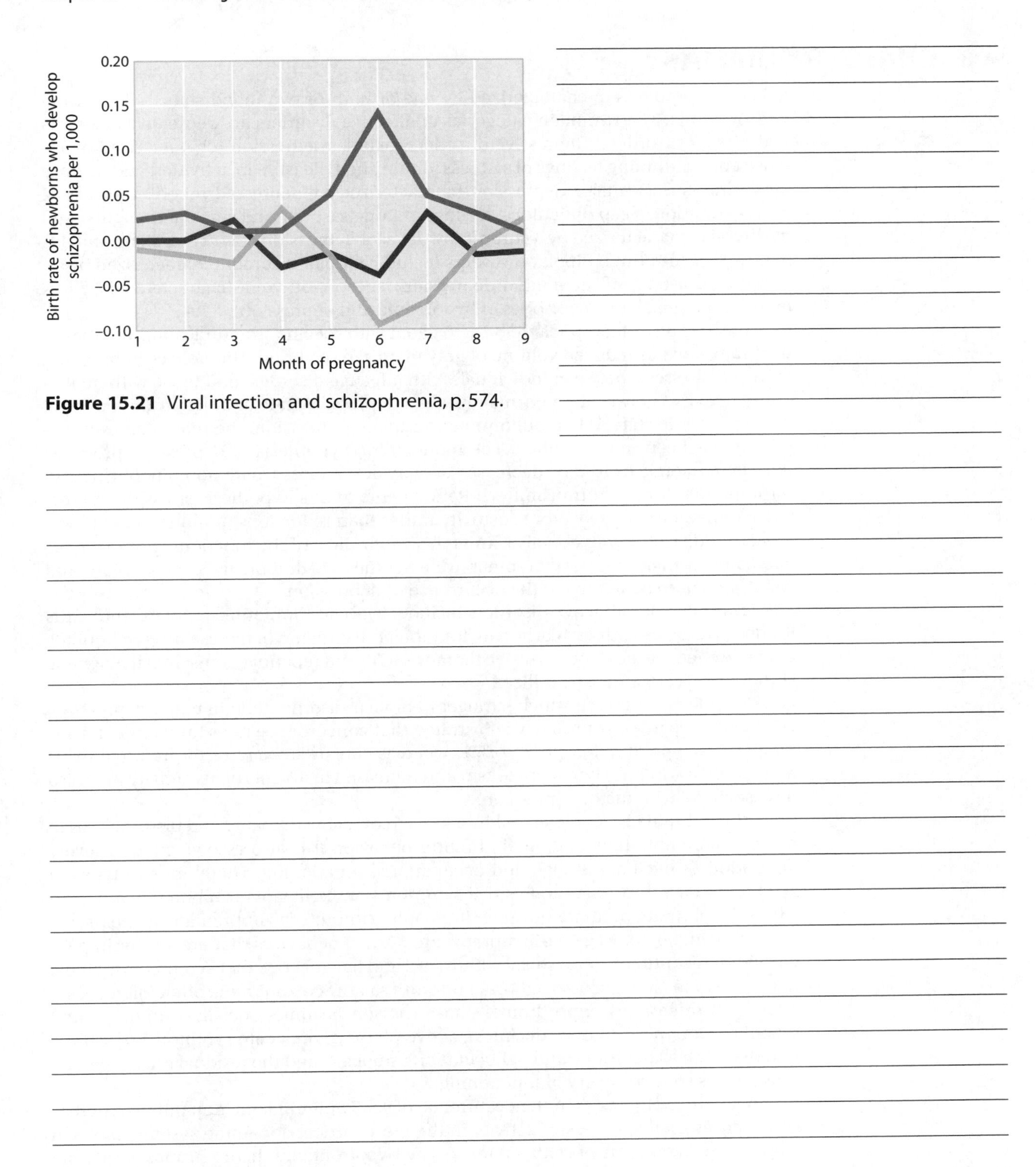

Figure 15.21 Viral infection and schizophrenia, p. 574.

CHAPTER SUMMARY

Affective disorders are characterized by one or both of two mood states—depression and/or mania. The two main categories of affective disorders are depressive disorders and bipolar disorders. Depressive disorders include: depression (characterized by intense and continuing feelings of sadness, diminished pleasure in activities, and feelings of worthlessness), major depression (characterized by depressed mood of at least 2 weeks' duration, sleep difficulties, feelings of hopelessness, and suicidal thoughts) and dysthymia (characterized by a chronic low-level of depression, low self-esteem, and difficulty concentrating). Bipolar disorders include: bipolar disorder (characterized by alternating episodes of mania and depression) and cyclothymia (characterized by less intense, but long lasting episodes of hypomania and depression).

Affective disorders appear to be associated with specific structural abnormalities in the brain, such as reduced volume of gray matter in the brain. Differences in brain activity are also seen between individuals with affective disorders and those with no disorder; activity is lower than normal during a depressive state and higher than normal during a manic state. When attempting to explain depression, the role of neurotransmitters has been much studied. The monoamine hypothesis of depression proposes that depression is caused by decreased activity at synapses where norepinephrine and serotonin are the neurotransmitters. Refinements to this hypothesis stress the importance of monoamine receptor sensitivity rather than reductions in monoamine levels. Newer models of depression also stress the importance of the functioning of the locus coeruleus, a major site of norepinephrine synthesis. Additionally, acetylcholine and GABA appear to be related to the occurrence of depression.

Treatments for affective disorders include: tricyclic compounds, MAOIs, and SSRIs for depression and lithium carbonate for bipolar disorder. When these drug treatments fail to be effective, electroconvulsive therapy (ECT) and repetitive transcranial magnetic stimulation (rTMS) may be utilized.

The role of genetics is much stronger in bipolar disorder than in major depression. For bipolar disorder, studies have illustrated that concordance rates for identical twins range from approximately 20% to 75%, whereas concordance rates for fraternal twins range from 0% to 8%. Hypercortisolism and increased locus coeruleus activity may also be associated with major depression.

Schizophrenia is characterized by a loss of contact with reality and disturbances in perception, emotion, cognition, and motor behavior. It is also associated with severe disruption of personal, social, and occupational functioning. There are two types of symptoms for schizophrenia. Positive symptoms are behaviors exhibited by a person with schizophrenia that are not seen in people without schizophrenia (e.g., delusions and hallucinations). Negative symptoms are normal behaviors that are absent in people with schizophrenia (e.g., social withdrawal and flat affect). Other symptoms include: neologism, loosening of associations, and word salad. Schizophrenia often follows a sequence of three phases: prodromal phase (person becomes socially withdrawn and school or work performance declines), active phase (more acute symptoms of schizophrenia, such as delusions and hallucinations, appear), and the residual phase (person experiences some recovery of functioning).

In an attempt to explain the occurrence of schizophrenia, the dopamine hypothesis proposes that an excess of activity in the mesocortical dopamine system results in the positive symptoms of schizophrenia. The hypofrontality theory proposes that the negative symptoms of schizophrenia are caused by decreased activity in the prefrontal cortex. Other brain abnormalities associated with schizophrenia include enlarged lateral ventricles and neuronal disorganization in the cerebral cortex and hippocampus, which may be caused by a failure of normal neural development.

In the general population, the occurrence of schizophrenia is approximately 1%. Twin studies have found a much higher concordance rate for schizophrenia in identical twins (about 48%) than in fraternal twins (about 17%), suggesting a genetic predisposition to developing schizophrenia. Additionally, family studies have illustrated that the risk of a person developing schizophrenia seems to be directly related to the closeness of the person's relationship to a family member with schizophrenia, and adoption studies have shown that the probability of an adopted child developing schizophrenia increases if a biological parent has schizophrenia, both of which provide further support for a genetic predisposition for developing schizophrenia.

◆ KEY TERMS

The following is a list of important terms introduced in Chapter 15. Give the definition of each term in the space provided.

active phase

affective disorder

bipolar disorder

concordance rate

cyclothymia

delusion

dementia praecox

depression

depressive disorder

dexamethasone suppression test (DST)

dopamine hypothesis of schizophrenia

dysthymia

electroconvulsive therapy (ECT)

hallucination

hypercortisolism

hypofrontality theory

hypomania

learned helplessness

loosening of associations

major depression

mania

monoamine oxidase inhibitor (MAOI)

monoamine hypothesis of depression

negative symptom

neologism

positive symptom

prodromal phase

residual phase

schizophrenia

serotonin-specific reuptake inhibitor (SSRI)

tardive dyskinesia

tricyclic compound

word salad

◆ LABELING EXERCISES

1. In the figure below, label the mechanisms of actions of antidepressants (MAOIs, tricyclics, and SSRIs).

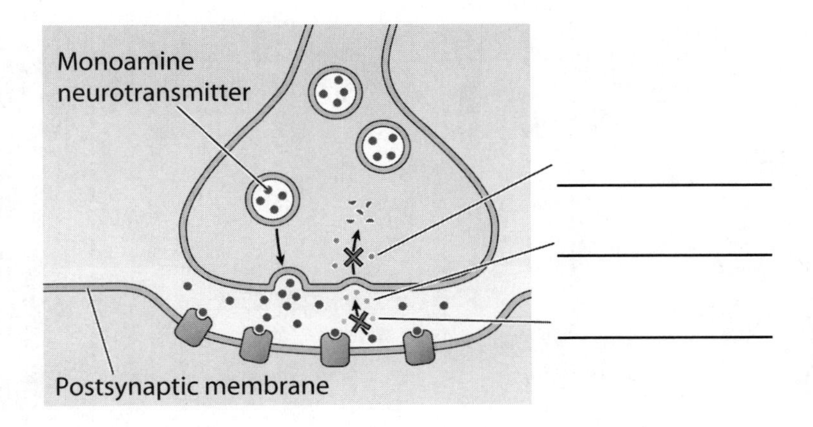

2. In the figure below, label the synaptic effect of chlorpromazine.

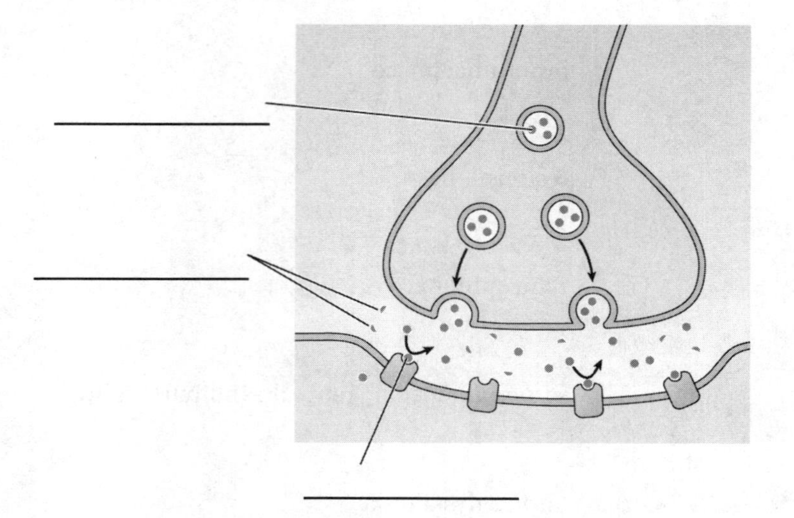

Answers

CHAPTER 1

Key Terms with Definitions

- **ablation** (p. 13): the experimental destruction of neurons or the surgical removal of a part of the brain.
- **autoradiography** (p. 19): the injection of radioactive chemicals into the bloodstream and subsequent analysis of neural tissue to determine where a specific chemical is found in the nervous system.
- **behavior** (p. 2): anything that an organism does that involves action and response to stimulation.
- **behavior genetics** (p. 24): the study of how inheritance affects the behavior of a species.
- **Bell-Magendie law** (p. 6): the principle that the dorsal root of a spinal nerve carries sensory information to the spinal cord and the ventral root conveys commands to the muscles.
- **biological psychology** (p. 2): the study of the influence of biological systems on behavior.
- **Broca's area** (p. 9): an area in the frontal lobe of the left hemisphere of the brain that contributes to speech production.
- **cerebrum** (p. 7): the uppermost portion of the brain.
- **cognitive neuroscience** (p. 18): the study of the relationship between the nervous system and mental processes.
- **comparative psychology** (p. 24): the comparative study of the behavior of different species of animals, generally in a laboratory setting.
- **computerized axial tomography (CT)** (p. 15): a technique that produces a static image of the brain by shooting a narrow beam of x-rays from all angles to produce a cross-sectional image, referred to as a CT scan or CAT scan.
- **doctrine of specific nerve energies** (p. 6): the theory that the message detected by the nervous system is determined by which nerve carries the message.
- **dualism** (p. 3): the idea that both body and mind exist.
- **electroencephalogram (EEG)** (p. 16): a graphical record of the electrical activity of the cerebral cortex.
- **engram** (p. 10): a memory trace, or the physical location of specific memories.
- **equipotentiality** (p. 10): the idea that any part of a functional area can carry out the function of that area.
- **ethology** (p. 24): the study of the behavior of animals, usually in their natural environments.
- **evoked potential** (p. 16): a neural response to sensory stimulation introduced by an experimenter.
- **functional MRI (fMRI)** (p. 18): a technique that uses high-powered, rapidly oscillating magnetic fields and powerful computation to measure cerebral blood flow in the brain and obtain an image of the neural activity in a specific brain area.
- **macroelectrode** (p. 16): an electrode designed to record from many neurons at once.
- **magnetic resonance imaging (MRI)** (p. 15): a technique that produces a static image of the brain by passing a strong magnetic field through the brain, followed by a radio wave, then measuring the radiation emitted from hydrogen atoms.
- **mass action** (p. 10): Lashley's finding that the greater the brain area destroyed, the more severe the impact on learning.
- **microdialysis** (p. 19): a technique for identifying the neurotransmitter in a specific area of the nervous system by measuring the chemical constituents of fluid from neural tissue.
- **microelectrode** (p. 16): an electrode designed to record the activity of one or a few neurons.

- **monism** (p. 3): the idea that there is only one underlying reality, either body or mind.
- **nerve net theory** (p. 12): the idea that the nervous system consists of a network of connected nerves.
- **neuron** (p. 12): a nerve cell.
- **neuronal theory** (p. 12): the idea that the nervous system is made up of individual nerve cells.
- **neuropsychology** (p. 23): the study of the behavioral effects of brain damage in humans.
- **neuroscience** (p. 21): the study of the nervous system.
- **phrenology** (p. 7): Gall's "science of the mind," which assumed that mental functions are localized in certain brain areas and that the moral and intellectual character of a person can be determined by studying the bumps and indentations on the skull.
- **physiological psychology** (p. 22): the study of the relationship between the nervous system and behavior by experimentally altering specific nervous system structures and observing the effects on behavior.
- **positron emission tomography (PET)** (p. 17): a technique that measures the metabolic activity of a specific structure in the nervous system in order to determine neural functioning.
- **pressure phosphene** (p. 6): a visual sensation caused by pressure on the optic nerve.
- **psychoactive drug** (p. 23): a drug that influences mental functioning.
- **psychopharmacology** (p. 23): the study of the effects of psychoactive drugs on behavior.
- **psychophysiology** (p.23): the study of the relationship between behavior and physiology through the analysis of the physiological responses of human subjects engaged in various activities.
- **reflex** (p. 5): an involuntary response to a stimulus, caused by a direct connection between a sensory receptor and a muscle.
- **stereotaxic apparatus** (p. 14): a surgical instrument that allows a neuroscientist to create a lesion in a specific region of the brain.
- **synapse** (p. 12): the point of functional contact between a neuron and its target.
- ***vagusstoff*** (p. 13): Loewi's term for the chemical that acts to decrease the heart rate.
- **Wernicke's area** (p. 10): an area in the temporal lobe of the left hemisphere of the brain that contributes to understanding language and producing intelligible speech.

Answers to Labeling Exercises

1.

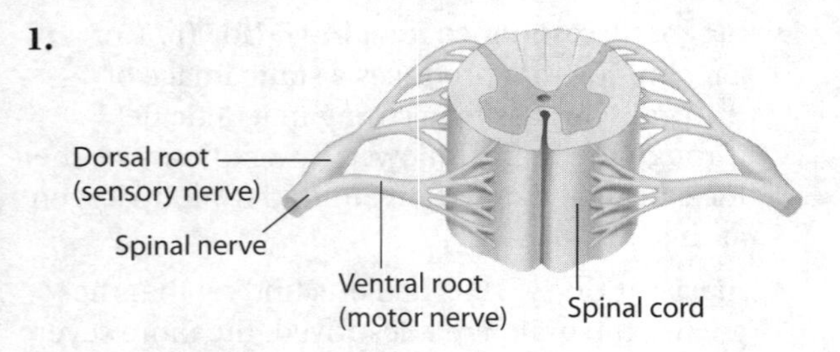

Figure 1.3, p. 5.

2.

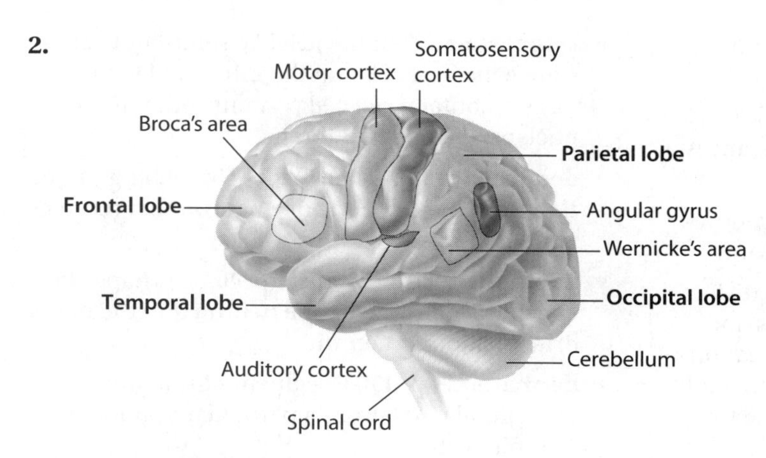

Figure 1.6, p. 9.

CHAPTER 2

Key Terms with Definitions

- **adrenocorticotropic hormone (ACTH)** (p. 60): an anterior pituitary hormone that stimulates the production and release of hormones by the adrenal cortex.
- **afferent neuron** (p. 45): a neuron that transmits messages from sensory receptors to the CNS, unless the receptors are already part of the CNS.
- **amygdala** (p. 61): a limbic system structure at the base of the temporal lobe that processes the emotions of anger and fear.
- **anterior** (p. 36): toward the front end.
- **anterior pituitary gland** (p. 60): the part of the pituitary gland that manufactures and secretes releasing hormones; also called the adenohypophysis.
- **antidiuretic hormone (ADH)** (p. 60): a posterior pituitary hormone that helps conserve bodily fluids by concentrating urine; also called vasopressin.
- **arachnoid mater** (p. 50): a thin, weblike sheet of tissue that is the middle layer of meninges.
- **astrocyte** (p. 42): a star-shaped glial cell that provides physical support for a neuron, transports nutrients into and waste products out of the neuron, regulates blood flow, and guides neural development.
- **autonomic nervous system** (p. 35): the division of the PNS containing the nerves that regulate the functioning of internal organs.
- **axoaxonic synapse** (p. 40): a synapse between the axon of one neuron and the axon of another neuron.
- **axodendritic synapse** (p. 40): a synapse between the axon of one neuron and the dendrite of another neuron.
- **axon** (p. 39): a long, relatively thick fiber that transmits neural impulses away from the neural cell body.
- **axon hillock** (p. 39): the area between the cell body and axon of a neuron where neural impulses are generated.
- **axosomatic synapse** (p. 40): a synapse between the axon of one neuron and the cell body of another neuron.
- **basal ganglia** (p. 62): a collective forebrain structure that integrates voluntary movement; consists of three nuclei: the caudate nucleus, the putamen, and the globus pallidus.
- **brain** (p. 36): the division of the CNS within the vertebrate skull, which interprets sensory messages and determines the appropriate behavioral response.
- **brain stem** (p. 57): a group of structures consisting of the hindbrain (minus the cerebellum) and the midbrain.
- **caudal** (p. 37): toward the tail.

- **cell body** (p. 39): soma; the body of a neuron from which the dendrites and axon project.
- **cell membrane** (p. 38): the structure that surrounds a cell and controls the flow of substances into and out of the cell.
- **central canal** (p. 52): the chamber of the ventricular system that runs through the spinal cord.
- **central nervous system (CNS)** (p. 36): the division of the nervous system that recognizes and analyzes the significance of sensory information, decides how to respond to that information, and sends the message to execute that response to the PNS.
- **central sulcus** (p. 64): a deep groove that separates the anterior and posterior halves of the cerebral cortex.
- **cerebellum** (p. 56): a hindbrain structure located posterior to the medulla; develops and coordinates complex movement.
- **cerebral commissure** (p. 64): a fiber tract that connects the two hemispheres of the brain.
- **cerebral cortex** (p. 62): the outer layer of the forebrain that processes sensory information, controls thinking and decision making, stores and retrieves memories, and initiates motor responses.
- **cerebrospinal fluid (CSF)** (p. 52): the clear fluid contained in the ventricular system and arachnoid space that supports and protects the CNS and provides it with nutrients.
- **choroid plexus** (p. 52): a rich network of blood vessels in the ventricles that manufactures CSF.
- **cingulate gyrus** (p. 61): a limbic system structure involved in positive and negative emotional response.
- **congenital disorder** (p. 50): a disorder that is present at birth.
- **contralateral control** (p. 64): the process by which one side of the brain controls movements on the opposite side of the body.
- **coronal section** (p. 38): a view of a structure from the front.
- **corpus callosum** (p. 64): the largest of the cerebral commissures.
- **cranial nerve** (p. 45): a group of axons that directly links sensory receptors to the brain, and the brain to certain muscles.
- **cytoplasm** (p. 38): the jellylike semi-liquid substance inside a cell and the intracellular structures it contains; all cell contents other than the nucleus and cell membrane.
- **dendrite** (p. 39): a thin, widely branching projection from the cell body of a neuron that receives neural impulses.
- **dendrodendritic synapse** (p. 40): a synapse between the dendrite of one neuron and the dendrite of another neuron.
- **dermatome** (p. 45): a segment of skin innervated by a spinal nerve from a particular segment of the spinal cord.
- **deoxyribonucleic acid (DNA)** (p. 38): an organism's genetic material; controls the production of RNA.
- **diencephalon** (p. 58): the division of the forebrain containing the epithalamus, thalamus, hypothalamus, and the pituitary gland.
- **dorsal** (p. 36): toward the back.
- **dura mater** (p. 49): the thick, tough, and flexible outermost layer of the meninges.
- **efferent neuron** (p. 45): a neuron that transmits messages from the CNS to skeletal muscles.
- **epithalamus** (p. 58): an area of the diencephalon above the thalamus; contains the pineal gland and the habenula.
- **forebrain** (p. 58): the division of the brain located rostral to and surrounding the midbrain, containing the telencephalon and the diencephalon.
- **frontal lobe** (p. 65): the lobe in the most anterior part of the cerebral cortex; responsible for executive functioning and the control of movement.
- **ganglion** (p. 39): a collection of neuronal cell bodies outside the CNS.
- **glial cell** (p. 42): a nervous system cell that has a support function.
- **gonadotropin** (p. 60): an anterior pituitary hormone that regulates the activities of the gonads.
- **gray matter** (p. 53): the cell bodies of neurons.
- **habenula** (p. 58): a structure of the epithalamus with olfactory functions.
- **hindbrain** (p. 56): the division of the brain just above the spinal cord that contains the medulla oblongata, the pons, the cerebellum, and the raphé system.

- **hippocampus** (p. 62): a limbic system structure that processes or contributes to memory storage and retrieval.
- **horizontal section** (p. 37): a view of a structure from above.
- **hydrocephalus** (p. 50): a blockage of CSF flow from the brain.
- **hypothalamus** (p. 59): a forebrain structure that detects need states and controls pituitary hormone production and release.
- **inferior** (p. 37): below a structure.
- **inferior colliculus** (p. 57): a structure in the tectum that relays auditory information.
- **interneuron** (p. 40): a neuron that connects a sensory and a motor neuron or communicates with other neurons.
- **lateral** (p. 37): away from the midline.
- **lateral geniculate nucleus (LGN)** (p. 59): a structure in the thalamus that relays visual information to the cortex.
- **lateralization of function** (p. 64): the differentiation of the functions of the two hemispheres of the brain.
- **lateral sulcus** (p. 64): a deep groove that separates the temporal from the frontal and parietal lobes of the cerebral cortex.
- **limbic system** (p. 61): a group of forebrain structures, surrounding the brain stem, that processes emotional expression and the storage and retrieval of memories.
- **longitudinal fissure** (p. 63): a deep groove that separates the right and left hemispheres.
- **medial** (p. 37): toward the midline.
- **medial geniculate nucleus (MGN)** (p. 58): a structure in the thalamus that relays auditory information to the cortex.
- **medulla oblongata** (p. 56): a hindbrain structure located just rostral to the spinal cord; controls essential functions such as respiration and heart rate.
- **melatonin** (p. 58): a hormone secreted by the pineal gland in response to daylight and darkness.
- **meninges** (p. 49): the three layers of tissue between the skull and brain and between the vertebral column and spinal cord.
- **metencephalon** (p. 56): one of two divisions of the hindbrain; contains the cerebellum and the pons.
- **microglial cell** (p. 42): a type of glial cell that removes the debris of dead neurons.
- **midbrain** (p. 57): a division of the CNS that contains the tectum and tegmentum.
- **motor cortex** (p. 65): an area in the frontal lobe involved in the control of voluntary body movements.
- **motor neuron** (p. 40): a specialized neuron that carries messages from the CNS to muscles.
- **myelencephalon** (p. 56): one of two divisions of the hindbrain; contains the medulla oblongata.
- **myelin** (p. 42): a fatlike substance that surrounds and insulates the axons of certain neurons.
- **nerve** (p. 39): a collection of axons outside the CNS, within the PNS.
- **neuromuscular junction** (p. 40): the point of contact between a neuron and a muscle.
- **neurotransmitter** (p. 40): a chemical stored in the synaptic vesicles that is released into the synaptic cleft and transmits messages to other neurons, blood vessels, or muscles.
- **nucleus (of cell)** (p. 38): the part of a cell containing chromosomes, genes, and DNA.
- **nucleus (of CNS)** (p. 39): a collection of neuronal cell bodies within the CNS.
- **occipital lobe** (p. 64): the lobe located in the most posterior part of the cerebral cortex; responsible for the analysis of visual stimuli.
- **oligodendrocyte** (p. 42): a type of glial cell that myelinates certain neurons in the CNS.
- **oxytocin** (p. 60): a posterior pituitary hormone that stimulates uterine contractions and milk secretion in females and causes prostate gland contractions in males.
- **parasympathetic nervous system** (p. 46): a division of the autonomic nervous system that is activated by conditions of recovery or the termination of stress.
- **parietal lobe** (p. 64): the lobe of the cerebral cortex located between the central sulcus and the occipital lobe; responsible for the analysis of somatosensory stimuli.
- **peripheral nervous system** (p. 35): the division of the nervous system that detects environmental

information, transmits that information to the CNS, and executes CNS decisions.

- **pia mater** (p. 51): a thin membrane that adheres closely to the surface of the brain and is the innermost layer of the meninges.
- **pineal gland** (p. 58): a structure of the epithalamus that controls seasonal rhythms in behavior through its release of melatonin.
- **pituitary gland** (p. 60): a gland located just ventral to the hypothalamus; divided into two lobes: the anterior pituitary gland and the posterior pituitary gland; also called the hypophysis.
- **pons** (p. 56): a hindbrain structure located superior to the medulla; relays sensory information to the cerebellum and thalamus.
- **posterior** (p. 36): toward the rear end.
- **posterior pituitary gland** (p. 60): the part of the pituitary gland, considered an extension of the hypothalamus, that produces and releases oxytocin and antidiuretic hormone; also called the neurohypophysis.
- **postsynaptic membrane** (p. 40): the outer surface of a target cell that receives messages from the presynaptic membrane.
- **prefrontal cortex** (p. 66): an area in the anterior part of the frontal lobe that controls complex intellectual functions.
- **prefrontal lobotomy** (p. 66): a surgical procedure that severs the connections of the prefrontal cortex to the rest of the brain.
- **presynaptic membrane** (p. 40): the outer surface of the presynaptic terminal; the site of release of neurotransmitters into the synaptic cleft.
- **presynaptic terminal** (p. 39): a swelling at the end of an axon.
- **primary auditory cortex** (p. 65): an area in the temporal lobe that receives auditory information from the thalamus.
- **primary visual cortex** (p. 64): an area in the occipital lobe that receives visual information from the thalamus.
- **raphé system** (p. 56): a group of nuclei located along the midline of the hindbrain between the medulla and midbrain; controls the sleep-wake cycle.
- **red nucleus** (p. 57): a structure in the tegmentum that controls basic body and limb movements.
- **reticular formation** (p. 56): a network of neurons that controls arousal and consciousness.
- **ribonucleic acid (RNA)** (p. 38): a substance that controls the manufacture of proteins, which regulate cell functioning.
- **rostral** (p. 37): toward the head.
- **sagittal section** (p. 37): a view that divides a structure into left and right parts.
- **Schwann cell** (p. 42): a type of glial cell that myelinates certain neurons in the PNS.
- **sensory neglect** (p. 64): a condition resulting from parietal lobe damage (usually on the right side) in which a person shows clumsiness or neglect of the side of their body opposite the damage.
- **sensory neuron** (p. 40): a specialized neuron that detects information from inside the body or from the outside world.
- **skull** (p. 49): the outer bony covering that protects the brain.
- **soma** (p. 39): cell body; the body of a neuron from which the dendrites and axon project.
- **somatic nervous system** (p. 35): the division of the PNS containing sensory receptors that detect environmental stimuli and motor nerves that activate skeletal muscles.
- **somatosensory cortex** (p. 64): an area in the anterior part of the parietal lobe that receives information about touch, pain, pressure, temperature, and body position from the thalamus.
- **somatotropin** (p. 60): a growth-promoting hormone released by the anterior pituitary; also called growth hormone.
- **spinal cord** (p. 36): the division of the CNS located within the vertebrate spinal column, which receives sensory messages from the body below the head and sends motor commands to the PNS. Most sensory messages are sent to the brain and most motor commands originate in the brain.
- **spinal nerve** (p. 45): a group of axons that transmits messages to and from the brain through the spinal cord.
- **spinal reflex** (p. 53): a reflex in which afferent sensory input enters the spinal cord and then directly innervates an efferent motor neuron.
- **subarachnoid space** (p. 51): the space between the arachnoid mater and pia mater that is filled with cerebrospinal fluid.

- **substantia nigra** (p. 57): a structure in the tegmentum that is involved in the integration of voluntary movements.
- **superior** (p. 37): above a structure.
- **superior colliculus** (p. 57): a structure in the tectum that relays visual information.
- **sympathetic nervous system** (p. 45): a division of the autonomic nervous system that is activated by challenging, stimulating, or dangerous situations.
- **synapse** (p. 40): the point of functional contact between a neuron and its target.
- **synaptic cleft** (p. 40): the space between the presynaptic and postsynaptic membranes.
- **synaptic vesicle** (p. 40): a sac within the presynaptic terminal that contains neurotransmitters.
- **tectum** (p. 57): a midbrain structure that controls simple reflexes and orients eye and ear movements.
- **tegmentum** (p. 57): a division of the midbrain that contains the substantia nigra, the red nucleus, and the reticular formation.
- **telencephalon** (p. 61): the division of the forebrain that consists of the cerebral cortex, limbic system, and basal ganglia.
- **telodendron** (p. 39): a branch at the end of an axon.
- **temporal lobe** (p. 65): the lobe of the cerebral cortex that is ventral to the lateral sulcus; responsible for the analysis of auditory stimuli, language, and some visual information.
- **thalamus** (p. 58): a forebrain structure that relays information from sensory receptors to the cerebral cortex.
- **thyroid-stimulating hormone (TSH)** (p. 60): an anterior pituitary hormone that regulates the thyroid gland.
- **tract** (p. 39): a collection of axons within the CNS, outside the PNS.
- **tumor** (p. 50): an abnormal proliferation of cells.
- **ventral** (p. 36): toward the belly.
- **ventricle** (p. 52): one of four chambers of the ventricular system in the brain.
- **ventricular system** (p. 52): a series of interconnected hollow chambers in the brain and spinal cord that contain cerebrospinal fluid.
- **ventrolateral nucleus** (p. 59): a structure in the thalamus that receives information from the cerebellum and relays this information to the motor cortex so the brain can determine whether its intended movement corresponds to the actual movement executed.
- **vertebral column** (p. 49): the outer bony covering that protects the spinal cord; also called the spinal column, spine, or backbone.
- **white matter** (p. 53): myelinated axons of neurons.

Answers to Labeling Exercises

1.

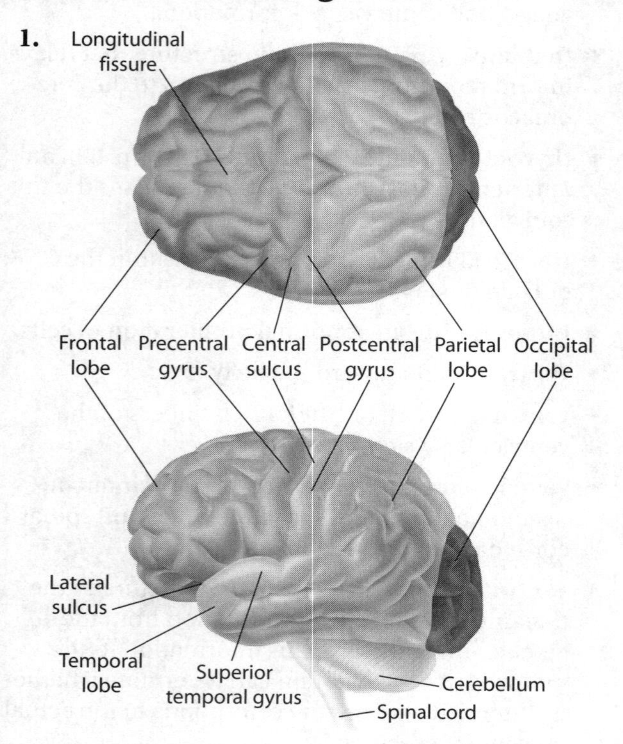

Figure 2.5, p. 39.

2.

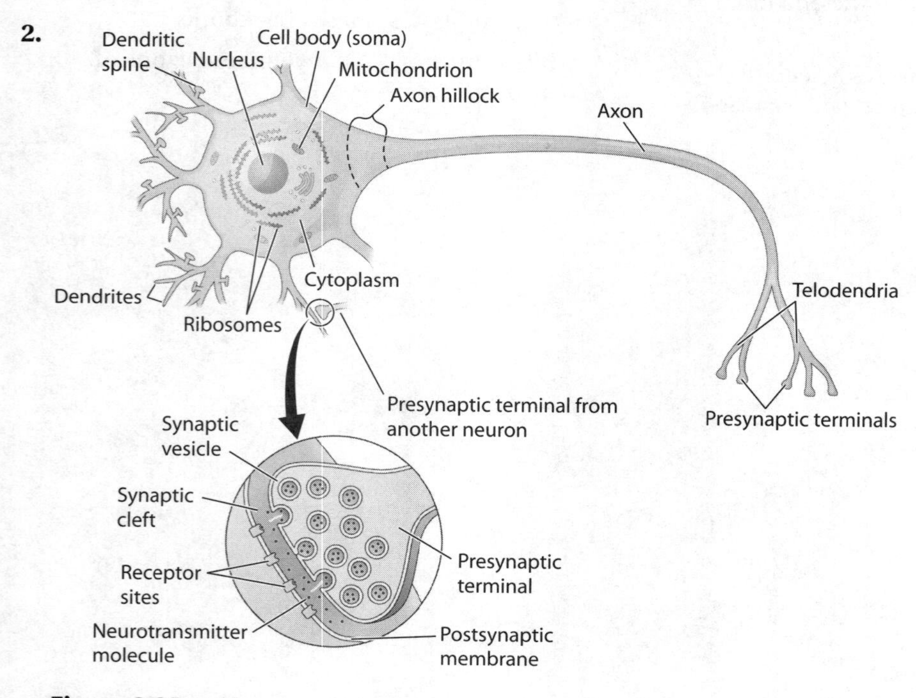

Figure 2.25, p 63.

CHAPTER 3

Key Terms with Definitions

- **alar plate** (p. 86): a zone of cells in the dorsal portion of the neural tube that develops into the sensory neurons and the interneurons of the dorsal horn of the spinal cord.
- **allele** (p. 76): an alternative form of a gene.
- **anencephaly** (p. 85): a neural tube defect that results when the brain or a major part of it fails to develop.
- **anterograde degeneration** (p. 98): the breakdown of an axon from the site of damage to the presynaptic terminals.
- **basal plate** (p. 86): a zone of cells in the ventral portion of the neural tube that develops into motor neurons and interneurons of the ventral horn of the spinal cord and the sympathetic and parasympathetic nervous systems.
- **cell-autonomous differentiation** (p. 89): the process by which neurons develop without outside influence; develop by genetic programming that directs them to develop in a particular way.
- **cephalization** (p. 81): the evolutionary process of concentrating neurons in the head region; the fusion of many ganglion pairs to form an increasingly larger and more complex brain.
- **chemotropism** (p. 91): the process by which a target cell releases chemicals that attract filopodia and guide the axon to its appropriate location in the nervous system.
- **chromatolysis** (p. 98): the breakdown of a neuronal cell body following damage to the axon.
- **chromosome** (p. 74): the structure in the nucleus of each cell that contains genes.
- **collateral sprouting** (p. 100): a process by which neighboring neurons of a degenerating neuron sprout new axonal endings to connect to the receptor sites left vacated by the degenerated neuron.
- **conception** (p. 83): the moment of fertilization of an egg by a sperm.
- **cortical plate** (p. 88): a layer of daughter cells between the intermediate and marginal layers that develop into the neurons and glial cells of the cerebral cortex.
- **crossing over** (p. 76): the exchange of genetic material between chromosomes of a chromosome pair during meiosis.
- **deoxyribonucleic acid (DNA)** (p. 74): a large, double-stranded molecule consisting of the nitrogen-containing bases adenine, guanine, cytosine, and thymine, which are attached to the sugar deoxyribose; the hereditary material.
- **diencephalon** (p. 85): the division of the forebrain that becomes the epithalamus, the thalamus, and the hypothalamus.
- **differentiation** (p. 84): the creation of different cell types.
- **dominant allele** (p. 76): a form of a gene that determines the expression of a physical characteristic, regardless of whether it is present as one or both members of a pair of alleles.
- **Down syndrome** (p. 95): a genetic disorder caused by an extra copy of chromosome 21; characterized by altered facial features, decreased mental functioning, and abnormalities in several internal organs.
- **ectoderm** (p. 84): the outermost layer of the embryo, which will become the nervous system, the skin, and parts of the eyes and ears.
- **embryo** (p. 84): the human developmental stage for the first 8 weeks after conception.
- **endoderm** (p. 84): the innermost layer of the embryo, which will form linings of the intestines, lungs, and liver.
- **evolution** (p. 79): the process by which succeeding generations of organisms change in physical appearance, function, and behavior through a process of natural selection.
- **fertilization** (p. 83): the fusion of an egg nucleus and sperm nucleus.
- **fetal alcohol syndrome (FAS)** (p. 96): a disorder caused by alcohol consumption by the mother during pregnancy; characterized by low birth weight and diminished height, distinctive facial features, mental retardation, and behavioral problems (hyperactivity and irritability).

- **fetus** (p. 84): the human developmental stage beginning at 8 weeks and continuing for the remainder of the pregnancy.
- **filopodia** (p. 91): spinelike extensions from the growth cone that pull the axon to the target cell.
- **fragile X syndrome** (p. 95): a disorder caused by a fragile gene at one site on the large arm of the X chromosome that can cause the chromosome to break; characterized by an abnormal facial appearance and mental retardation.
- **ganglion** (p. 80): a group of neurons with a specialized function.
- **gene** (p. 74): a unit of heredity; a region of DNA that directs the making of a protein.
- **genetics** (p. 74): the science of heredity.
- **glycoprotein** (p. 89): a class of compounds in which a protein is combined with a carbohydrate group.
- **growth cone** (p. 91): the swollen end of the developing neuron from which an axon emerges.
- **guidepost cell** (p. 91): a cell that redirects the growth of the axon toward the target cell.
- **heterozygous** (p. 77): describes an allele pair in which the two alleles are different.
- **homozygous** (p. 76): describes an allele pair with identical alleles.
- **Huntington's disease** (p. 78): a progressive neurological disorder characterized by psychiatric symptoms, dementia, and a slow deterioration of muscle control; caused by a single dominant gene.
- **induction** (p. 90): a process in which neurons rely on the influence of other cells to determine their final form.
- **invertebrate** (p. 80): an animal without a backbone.
- **locus** (p. 76): the location of a gene on a chromosome.
- **meiosis** (p. 76): the process by which gametes, sperm and egg cells with half the number of chromosomes found in other cells, are formed.
- **mesencephalon** (p. 85): another name for the midbrain.
- **mesoderm** (p. 84): the middle layer of the embryo, which will form the connective tissue, muscle, and blood and blood vessel linings.
- **metencephalon** (p. 85): the division of the hindbrain that becomes the pons and the cerebellum.
- **myelencephalon** (p.85): the division of the hindbrain that becomes the medulla oblongata.
- **neural crest** (p. 85): a specialized group of cells that migrate away from the neural tube to form several types of tissue, including the sensory and autonomic neurons of the peripheral nervous system (PNS).
- **neural fold** (p. 84): the lateral edge of the neural plate.
- **neural groove** (p. 85): the space formed between the edges of the neural fold.
- **neural plate** (p. 84): the thickened ectodermal layer of the embryo.
- **neural regeneration** (p. 99): the regrowth of a neuron and the re-establishment of its connections to other neurons.
- **neural tube** (p. 85): the closed space that is formed when the neural folds meet and close the neural groove.
- **neurogenesis** (p. 88): the formation of new neurons.
- **neuroplasticity** (p. 88): the ability of cognitive areas of the brain to form new neurons.
- **neurotrophin** (p. 91): a chemical released by a target cell that attracts the filopodia of a developing neuron.
- **phenylketonuria (PKU)** (p. 95): a genetic disorder involving the absence of an enzyme needed to break down phenylalanine; the resulting buildup of phenylalanine can lead to mental retardation.
- **prosencephalon** (p. 85): another name for the forebrain, which divides into the telencephalon and the diencephalon.
- **radial glial cell** (p. 88): a glial cell that guides the migration of daughter cells during the embryonic development of the nervous system.
- **recessive allele** (p. 76): a form of a gene that can determine the expression of a specific physical characteristic only when it is present as both members of a pair of alleles.
- **rehabilitation** (p. 103): the process of developing compensatory behaviors that substitute for lost functions.

- **retrograde degeneration** (p. 98): the progressive breakdown of an axon between the site of the break and the cell body.
- **rhombencephalon** (p. 85): another name for the hindbrain.
- **ribonucleic acid** (p. 75): a single-stranded molecule consisting of four nitrogenous bases—adenine, guanine, cytosine, and uracil; directs the synthesis of proteins.
- **spina bifida** (p. 85): a neural tube defect that results when some part of the neural folds fails to close.
- **subventricular layer** (p. 88): a layer of daughter cells between the intermediate and marginal layers that become either glial cells or interneurons.
- **supraesophageal ganglion** (p. 81): a primitive brain above the esophagus, formed by the fusion of several ganglion pairs in certain invertebrates.
- **target cell** (p. 91): a cell with which a neuron establishes synaptic connections.
- **telencephalon** (p. 85): the division of the forebrain that becomes the cerebral cortex, the basal ganglia, and the limbic system.
- **transneuronal degeneration** (p. 99): damage to neurons with which a degenerating neuron has synaptic connections.
- **ventricular layer** (p. 88): the innermost layer of the developing nervous system; its cells become daughter cells, some of which become neurons or glial cells.
- **vertebrate** (p. 81): an animal with a protective covering over its spinal cord and brain.
- **zygote** (p. 84): a single cell formed when the sperm fertilizes the egg.

Answers to Labeling Exercises

1.

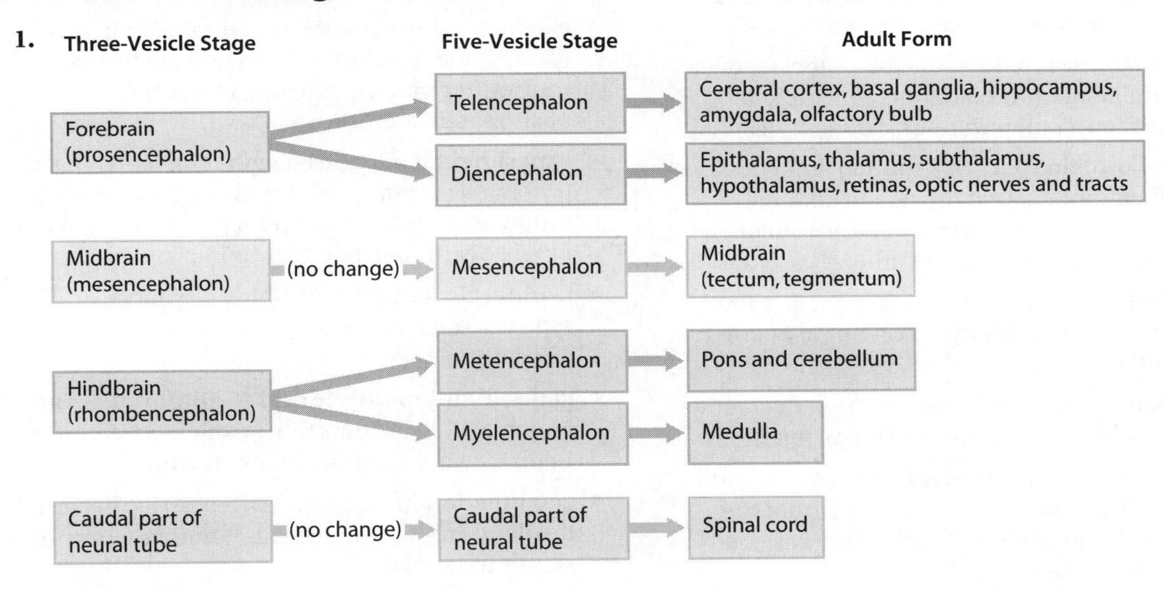

Figure 3.17, p. 86.

CHAPTER 4

Key Terms with Definitions

- **absolute refractory period** (p. 115): the time during which the neuron is insensitive to further stimulation.
- **acetylcholine (ACh)** (p. 133): a neurotransmitter synthesized from acetyl CoA and choline by the enzyme choline acetyltransferase.

- **acetylcholinesterase (AChE)** (p. 133): an enzyme present in the synaptic cleft that quickly deactivates ACh after it is released.
- **action potential** (p. 114): the changes that occur within the neuron in response to a stimulus, also called the spike potential or firing of the neuron.
- **adrenergic** (p. 130): describing a synapse or synaptic transmission with norepinephrine as the neurotransmitter.
- **all-or-none law** (p. 116): a principle stating that the strength of an action potential is independent of the intensity of the stimulus that elicits it.
- **anaxonic neuron** (p. 139): a neuron without an axon.
- **autoreceptor** (p. 125): a presynaptic receptor whose stimulation decreases the amount of neurotransmitter released by that presynaptic neuron.
- **axon hillock** (p. 117): the part of the neuron where the axon and the action potential begin.
- **blood-brain barrier** (p. 140): a barrier between the blood and the brain that prevents the free flow of substances between the two.
- **catecholamines** (p. 130): one of a subclass of monoamine neurotransmitters that includes epinephrine, norepinephrine, and dopamine.
- **channel protein** (p. 111): a protein embedded in the cell membrane that provides a channel through which substances can pass from one side of the membrane to the other.
- **cholinergic** (p. 133): describing a synapse or synaptic transmission with ACh as the neurotransmitter.
- **connexon** (p. 139): a specialized protein channel through which ions move across gap junctions.
- **dendrodendritic transmission** (p. 139): communication between anaxonic neurons from the dendrites of one neuron to the dendrites of another neuron.
- **depolarization** (p. 114): a reduction in electrical charge across the neuronal cell membrane.
- **diffusion** (p. 111): the tendency of molecules to move from areas of higher concentration to areas of lower concentration.
- **dopamine** (p. 130): a neurotransmitter synthesized from the amino acid tyrosine; closely related to norepinephrine.
- **dopaminergic** (p. 130): describing a synapse or synaptic transmission with dopamine as the neurotransmitter.
- **electrical synapse** (p. 139): the junction between the dendrites of two neurons where localized depolarization or hyperpolarization is produced.
- **electrostatic pressure** (p. 112): the attraction of opposite-polarity (+/-) particles and the repulsion of same-polarity (+/+ or −/−) particles.
- **endocrine system** (p. 136): the system of glands that releases hormones into the bloodstream, where they are carried to distant target areas.
- **endogenous opioid** (p. 135): one of a class of neurotransmitters that have opiate-like characteristics.
- **enzymatic degradation** (p. 126): breakdown and thus deactivation of neurotransmitter molecule by an enzyme.
- **epinephrine** (p. 130): a neurotransmitter closely related to norepinephrine; also called adrenalin (adrenaline).
- **excitatory postsynaptic potential (EPSP)** (p. 122): the depolarization produced by neurotransmitter molecules acting on receptors on the postsynaptic membrane.
- **experimental allergic encephalomyelitis (EAE)** (p. 141): a neurological disorder resembling MS produced by injecting myelin proteins into the bloodstreams of laboratory animals.
- **GABAergic** (p. 129): describing a synapse or synaptic transmission with GABA as the neurotransmitter.
- **gamma-aminobutyric acid (GABA)** (p. 129): an amino acid neurotransmitter, the most common inhibitory neurotransmitter in the brain.
- **gap junction** (p. 139): the narrow space between the dendrites of two neurons; another name for an electrical synapse.
- **glutamate** (p. 129): an amino acid neurotransmitter, the most common excitatory neurotransmitter in the CNS.
- **glutamatergic** (p. 129): describing a synapse or synaptic transmission with glutamate as the neurotransmitter.
- **graded potential** (p. 123): an EPSP or IPSP received by the dendrites and cell body that can have a different value at different times.

- **hormone** (p. 136): a chemical produced by the endocrine glands that is circulated widely throughout the body via the bloodstream.
- **hyperpolarized** (p. 115): having an electrical charge across the cell membrane that is more negative than normal.
- **indoleamine** (p. 130): one of a subclass of monoamine neurotransmitters that includes serotonin and melatonin.
- **inhibitory postsynaptic potential (IPSP)** (p. 122): the hyperpolarization produced by neurotransmitter molecules acting on receptors on the postsynaptic membrane.
- **ion** (p. 111): a charged particle, such as a sodium (Na^+), potassium (K^+), or chloride (Cl^-) ion.
- **ionotropic receptor** (p. 125): a receptor whose ion channels are rapidly opened by the direct action of a neurotransmitter.
- **metabotropic receptor** (p. 125): a receptor whose ion channels are opened indirectly by a second messenger.
- **monoamine** (p. 130): one of a class of neurotransmitters that contain an amino group (NH_2); includes epinephrine, norepinephrine, dopamine, and serotonin.
- **monoamine oxidase (MAO)** (p. 130): an enzyme that deactivates norepinephrine, dopamine, and serotonin.
- **monoamine oxidase inhibitor (MAOI)** (p. 132): a type of drug that increases monoamine levels by preventing MAO from degrading excess monoamine neurotransmitters.
- **multiple sclerosis (MS)** (p. 120): a progressive neurological disorder caused by the degeneration of the myelin sheath in the central nervous system.
- **myelin sheath** (p. 119): the segments of myelin covering certain axons; myelinated axons transmit a neural impulse faster than unmyelinated axons.
- **negative feedback loop** (p. 137): the release of a substance that acts to inhibit its subsequent release.
- **neural impulse** (p. 117): the propagation of an action potential along an axon.
- **neuromodulator** (p. 135): a type of chemical that modifies the sensitivity of groups of cells to neurotransmitters or the amount of neurotransmitter released.
- **neuropeptide** (p. 134): a peptide that functions as a neurotransmitter.
- **neurotransmitter reuptake** (p. 126): the return of neurotransmitter to the presynaptic neuron.
- **nitric oxide (NO)** (p. 133): a soluble gas neurotransmitter involved in such disparate functions as penile erection and learning.
- **node of Ranvier** (p. 119): the space between myelinated segments of a myelinated axon.
- **noradrenergic** (p. 130): describing a synapse or synaptic transmission with norepinephrine as the neurotransmitter.
- **norepinephrine** (p. 130): a neurotransmitter synthesized from the amino acid tyrosine; sometimes called noradrenalin (noradrenaline).
- **pheromone** (p. 138): a chemical released into the air, rather than into the bloodstream, that affects other members of a species.
- **positive feedback loop** (p. 137): the release of a substance that acts to promote its further release.
- **presynaptic facilitation** (p. 125): the enhanced release of neurotransmitter from the presynaptic membrane caused by the action of another neuron.
- **presynaptic inhibition** (p. 124): a decrease in the release of neurotransmitter from the presynaptic membrane (despite the occurrence of an action potential) caused by the action of another neuron.
- **pump protein** (p. 111): a protein in the cell membrane that exchanges one type of ion on one side of the membrane for another ion on the other side of the membrane.
- **rate law** (p. 116): a principle stating that the greater the stimulus intensity, the faster the rate of neural firing (up to the maximum rate possible for the neuron).
- **receptor protein** (p. 111): a protein in the cell membrane that recognizes and binds a specific neurotransmitter.
- **relative refractory period** (p. 115): the time following the absolute refractory period during which a neuron can be activated but only by a more intense stimulus than normal.

- **repolarization** (p. 115): the process of recovery of the resting membrane potential.
- **resting membrane potential** (p. 111): the difference in polarity between the inside and the outside of the cell membrane when the neuron is at rest.
- **saltatory conduction** (p. 119): the propagation of an action potential from node to node in myelinated axons.
- **second messenger** (p. 125): a chemical that causes changes inside the cell in response to a neurotransmitter that leads to ion channel changes.
- **selective serotonin reuptake inhibitor (SSRI)** (p. 132): a type of drug that increases the availability of serotonin by inhibiting its reuptake.
- **serotonergic** (p. 131): describing a synapse or synaptic transmission with serotonin as the neurotransmitter.
- **serotonin** (p. 131): a neurotransmitter synthesized from the amino acid tryptophan; also known as 5-HT.
- **sodium-potassium pump** (p. 112): a protein in the cell membrane that expels three Na^+ ions for every two K^+ ions it conveys into the cell.
- **soluble gas** (p. 133): a class of neurotransmitters that includes nitric oxide and carbon monoxide.
- **spatial summation** (p. 123): the combined effects of neurotransmitters binding to different locations on the postsynaptic membrane at a particular moment in time.
- **temporal summation** (p. 123): the combined effects of neurotransmitter binding over time.
- **threshold** (p. 114): the level of cell membrane depolarization required for an action potential to occur.
- **transmitter-gated ion channel** (p. 122): an ion channel sensitive to a specific neurotransmitter.
- **tricyclic compound** (p. 132): a type of drug that increases brain levels of norepinephrine and serotonin by interfering with neurotransmitter reuptake.
- **voltage-gated ion channel** (p. 115): an ion channel sensitive to changes in the cell membrane potential.

Answers to Labeling Exercises

1.

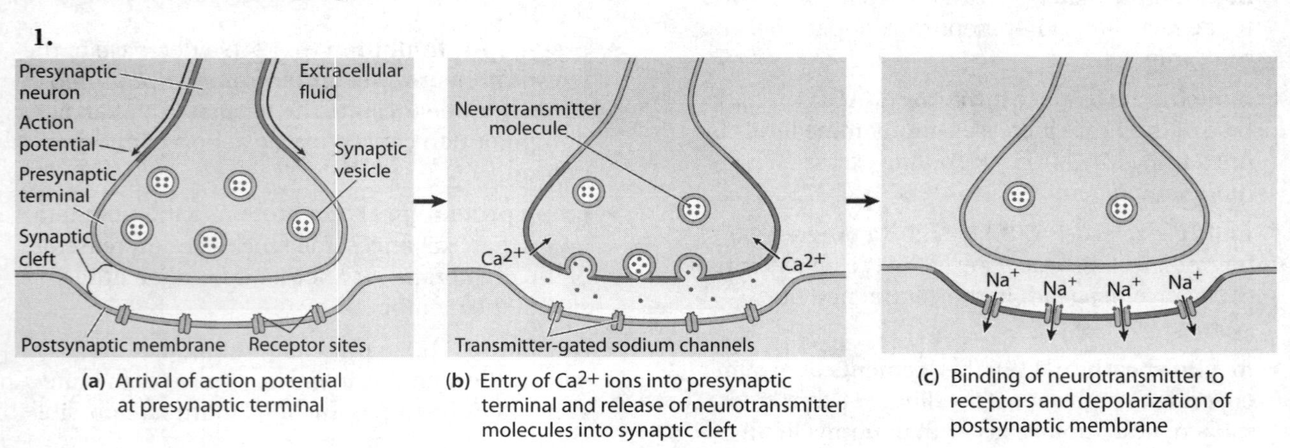

(a) Arrival of action potential at presynaptic terminal

(b) Entry of Ca^{2+} ions into presynaptic terminal and release of neurotransmitter molecules into synaptic cleft

(c) Binding of neurotransmitter to receptors and depolarization of postsynaptic membrane

Figure 4.11, p. 121.

2.

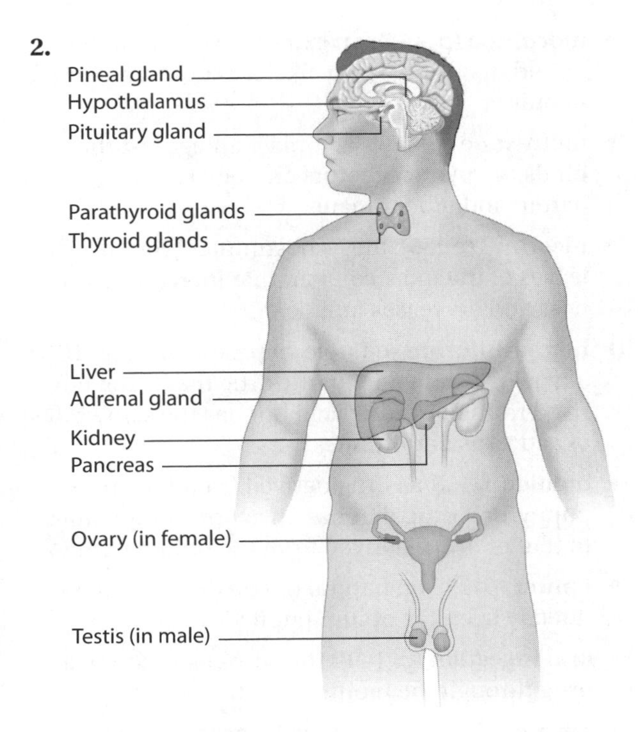

Figure 4.25, p. 136.

CHAPTER 5

Key Terms with Definitions

- **agonist** (p. 152): a drug that mimics or enhances the activity of a neurotransmitter.
- **alcohol** (p. 159): ethyl alcohol (ethanol); a powerful depressant that strongly influences consciousness and the ability to respond effectively to the environment.
- **alcoholism** (p. 161): a dependence on alcohol.
- **amphetamine** (p. 164): a collective term for psychostimulant drugs typically used to treat attention deficit hyperactivity disorder and sleep disorders.
- **anandamide** (p. 174): a naturally occurring THC-like substance.
- **antagonist** (p. 152): a drug that blocks the activity of a neurotransmitter.
- **anxiolytic** (p. 162): a sedative-hypnotic drug often used to reduce nervousness, anxiety, or fear.
- **barbiturate** (p. 161): a type of sedative-hypnotic drug that is a derivative of barbituric acid.
- **benzodiazepine** (p. 162): a widely prescribed subclass of antianxiety drugs.
- **caffeine** (p. 164): a psychostimulant found in various plants that increases alertness and decreases fatigue.
- **cocaine** (p. 164): a psychostimulant extracted from the leaves of the coca plant that increases alertness, decreases fatigue, and produces a pleasurable emotional state.
- **codeine** (p. 156): an alkaloid found in opium that is less potent than morphine.
- **depressant** (p. 159): a type of psychoactive drug that acts on the CNS to slow down mental and physical functioning.
- **false transmitter** (p. 153): a drug that prevents a neurotransmitter from binding to a receptor by attaching to the receptor on the postsynaptic membrane.
- **half-life** (p. 150): the amount of time it takes the body to eliminate half of a drug.

- **heroin** (p. 156): a powerful semisynthetic opioid made by reacting acetic anhydride with morphine.
- **inhalation** (p. 150): the administration of a drug through the lungs.
- **intracerebral injection** (p. 149): an injection of a drug directly into the brain.
- **intramuscular (IM) injection** (p. 149): an injection of a drug into a muscle.
- **intraperitoneal (IP) injection** (p. 149): an injection of a drug through the abdominal wall into the peritoneal cavity, or space surrounding major organs.
- **intravenous (IV) injection** (p. 149): an injection of a drug into a vein.
- **intraventricular injection** (p. 150): an injection of a drug into the cerebral ventricles in order to achieve widespread distribution in the brain and bypass the blood-brain barrier.
- **lysergic acid diethylamide (LSD)** (p. 170): a powerful synthetic psychedelic drug, also known as acid.
- **marijuana** (p. 173): a drug obtained from a mixture of crushed leaves, flowers, stems, and seeds of the hemp plant *Cannabis sativa.*
- **MDMA** (p. 171): the abbreviation for 3, 4-methylenedioxymethamphetamine, a synthetic psychoactive drug, known as ecstasy, that induces a state of consciousness that facilitates communication.
- **medial forebrain bundle (MFB)** (p. 176): a pathway of nerve fibers that interconnects structures in the limbic system with brainstem areas; considered part of the reinforcement system of the brain.
- **mescaline** (p. 170): the psychoactive ingredient in peyote.
- **mesolimbic reinforcement system (MRS)** (p. 178): the brain reinforcement system traveling from the ventral tegmental area through the MFB to end in limbic structures, particularly the nucleus accumbens.
- **metabolite** (p. 150): a component molecule of a drug, produced by enzymatic breakdown, that typically has little or none of the effect of the parent compound.
- **methadone** (p. 182): an opioid drug with pleasurable effects similar to those of heroin, used to treat heroin addiction.
- **morphine** (p. 156): an extremely potent natural opioid that is the main alkaloid compound found in opium.
- **naltrexone** (p. 183): an opiate antagonist that binds to opiate receptors and blocks the action of heroin and other opiates.
- **nicotine** (p. 165): a psychostimulant found in the leaves of the tobacco plant that increases alertness and decreases fatigue.
- **nonbarbiturate sedative-hypnotic drug** (p. 161): a type of sedative-hypnotic drug that is not derived from barbituric acid but has the same mode of action as barbiturates.
- **opioid** (p. 156): a drug derived from the opium poppy, or a drug that has an action comparable to that of drugs derived from the opium poppy.
- **opium** (p. 156): a natural opiate drug obtained directly from the opium poppy.
- **oral ingestion** (p. 149): the administration of a drug through the mouth.
- **peyote** (p. 170): a psychedelic drug obtained from the peyote cactus plant.
- **pharmacodynamics** (p. 149): the study of the effects of a drug on the living organism, on the organs of the body.
- **pharmacokinetics** (p. 149): the study of how a drug moves through the body, including absorption, metabolism, distribution to tissues, and elimination.
- **phencyclidine (PCP)** (p. 171): a powerful synthetic psychedelic drug, also known as angel dust.
- **psychedelic drug** (p. 170): a drug that profoundly alters a person's state of consciousness.
- **psychoactive drug** (p. 148): a drug that affects mental functioning.
- **psychopharmacology** (p. 149): the study of the effects of drugs on behavior.
- **psychostimulant** (p. 163): a drug that produces alertness by enhancing the functioning of the sympathetic nervous system and the reticular formation.
- **sedative-hypnotic drug** (p. 159): a drug that has a calming (sedative) effect at low doses and a sleep-inducing effect at higher doses.
- **stimulus-bound behavior** (p. 177): behavior motivated by brain stimulation in the presence of appropriate environmental stimuli.

- **subcutaneous (SC) injection** (p. 149): an injection of a drug under the skin.
- **substance abuse** (p. 151): a pattern of drug use that results in negative effects.
- **substance dependence** (p. 151): the compulsive use of a substance; also known as addiction.
- **THC** (p. 173): the abbreviation and commonly used name for delta-9-tetrahydrocannabinol, the psychoactive ingredient in marijuana.
- **tolerance** (p. 151): a decrease in the effects of a drug as a result of repeated use.
- **withdrawal symptom** (p. 151): a physical or psychological problem that results from stopping the use of a drug.

Answers to Labeling Exercises

1.

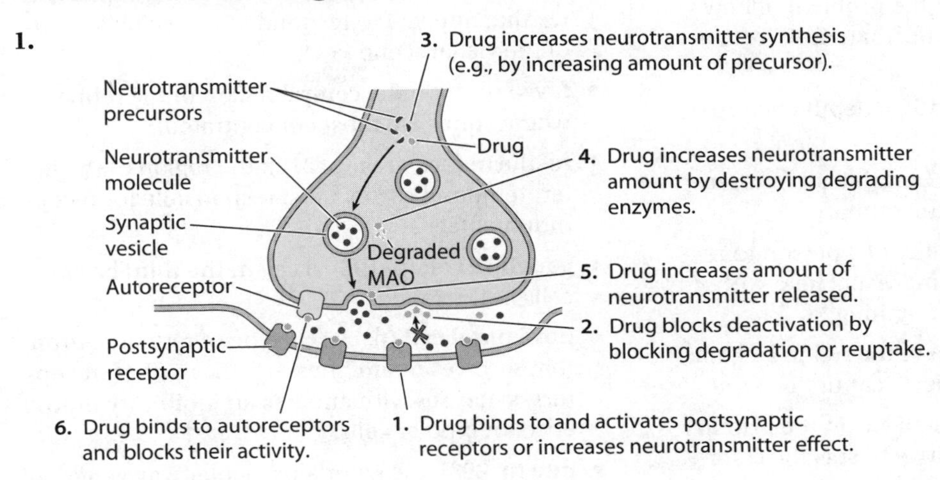

Figure 5.2, p. 152.

2.

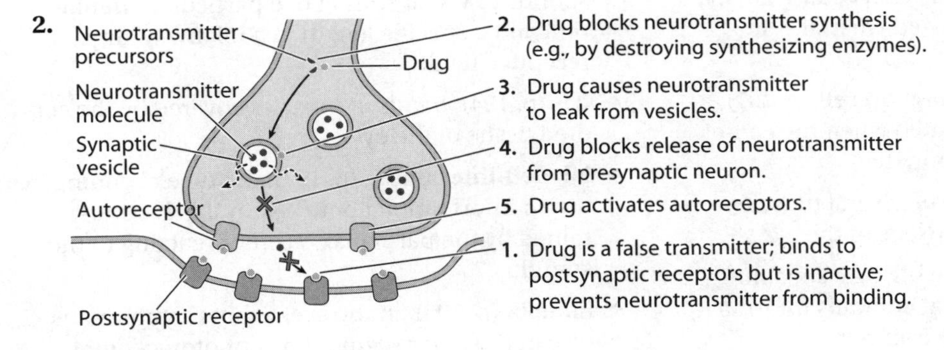

Figure 5.3, p. 153.

CHAPTER 6

Key Terms with Definitions

- **accommodation** (p. 194): the change of the shape of the lens to maintain the focus of an image on the retina.
- **across-fiber pattern coding** (p. 193): the type of coding in which information about a stimulus is determined by the pattern of neural impulses.

- **amacrine cell** (p. 204): a type of retinal neuron that receives neural messages from bipolar cells; synapses with and inhibits both bipolar and ganglion cells.
- **aqueous humor** (p. 194): a clear fluid that fills the anterior chamber of the eye.
- **Balint's syndrome** (p. 221): a disorder caused by damage to the dorsal stream; characterized by difficulty in recognizing two or more objects that appear simultaneously, difficulty in visually guided reaching for objects, and impaired eye movements.
- **binding problem** (p. 220): the problem of how the brain binds together information to form a unified perception.
- **binocular depth cue** (p. 215): a depth cue provided by both eyes.
- **bipolar cell** (p. 195): a cell between a photoreceptor and a ganglion cell in the retina.
- **blindsight** (p. 200): the ability of a person to respond to objects in a missing visual field without being conscious of seeing anything.
- **blind spot** (p. 197): an area of the retina lacking photoreceptors, where objects cannot be seen.
- **blob** (p. 199): a cluster of neurons in the primary visual cortex that are sensitive to specific colors.
- **brightness** (p. 202): the intensity of a light stimulus.
- **center-off, surround-on ganglion cell** (p. 207): a type of ganglion cell stimulated when the surround is illuminated.
- **center-on, surround-off ganglion cell** (p. 207): a type of ganglion cell stimulated when the center of the receptive field is illuminated.
- **ciliary muscle** (p. 194): one of several muscles that control the shape of the lens of the eye.
- **coding** (p. 193): a process involving a specific pattern of neural activity that contains information about stimuli in the environment.
- **color constancy** (p. 219): the perception that the color of an object remains the same even under different lighting conditions.
- **complex cell** (p. 209): a neuron in areas V1 and V2 that is sensitive to a line stimulus oriented in a particular direction and occurring anywhere in the receptive field.
- **component direction-selective neuron** (p. 215): a neuron in area V1 that responds to movement in one direction.
- **cone** (p. 196): a type of photoreceptor relatively concentrated in the center of the retina; detects fine details and colors in bright light.
- **cornea** (p. 194): the transparent outer layer of the eyeball.
- **duplex theory** (p. 196): a theory of vision proposed by Max Schultze that summarizes the differences between rods and cones.
- **feature detector** (p. 210): a cell in the visual cortex that appears to respond to a specific feature of the visual scene.
- **fovea** (p. 196): the central region of the retina, where cones are most concentrated.
- **fusiform face area** (p. 212): the region of the inferotemporal cortex most responsible for recognition of faces.
- **ganglion cell** (p. 195): a cell in the third layer of cells in the retina.
- **horizontal cell** (p. 204): a type of retinal neuron that receives neural messages from photoreceptors; synapses with and has an inhibitory influence on bipolar cells.
- **hue** (p. 202): the color a particular wavelength of light is perceived to be.
- **hypercomplex cell** (p. 209): a neuron that responds to visual stimuli of a particular orientation and a specific length in a relatively large receptive field.
- **iris** (p. 194): bands of muscles covered by the colored tissue of the eye.
- **labeled-line coding** (p. 193): the type of coding in which information about a stimulus is determined by the particular receptor reacting to the stimulus.
- **lamella** (p. 203): in the eye, a thin membranous disc in the outer segment of a photoreceptor.
- **lateral geniculate nucleus (LGN)** (p. 198): a group of neurons in the thalamus that receive neural impulses from the ganglion cells of the retina.
- **lateral inhibition** (p. 206): a decrease in activity of one neuron caused by the stimulation of its neighbors.

- **lens** (p. 194): a structure made of a series of transparent, onionlike layers of tissue that changes shape to focus images on the retina.
- **magnocellular layer** (p. 198): one of the bottom two layers of the LGN, consisting of neurons with large cell bodies.
- **monocular depth cue** (p. 214): a depth cue requiring only one eye for detection.
- **negative afterimage** (p. 218): the brief perception of a complementary color after extended stimulation with a particular color.
- **ocular dominance column** (p. 209): a column of cells in the visual cortex all having the same amount of dominance of input from either the left or the right eye.
- **off ganglion cell** (p. 204): a type of ganglion cell excited when a light stimulus is removed and inhibited by amacrine cells in the presence of light.
- **on ganglion cell** (p. 204): a type of ganglion cell excited by bipolar cells in response to a light stimulus.
- **on-off ganglion cell** (p. 204): a type of ganglion cell excited by both the presence and removal of a light stimulus.
- **opponent-process theory** (p. 218): the theory that there are three receptor complexes operating in opponent fashion to yield a perception of color and brightness.
- **opsin** (p. 203): the protein component of a photopigment.
- **optic chiasm** (p. 198): the place where the two optic nerves meet and some or all of the optic nerve fibers cross to the opposite side of the brain.
- **optic disk** (p. 197): the point at the back of the eye where axons from ganglion cells converge.
- **optic nerve** (p. 198): a nerve formed by the axons of ganglion cells after leaving the optic disk.
- **optic tract** (p. 198): the continuation of the optic nerve fibers beyond the optic chiasm.
- **orientation column** (p. 209): a column of cells in the visual cortex all responding to the same orientation of a line stimulus (line-tilt).
- **parvocellular layer** (p. 198): one of the top four layers of the LGN, consisting of neurons with small cell bodies.
- **pattern direction-selective neuron** (p. 215): a neuron in the middle temporal cortex that combines the information arriving from the primary visual cortex to recognize the direction in which an object is moving.
- **photopigment** (p. 203): a chemical molecule in the lamellae of the eye that absorbs light.
- **photoreceptor** (p. 194): the receptor cell located at the back of the eye that transduces light into a neural impulse.
- **primary visual cortex** (p. 199): the area of the cerebral cortex that detects features of the visual environment; also called area V1 or striate cortex.
- **prosopagnosia** (p. 212): an impaired ability to recognize familiar faces visually.
- **pupil** (p. 194): the opening in the iris through which light passes.
- **pursuit movement** (p. 205): the smooth movement of the eyes following a moving object.
- **receptive field** (p. 207): the part of the retina that, when stimulated, causes a change in the activity of the cell.
- **retina** (p. 194): the interior lining at the back of the eye that contains the photoreceptors.
- **retinal** (p. 203): the lipid component of a photopigment, synthesized from vitamin A.
- **retinal image** (p. 194): the image focused on the retina; it is upside down and reversed relative to the stimulus that created it.
- **rhodopsin** (p. 203): the photopigment in rods; consists of rod opsin and retinal.
- **rod** (p. 196): a type of photoreceptor concentrated in the periphery of the retina; operates in low light.
- **rod opsin** (p. 203): the form of opsin found in rods.
- **saccadic movement** (p. 204): the rapid, jerky movement of the eye from one point to another as the physical environment is scanned.
- **saturation** (p. 202): the purity of a light stimulus.
- **secondary visual cortex** (p. 201): the area of the cerebral cortex that combines visual features into a recognizable visual perception; also called area V2 or prestriate cortex.
- **sense** (p. 192): the mechanism we use to detect and react to stimuli, so as to transform

environmental stimulation into information the nervous system can use.

- **simple cell** (p. 208): a neuron in area V1 that responds to lines (edges) in a specific part of the visual field having a specific orientation.
- **sine-wave grating** (p. 210): the alternating lighter and darker intensities in a light stimulus.
- **spatial-frequency theory** (p. 210): the theory that cells in the visual cortex are responding to spatial frequencies of lightness and darkness in a visual scene.
- **transduction** (p. 192): the conversion of physical energy into a neural impulse.
- **visual agnosia** (p. 212): a perceptual problem involving the inability to name an object when it is presented visually but not when it is presented in another sensory modality.
- **visual field deficit** (p. 200): an inability to see objects in a specific part of the visual field, caused by damage to a region of the occipital lobe or the pathways leading to it.
- **vitreous humor** (p. 194): a clear, jelly-like fluid between the lens and the retina.
- **X ganglion cell** (p. 198): a type of ganglion cell that originates mostly from the central part of the retina.
- **Y ganglion cell** (p. 198): a type of ganglion cell that originates mostly from the peripheral part of the retina.
- **Young-Helmholtz trichromatic theory** (p. 218): the theory that color perceptions come from a pattern of stimulation of three sets of color receptors in the eye.

Answers to Labeling Exercises

1.

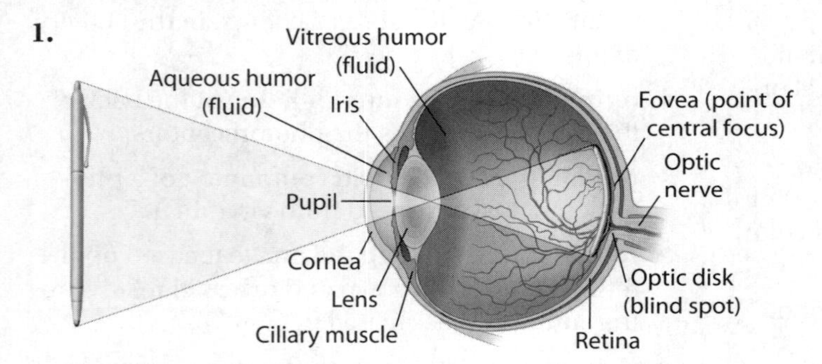

Figure 6.1, p. 194.

2.

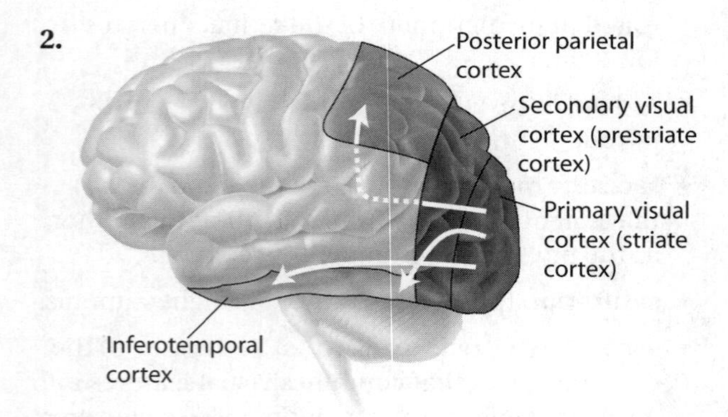

Figure 6.8, p. 202.

CHAPTER 7

Key Terms with Definitions

- **anterolateral system** (p. 247): the somatosensory pathway that begins in the spinal cord and transmits information about temperature and pain to the brain stem reticular formation and the primary and secondary somatosensory cortices.
- **auditory agnosia** (p. 239): an inability to recognize language and nonlanguage sounds because of damage to the secondary auditory cortex.
- **auditory nerve** (p. 232): cranial nerve VIII, the nerve that extends from the merging of the cochlear nerve and vestibular nerve.
- **basilar membrane** (p. 231): a membrane in the organ of Corti to which auditory receptors are attached by Deiter's cells.
- **capsaicin** (p. 245): the ingredient that gives chili peppers their hot taste by causing free nerve endings to release substance P.
- **chorda tympani** (p. 255): a branch of cranial nerve VII that conveys taste information from the posterior tongue and the palate and throat to the nucleus of the solitary tract.
- **cochlea** (p. 230): a snail-shaped structure in the inner ear that contains the auditory receptors.
- **cochlear implant** (p. 238): a device that transmits electrical impulses along cranial nerve VIII to the brain.
- **cochlear nerve** (p. 232): a nerve formed by the axons of bipolar cells in the spiral ganglion that synapse with the hair cells.
- **cochlear nucleus** (p. 232): the first neurons in the medulla that receive neural messages from auditory receptors via the auditory nerve.
- **dorsal column-medial lemniscal system** (p. 246): a somatosensory pathway that begins in the spinal cord and transmits information about touch and proprioception to the primary somatosensory cortex.
- **dorsal column nucleus** (p. 246): a group of neurons in the medulla that receives neural messages about touch and proprioception via the dorsal column-medial lemniscal system.
- **eustachian tube** (p. 230): a tube connecting the middle ear with the back of the throat.
- **fast pain** (p. 245): the type of pain carried by myelinated type A fibers that quickly reaches the spinal cord.
- **free nerve ending** (p. 244): a type of skin receptor located just below the surface in both hairy and hairless skin; detects temperature and pain stimuli.
- **frequency theory of pitch perception** (p. 234): the view that the firing rate in the auditory nerve matches the frequency of the sound.
- **gate-control theory of pain** (p. 248): the view that input from pain receptors will produce the perception of pain only if the message first passes through a "gate" in the spinal cord and lower brain stem structures.
- **gustatory sense** (p. 252): the sense of taste.
- **hair cell** (p. 231): an auditory receptor involved in transducing eardrum vibrations into neural impulses.
- **incus (anvil)** (p. 229): the bone of the middle ear attached to the malleus and stapes.
- **inferior colliculus** (p. 232): an area of the tectum of the midbrain that receives neural messages from both the cochlear nucleus and the superior olivary nucleus.
- **intensity difference** (p. 237): a cue to the localization of high-pitched sounds; a sound is louder in the ear closer to it than in the ear farther away.
- **loudness** (p. 228): the perception of the amplitude of a sound wave, measured in decibels.
- **malleus (hammer)** (p. 229): the bone of the middle ear attached to the tympanic membrane and the incus.
- **medial geniculate nucleus (MGN)** (p. 232): a group of neurons in the thalamus that receives neural impulses from the inferior colliculus.
- **medial lemniscus** (p. 246): a ribbon-like band of fibers in the dorsal column-medial lemniscal system that conveys neural messages from the dorsal column nuclei to the ventral posterolateral thalamic nuclei.
- **Meissner's corpuscle** (p. 245): a type of skin receptor in hairy skin, located in the elevations of

the dermis into the epidermis; responds to pressure and low-frequency vibrations.

- **Merkel's disk** (p. 245): a type of skin receptor in the base of the epidermis near the sweat ducts; sensitive to pressure.
- **motion sickness** (p. 241): the feelings of dizziness and nausea that occur when the body is moved passively without motor activity and corresponding feedback to the brain.
- **neuromatrix theory of pain** (p. 249): a theory that accounts for types of pain unexplained by the gate-control theory of pain.
- **nucleus of the solitary tract** (p. 255): a group of neurons in the medulla that receives information from taste receptors.
- **nystagmus** (p. 241): the rapid side-to-side eye movements caused by inconsistent information from the visual and vestibular systems.
- **olfactory bulb** (p. 259): a structure at the base of the brain that receives information about odor from olfactory receptors.
- **olfactory epithelium** (p. 258): the mucous membrane in the top rear of the nasal passage, lined by olfactory receptors.
- **olfactory sense** (p. 257): the sense of smell.
- **olfactory tract** (p. 259): axons of olfactory bulb neurons that project to the primary olfactory cortex.
- **organ of Corti** (p. 231): a structure inside the cochlea that contains the basilar membrane, the hair cells, and the tectorial membrane.
- **oval window** (p. 229): the part of the inner ear attached to the stapes.
- **Pacinian corpuscle** (p. 243): the largest type of skin receptor, found in both hairy and hairless skin; detects high-frequency vibrations.
- **papilla** (p. 253): a small, visible bump on the tongue that contains taste buds.
- **periaqueductal gray (PAG)** (p. 248): an area of the midbrain that is the origin of a descending fiber tract that synapses with inhibitory interneurons in the lower brain stem and spinal cord to block messages about pain.
- **phantom limb pain** (p. 249): the sensation of pain in a missing limb experienced by up to 70% of people who lose a limb.
- **phase difference** (p. 237): a cue to localizing a low-pitched sound by the difference in the cycle of the sound wave when it reaches each ear.
- **pinna** (p. 229): the outer, visible portion of the ear.
- **pitch** (p. 228): the perception of the frequency of a sound wave, measured in hertz (Hz).
- **place theory of pitch perception** (p. 233): the view that different sounds activate nerve fibers at different locations on the basilar membrane.
- **posterior thalamic nucleus** (p. 247): a group of neurons in the thalamus that receives information about temperature and pain via the anterolateral pathway.
- **primary auditory cortex (Heschl's gyrus)** (p. 232): the part of the superior temporal gyrus that detects characteristics of sound (frequency, amplitude, complexity).
- **primary gustatory cortex** (p. 255): an area located just ventral and rostral to the area representing the tongue in the somatosensory cortex.
- **primary olfactory cortex** (p. 259): an area in the pyriform cortex in the limbic system that gives odors an emotional component.
- **primary somatosensory cortex** (p. 247): an area in the cortex that receives information about touch, proprioception, temperature, and pain.
- **proprioception** (p. 243): the somatosense that monitors body position and movement, acts to maintain body position, and ensures the accuracy of intended movements.
- **remapping** (p. 250): the modification of neurons after they no longer receive input from the body part they once represented.
- **round window** (p. 230): a membrane that bulges as a result of pressure on the fluid inside the cochlea, which results from the movement of the stapes against the oval window.
- **Ruffini's corpuscle** (p. 245): a type of skin receptor just below the surface; detects low-frequency vibrations.
- **saccule** (p. 240): one of the two vestibular sacs containing the vestibular receptor cells, or hair cells.
- **secondary auditory cortex** (p. 232): the area of the temporal lobe surrounding the primary auditory cortex, where pitch, loudness, and timbre are perceived and specific sounds are recognized.

- **secondary somatosensory cortex** (p. 247): an area of the cortex, lateral and slightly posterior to the primary somatosensory cortex, that receives information from the skin senses.
- **semicircular canal** (p. 240): one of three fluid-filled canals in the vestibular system.
- **slow pain** (p. 245): the type of pain propagated by unmyelinated type C fibers that slowly reaches the spinal cord.
- **somatosense** (p. 243): the skin sensations of touch, pain, temperature, and proprioception.
- **sound** (p. 228): vibrations in a material medium, such as air, water, or metal.
- **spinocerebellar system** (p. 247): the somatosensory pathway that begins in the spinal cord and transmits proprioceptive information to the cerebellum.
- **spiral ganglion** (p. 231): an auditory structure containing bipolar neurons that synapse with hair cells of the inner ear.
- **stapes (stirrup)** (p. 229): the bone of the middle ear attached to the incus and the oval window.
- **superior olivary nucleus** (p. 232): a group of neurons in the medulla that receives neural messages from the cochlear nuclei.
- **taste bud** (p. 253): a cluster of taste receptors that lie either near or within a papilla.
- **tectorial membrane** (p. 231): a membrane in the organ of Corti in which hair cell cilia are embedded or with which cilia make close contact.
- **timbre** (p. 229): the purity of a sound; the combination of frequencies that gives each sound its characteristic quality.
- **tonotopic distribution** (p. 235): the pattern of neurons responding to specific tones in particular places throughout the auditory system.
- **tympanic membrane** (p. 229): the membrane that divides the outer and middle parts of the ear; also called the eardrum.
- **utricle** (p. 240): one of the two vestibular sacs containing the vestibular receptor cells, or hair cells.
- **ventral posterolateral thalamic nucleus** (p. 247): a group of neurons that receives information about touch and proprioception via the dorsal column-medial lemniscal system and about temperature and pain via the anterolateral system.
- **ventral posteromedial thalamic nucleus** (p. 255): a group of neurons that receives taste information from the nucleus of the solitary tract and then transmits it to the primary gustatory cortex.
- **vestibular ganglion** (p. 241): a group of bipolar neurons that receive input from vestibular hair cells.
- **vestibular nerve** (p. 241): axons of the vestibular ganglion neurons.
- **vestibular nucleus** (p. 241): the part of the medulla with which most vestibular nerve fibers synapse.
- **vestibular sac** (p. 240): the part of the vestibular system that provides information about the position of the head relative to the body.
- **vestibular sense** (p. 240): the sense responsible for maintaining balance.
- **volley principle** (p. 234): the idea that groups of neurons in the auditory nerve fire asynchronously, in volleys, to match the frequency of the sound.

Answers to Labeling Exercises

1.

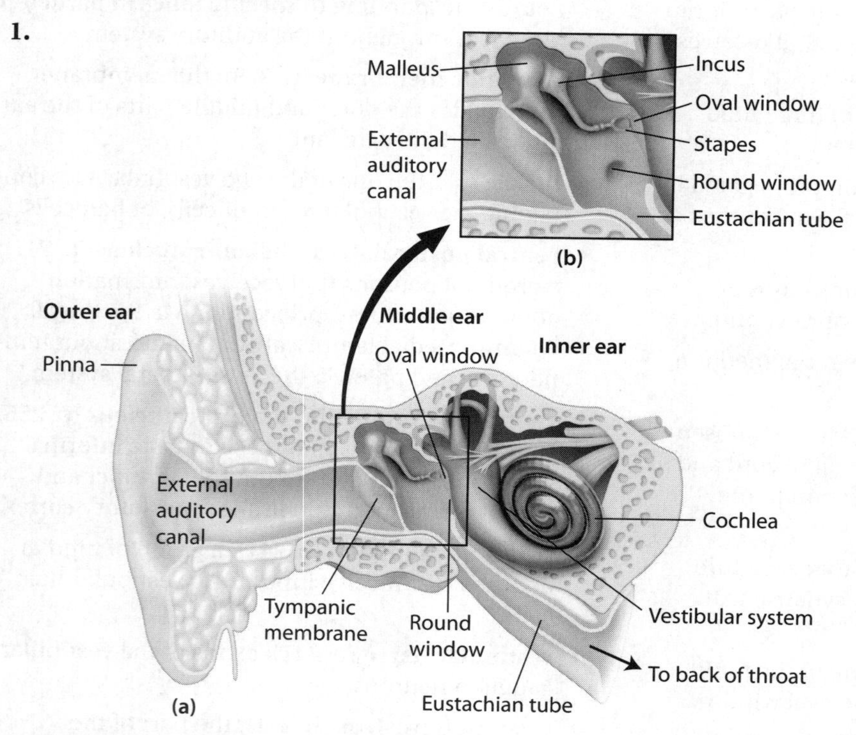

Figure 7.2, p. 229.

2.

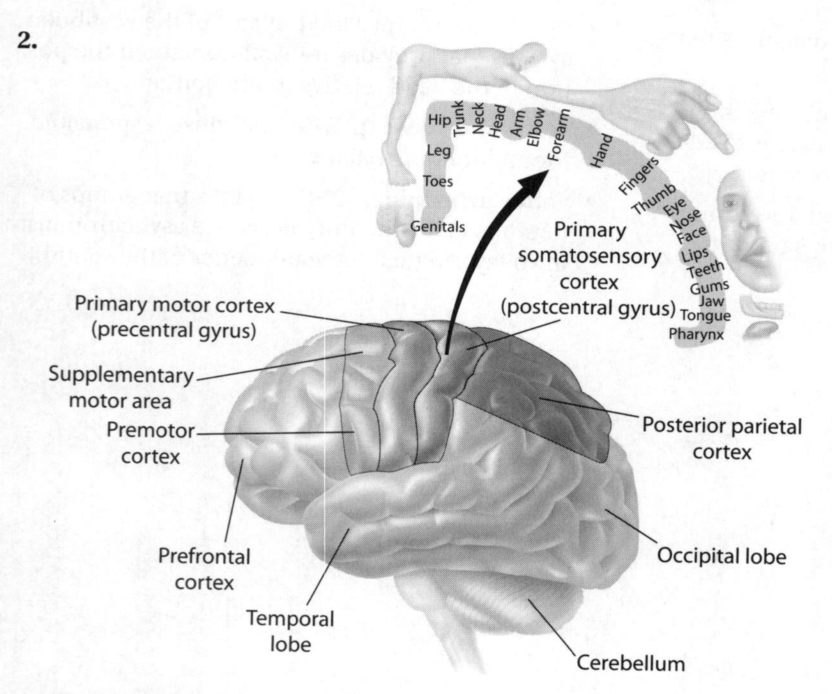

Figure 7.19, p. 247.

CHAPTER 8

Key Terms with Definitions

- **actin** (p. 272): the protein component of thin myofilaments.
- **alpha motor neuron** (p. 272): a motor neuron with a long axon that leaves the ventral root of the spinal cord or brain stem and synapses with individual muscle fibers.
- **amyotrophic lateral sclerosis (ALS)** (p. 288): a degenerative neuromuscular disease caused by degeneration of the corticospinal and corticobulbar tracts and the anterior (ventral) horns of the spinal cord.
- **annulospiral ending** (p. 275): a sensory receptor in the central part of an intrafusal muscle fiber.
- **apraxia** (p. 286): a movement disorder characterized by missing or inappropriate actions not caused by paralysis or any other motor impairment.
- **apraxia of speech** (p. 286): a disorder characterized by difficulty speaking clearly; caused by damage limited to Broca's area.
- **ballistic movement** (p. 290): a habitual, rapid movement that does not depend on sensory feedback.
- **basal ganglia** (p. 293): a group of three structures that integrates voluntary movements; consists of the caudate nucleus, the putamen, and the globus pallidus.
- **basket cell** (p. 292): a cerebellar neuron that has an inhibitory influence of Purkinje cells.
- **bradykinesia** (p. 296): a movement disorder characterized by slowed movement.
- **cerebral palsy** (p. 269): a congenital neurological motor disorder characterized by postural instability and extraneous movement.
- **constructional apraxia** (p. 286): a disorder characterized by difficulty drawing pictures or assembling objects.
- **contralateral neglect** (p. 285): a disturbance in the ability to respond to visual, auditory, or somatosensory stimuli on one side of the body; caused by damage to the contralateral posterior parietal cortex.
- **corpus striatum** (p. 294): the part of the basal ganglia consisting of the caudate nucleus and putamen.
- **corticobulbar tract** (p. 287): a motor pathway that controls movements of the face and tongue.
- **corticospinal tract** (p. 287): a motor pathway that controls movements of the fingers, hands, arms, trunk, legs, and feet.
- **deep cerebellar nucleus** (p. 291): a group of neurons that correct movements in progress.
- **dorsolateral prefrontal cortex** (p. 280): the top executive in the perception-action cycle; cells in this area integrate sensory information across time with motor actions needed to deal with the information.
- **extensor muscle** (p. 270): a muscle that produces movement of a limb away from the body.
- **extrafusal muscle fiber** (p. 272): a muscle fiber controlled by an alpha motor neuron.
- **fast-twitch muscle** (p. 274): a muscle fiber that contracts and fatigues quickly.
- **festination** (p. 296): a tendency in a movement disorder to speed up a walking pace to running.
- **flexor muscle** (p. 271): a muscle that produces movement of a limb toward the body.
- **gamma motor neuron** (p. 279): a neuron that synapses with intrafusal muscle fibers to produce continuous muscle tension.
- **Golgi tendon organ** (p. 277): a receptor located among the fibers of tendons that measures the total amount of force exerted by the muscle on the bone to which the tendon is attached.
- **Huntington's disease** (p. 299): an inherited neurological disorder characterized by a slow, progressive deterioration of motor control, cognition, and emotion.
- **Ia fiber** (p. 276): an axon from an annulospiral ending that enters the dorsal root of the spinal cord and synapses with an alpha motor neuron.
- **Ib fiber** (p. 277): an axon of a Golgi tendon organ that extends to the spinal cord and synapses with an interneuron that inhibits alpha motor neurons.

- **intermediate-twitch muscle** (p. 274): a muscle fiber that contracts at a lower rate than fast-twitch muscles and a higher rate than slow-twitch muscles.
- **intrafusal muscle fiber** (p. 275): a muscle fiber within the muscle spindle that is surrounded by annulospiral endings.
- **lateral reticulospinal tract** (p. 289): a ventromedial tract that activates the flexor muscles of the legs.
- **levodopa (L-dopa)** (p. 298): a drug converted to dopamine in the brain; used to treat Parkinson's disease.
- **limb apraxia** (p. 286): an impairment in the voluntary use of a limb caused by damage to the left parietal lobe or the corpus callosum.
- **medial reticulospinal tract** (p. 289): a ventromedial tract that activates the extensor muscles of the legs.
- **mirror neurons** (p. 281): discovered in monkeys; neurons in the primate premotor cortex that are activated both when the animal performs an action and when it watches another monkey or person performing that action.
- **monosynaptic stretch reflex** (p. 275): a spinal reflex with a single synapse between the sensory receptor and the muscle effector.
- **motor end plate** (p. 272): the flattened area of an extrafusal muscle fiber where a motor neuron and the muscle fiber synapse.
- **motor unit** (p. 274): an alpha motor neuron and all the muscle fibers it controls.
- **movement** (p. 268): a change in the place or position of the body or a body part.
- **muscle fiber** (p. 271): one of the units comprising a skeletal muscle.
- **muscle spindle** (p. 275): a structure embedded within an extrafusal muscle fiber that enables the CNS to contract a muscle to counteract the stretching of the extrafusal muscle fiber.
- **muscle tone** (p. 279): the resting tension of skeletal muscles caused by the activity of gamma motor neurons.
- **myasthenia gravis** (p. 273): a neuromuscular disorder characterized by muscle fatigue following exercise.
- **myofibril** (p. 271): one of the units comprising a muscle fiber.
- **myofilament** (p. 272): a component of a myofibril.
- **myosin** (p. 272): the protein component of thick myofilaments.
- **neuromuscular junction** (p. 272): a specialized synapse between an alpha motor neuron and an extrafusal muscle fiber.
- **pallidotomy** (p. 298): a psychosurgical treatment for Parkinson's disease that reduces tremors, rigidity, and bradykinesia.
- **Parkinson's disease** (p. 296): a degenerative neurological disorder characterized by rigidity of the limbs and muscle tremors.
- **patellar reflex** (p. 275): a reflex in which tapping the tendon of the knee stretches one of the muscles that extends the leg, and the resulting muscle contractions causes the leg to kick outward.
- **polysynaptic reflex** (p. 276): a spinal reflex with more than one synapse between the sensory receptor and the muscle effector.
- **posterior parietal cortex** (p. 285): a cortical area that integrates input from the visual, auditory, and skin senses and relays it to the primary motor cortex.
- **precentral gyrus** (p. 282): an area in the frontal lobe that contains the primary motor cortex.
- **premotor cortex** (p. 281): a part of the secondary motor cortex that receives input mostly from the visual cortex.
- **primary motor cortex** (p. 282): an area in the precentral gyrus of the frontal lobe that plays a major role in voluntary movements.
- **Purkinje cell** (p. 291): an output cell from the cerebellar cortex, which has an exclusively inhibitory effect.
- **pyramidal cell** (p. 282): a large, pyramid-shaped neuron in the primary motor cortex.
- **Renshaw cell** (p. 278): an inhibitory interneuron excited by an alpha motor neuron that causes it to stop firing, preventing excessive muscle contraction.
- **rubrospinal tract** (p. 289): a motor pathway that controls movements of the hands, lower arms, lower legs, and feet.

- **sarcomere** (p. 272): the functional unit of a myofibril, consisting of overlapping bands of thick myosin filaments and thin actin filaments.
- **secondary motor cortex** (p. 281): a cortical area consisting of the supplementary motor area and the premotor cortex; involved in the planning and sequencing of voluntary movements.
- **skeletal muscle** (p. 270): a type of muscle that produces the movements of bones.
- **slow-twitch muscle** (p. 274): a muscle fiber that contracts and fatigues slowly.
- **supplementary motor area** (p. 281): a part of the secondary motor cortex that receives input from the posterior parietal cortex and the somatosensory cortex.
- **tectospinal tract** (p. 289): a ventromedial tract that controls upper trunk (shoulder) and neck movements and coordinates the visual tracking of stimuli.
- **tendon** (p. 270): a strong band of connective tissue linking a muscle to a bone that causes the bone to move when the muscle contracts.
- **thalamotomy** (p. 298): a psychosurgical treatment for Parkinson's disease that relieves tremors and improves rigidity but does not relieve bradykinesia.
- **ventromedial tract** (p. 289): one of four motor pathways originating in different parts of the subcortex that control movements of the trunk and limbs.
- **vestibulospinal tract** (p. 289): a ventromedial tract that plays a central role in posture.
- **withdrawal reflex** (p. 276): the automatic withdrawal of a limb from a painful stimulus.

Answers to Labeling Exercises

1.

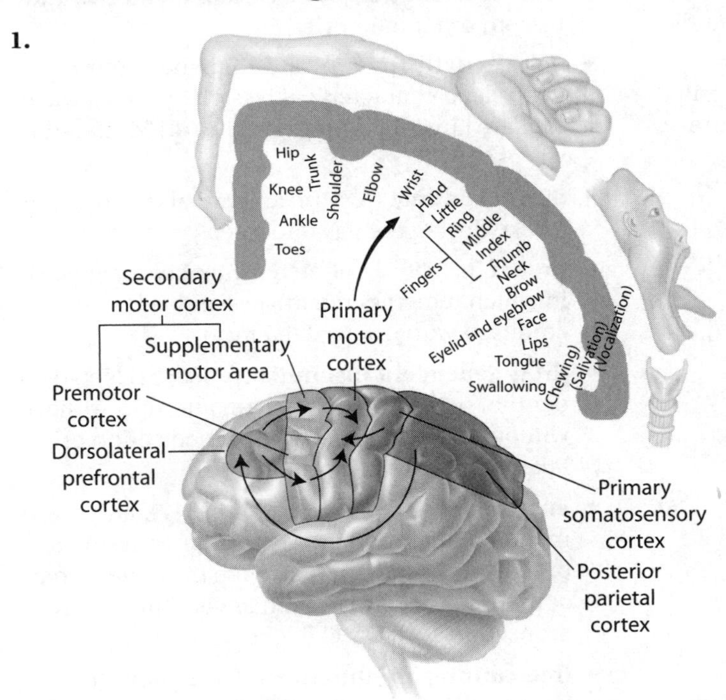

Figure 8.13, p. 281.

2.

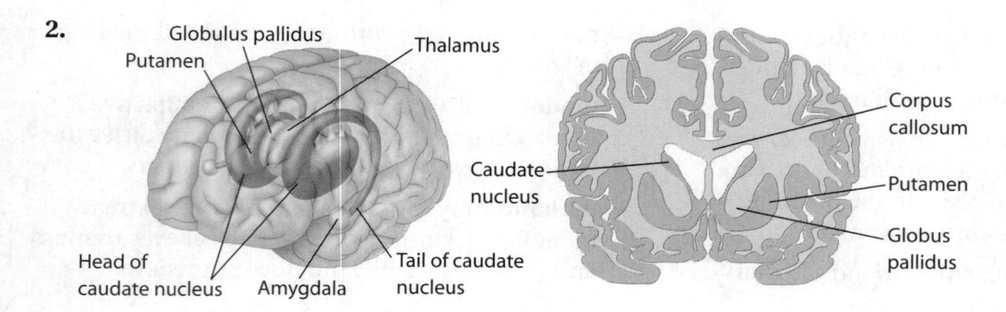

Figure 8.20, p. 293.

CHAPTER 9

Key Terms with Definitions

- **activation-synthesis theory** (p. 329): the view that dreams are a mental interpretation of the neural activity that occurs during sleep.
- **alpha activity** (p. 316): an EEG pattern of waves that are larger and more synchronized (8 to 12 Hz) than beta waves, which occurs when an individual is relaxed with eyes closed.
- **basal forebrain region** (p. 326): a brain area anterior to the hypothalamus and including the preoptic area; stimulation produces sleep and damage produces sleeplessness.
- **bedwetting** (p. 333) an NREM sleep disorder characterized by lack of bladder control during sleep.
- **beta activity** (p. 316): a rapid, desynchronized EEG pattern of small voltage changes (18 to 24 Hz) that occurs when a person is awake and active.
- **cataplexy** (p. 334): a sudden, complete lack of muscle tone that sometimes accompanies narcolepsy.
- **caudal reticular formation** (p. 327): an area within the reticular formation that produces REM sleep.
- **cerveau isolé preparation** (p. 316): an experimental preparation depriving higher brain areas of sensory information arriving from the spinal cord and brain stem; used to identify brain areas controlling arousal.
- **circadian cycle** (p. 308): a change in biological and behavioral functioning that occurs over a 24 hour period.
- **circadian rhythm** (p. 308): the intrinsic process that controls the circadian cycle.
- **cognitive perspective** (p. 328): in dream research, the view that dreams help solve everyday problems and may help store certain memories and discard other memories.
- **delta activity** (p. 319): an EEG pattern during deep sleep characterized by synchronized waves that are larger in amplitude (1 to 4 Hz) than theta waves.
- **diurnal animal** (p. 310): an animal that remains awake during the day and sleeps at night.
- **dream** (p. 328): an altered state of consciousness in which remembered images and fantasies are confused with external reality.
- **drug-dependent insomnia** (p. 332): a sleep disorder that occurs when a person attempts to sleep without previously used sleep medication or takes a lower-than-normal dose.
- **encéphale isolé preparation** (p. 317): an experimental preparation depriving higher brain areas of sensory information arriving from the spinal cord; used to identify brain areas controlling arousal.
- **free-running rhythm** (p. 311): a 25 hour (or more) sleep-wake cycle that develops in the absence of natural light-dark cycles.
- **hypersomnia** (p. 333): a sleep disorder characterized by too much sleep.
- **insomnia** (p. 331): a sleep disorder characterized by a long-term inability to obtain adequate sleep.

- **jet lag** (p. 308): the fatigue and sleep disturbance caused by traveling across several time zones.
- **K complex** (p. 319): a single large negative wave (upward spike) followed by a single large positive wave (downward spike) that occurs during stage 2 sleep.
- **lark** (p. 308): a person who is active and alert in the morning and becomes drowsy and inattentive in the evening.
- **light therapy** (p. 312): an increased exposure to intense broad-spectrum light that enhances mood in people with SAD.
- **locus coeruleus** (p. 318): a group of neurons within the reticular formation important for cortical activity and behavioral alertness.
- **lucid dream** (p. 329): a dream in which the person is conscious that he or she is dreaming.
- **melatonin** (p. 311): a hormone secreted by the pineal gland in response to daylight and darkness.
- **microsleep** (p. 322): a brief period during which a person appears to be awake, but the EEG patterns resemble stage 1 sleep.
- **narcolepsy** (p. 333): a sleep disorder characterized by a sudden, uncontrollable sleep attack, usually initiated by monotonous activity.
- **night terror** (p. 333): an abrupt awakening from NREM sleep, accompanied by intense autonomic arousal and feelings of panic.
- **nocturnal animal** (p. 310): an animal that sleeps during the day and is awake at night.
- **nonREM (NREM) sleep** (p. 319): sleep stages 1 to 4, in which the EEG patterns are markedly different from those in REM sleep.
- **nonvisual photoreceptor** (p. 311): a type of photoreceptor that detects the daily dawn-dusk cycle.
- **owl** (p. 309): a person who is drowsy and inattentive in the morning and active and alert in the evening.
- **PGO wave** (p. 320): a brief burst of neural activity during REM sleep that begins in the pons, is transmitted to the LGN, and ends in the occipital lobe.
- **phase-advance shift** (p. 313): a schedule that shortens the day by requiring a worker to start on the late shift and then rotate to an earlier shift the following week.
- **phase-delay shift** (p. 313): a schedule that lengthens the day by requiring a worker to rotate to a later shift each week.
- **pineal gland** (p. 311): a structure of the epithalamus that controls seasonal rhythms in behavior through its release of melatonin.
- **raphé nucleus** (p. 326): nucleus located in a thin strip of neurons running along the midline in the caudal part of the reticular formation; damage to this area produces insomnia.
- **rapid eye movement (REM) sleep** (p. 320): the phase of sleep in which the EEG pattern resembles the waking state, the eyes move behind closed lids, and muscle tone is absent.
- **REM behavior disorder** (p. 335): a sleep disorder in which the person acts out a dream because of a failure to lose muscle tone during REM sleep.
- **REM rebound** (p. 322): a greater proportion of sleep time spent in REM sleep after a period of REM-sleep deprivation.
- **reticular activating system (RAS)** (p. 317): a diffuse network of neurons originating in the hindbrain and extending through the midbrain; stimulation produces cortical arousal and behavioral alertness.
- **retinohypothalamic tract** (p. 311): a fiber tract that conveys information about the daily dawn-dusk cycle to the SCN.
- **seasonal affective disorder (SAD)** (p. 312): a form of depression caused by reduced daylight during the winter months.
- **sleep apnea** (p. 332): a sleep disorder characterized by repeated interruptions of sleep caused by the cessation of breathing.
- **sleep paralysis** (p. 334): a brief paralysis that occurs when a person with narcolepsy is going to sleep or awakening.
- **sleep spindle** (p. 319): a 1 to 2 second burst of activity of 12 to 14 Hz that occurs during stage 2 sleep.
- **sleepwalking** (p. 333): getting out of bed and walking during NREM sleep.
- **slow-wave sleep (SWS)** (p. 319): stages 3 and 4 of nonREM sleep.
- **stage 1 sleep** (p. 319): the first stage of light sleep, characterized by mostly theta activity.

- **stage 2 sleep** (p. 319): the second stage of sleep, characterized by sleep spindles and K complexes in addition to theta activity.
- **stage 3 sleep** (p. 319): the third sleep stage, characterized by the addition of delta activity.
- **stage 4 sleep** (p. 319): the deepest stage of sleep, in which delta activity predominates.
- **suprachiasmatic nucleus (SCN)** (p. 309): an area in the brain that regulates the circadian cycle.
- **theta activity** (p. 319): an EEG pattern during light sleep, characterized by synchronized waves that are larger in amplitude (4 to 7 Hz) than beta and alpha waves.
- **visual photoreceptor** (p. 311): a type of photoreceptor that codes the features of a light stimulus.
- **zeitgeber** (p. 311): an external time cue that resets an animal's biological clock every 24 hours.

Answers to Labeling Exercises

1.

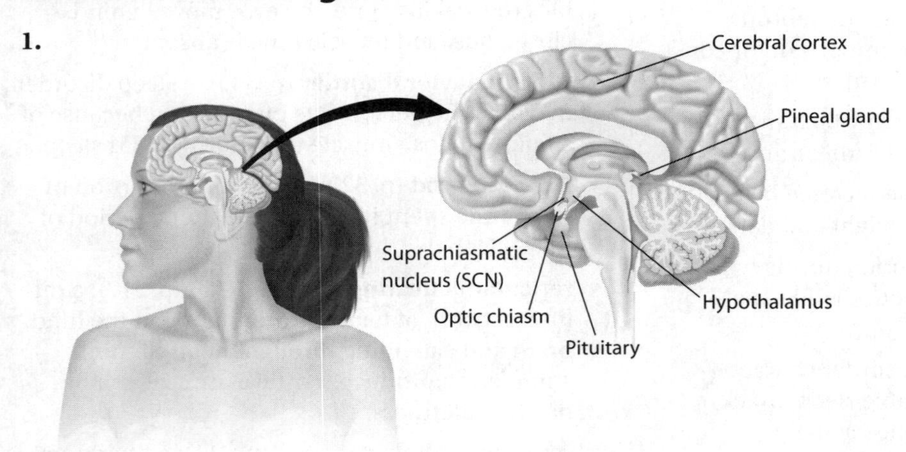

Figure 9.2, p. 309.

CHAPTER 10

Key Terms with Definitions

- **adipsia** (p. 344): the absence of drinking.
- **aldosterone** (p. 377): a hormone released by the adrenal cortex that causes increased water and salt retention by the kidneys.
- **allostasis** (p. 366): the maintenance of stability through change.
- **allostatic load** (p. 367): the cumulative cost to the body of repeated cycles of allostasis.
- **angiotensin** (p. 377): a hormone that stimulates the adrenal cortex to release aldosterone.
- **anorexia nervosa** (p. 371): an eating disorder in which adolescents or young adults diet and lose as much as 35% of their body weight, yet still feel fat.
- **antidiuretic hormone (ADH)** (p. 376): a hormone secreted by the posterior pituitary that causes fluid retention by the kidneys.
- **aphagia** (p. 344): the absence of eating.
- **arcuate nucleus** (p. 350): a hypothalamic nucleus that produces neuropeptide Y and releases it into the PVN and the lateral hypothalamic area.
- **binge eating disorder** (p. 374): an eating disorder characterized by recurrent episodes of binge eating without such compensatory weight-loss methods as vomiting, use of laxatives, and excessive exercise.
- **bulimia nervosa** (p. 372): an eating disorder characterized by recurrent episodes of binge eating, followed by self-induced vomiting and other forms of purging.
- **cephalic reflex** (p. 346): a response that prepares an animal to digest, metabolize, and store food; controlled by the CNS.

- **cholecystokinin (CCK)** (p. 359): a neuropeptide hormone that may serve as a satiety sensor.
- **conditioned hunger** (p. 362): hunger resulting from environmental factors, produced by conditioning.
- **conditioned satiety** (p. 362): satiety resulting from stimuli at the end of a meal, producing a short-term inhibition of eating.
- **critical set point** (p. 365): the critical level of stored fat their either activates or inhibits food-seeking behaviors.
- **diabetes mellitus** (p. 356): a disorder in which the pancreas makes too little insulin or insulin is unable to act effectively to remove glucose from the blood.
- **dorsal motor nucleus of the vagus** (p. 350): a group of neurons in the medulla that regulates insulin release by the parasympathetic nervous system.
- **fen-phen** (p. 352): a drug combination of fenfluramine and phentermine, once used in treating obesity.
- **ghrelin** (p. 360): a gastrointestinal peptide with an appetite-stimulating effect.
- **glucagon** (p. 357): a pancreatic hormone that increases blood glucose levels.
- **glucoprivation** (p. 358): the unavailability of glucose as an energy source.
- **glucoreceptor** (p. 356): a specialized receptor that monitors blood glucose levels.
- **glucostatic theory** (p. 356): a theory that hunger is caused by low blood glucose levels.
- **homeostasis** (p. 365): a tendency of an animal to maintain a constant internal state.
- **hyperphagia** (p. 345): excessive food intake; overeating.
- **hypovolemic thirst** (p. 377): a type of thirst caused by a loss of extracellular fluid.
- **ingestional neophobia** (p. 352): a reluctance to eat novel foods.
- **insulin** (p. 356): a pancreatic hormone that lowers blood glucose levels.
- **lateral hypothalamus (LH)** (p. 344): a hypothalamic area once thought to control hunger and the initiation of eating.
- **leptin** (p. 364): a hormone secreted by fat cells that appears to provide the brain with feedback about the level of stored fat in the body.
- **LH-lesion syndrome** (p. 344): the pattern of aphagic and adipsic behavior exhibited by rats following damage to the lateral hypothalamus.
- **lipid** (p. 364): a fat or fatty acid; fatty acid levels in the blood are involved in hunger.
- **lipoprivation** (p. 364): the unavailability of fats or fatty acids as an energy source.
- **lipostatic theory** (p. 364): a theory that proposes a relationship between fat deposits and hunger.
- **neuropeptide Y (NPY)** (p. 350): a peptide neurotransmitter involved in hunger.
- **nigrostriatal pathway** (p. 349): a dopaminergic system involved in voluntary eating and drinking behavior; begins in the substantia nigra, passes through the lateral hypothalamus, and ends in the basal ganglia.
- **nucleus medianus** (p. 378): a group of neurons in the brain involved in osmotic and hypovolemic thirst.
- **nucleus of the solitary tract** (p. 350): a structure in the medulla that influences the amount of food consumed.
- **organum vasculosum lamina terminalis (OVLT)** (p. 376): a structure outside the blood-brain barrier that contains osmoreceptors; plays a role in thirst.
- **osmoreceptor** (p. 376): a neuron that monitors osmotic pressure.
- **osmotic thirst** (p. 376): a condition of thirst caused by increased osmotic pressure that results from increased salt levels in the extracellular fluid.
- **paraventricular nucleus (PVN)** (p. 350): a hypothalamic area where damage may produce the VMH-lesion syndrome.
- **prandial drinking** (p. 345): drinking while eating.
- **preloading** (p. 355): an experimental procedure in which food is placed in the stomach before food becomes available to the subject.
- **primary drinking** (p. 375): drinking in response to loss of intracellular or extracellular fluid.
- **satiety** (p. 342): the state of feeling full or satisfied, relative to hunger or thirst.
- **secondary drinking** (p. 375): drinking that anticipates a bodily need.

- **subfornical organ (SFO)** (p. 376): a structure outside the blood-brain barrier that contains osmoreceptors; plays a role in thirst.
- **ventromedial hypothalamus (VMH)** (p. 344): a hypothalamic area once thought to control the inhibition of eating, or satiety.
- **VMH-lesion syndrome** (p. 345): the pattern of hyperphagia and obesity typically exhibited by rats following damage to the ventromedial hypothalamus.
- **VMH paradox** (p. 346): in VMH-lesioned rats, a motivational inconsistency between overeating in some situations and a reluctance to eat in others.

Answers to Labeling Exercises

1.

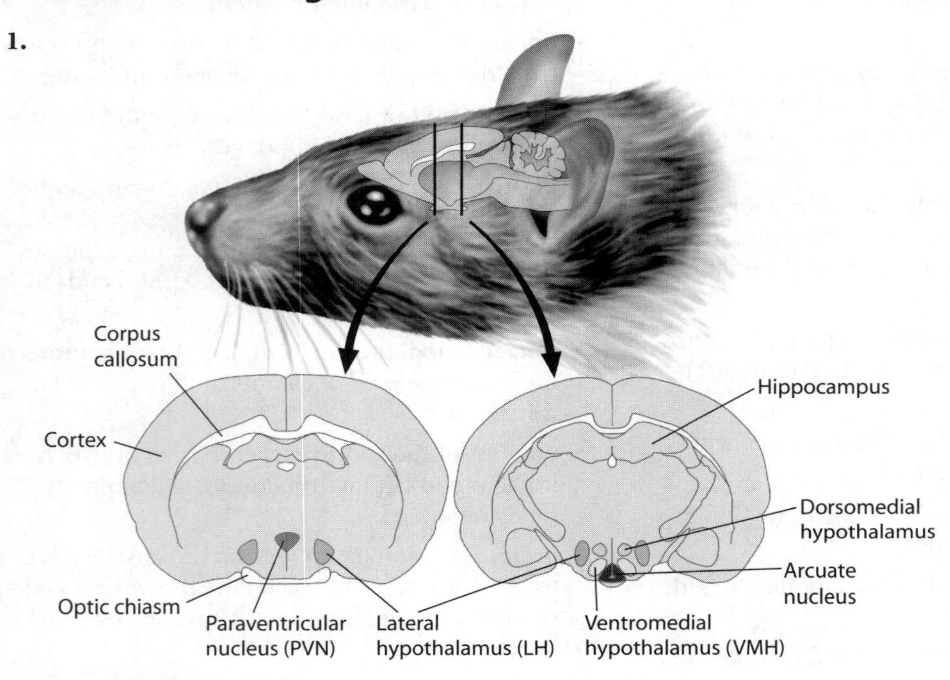

Figure 10.3, p. 344.

2.

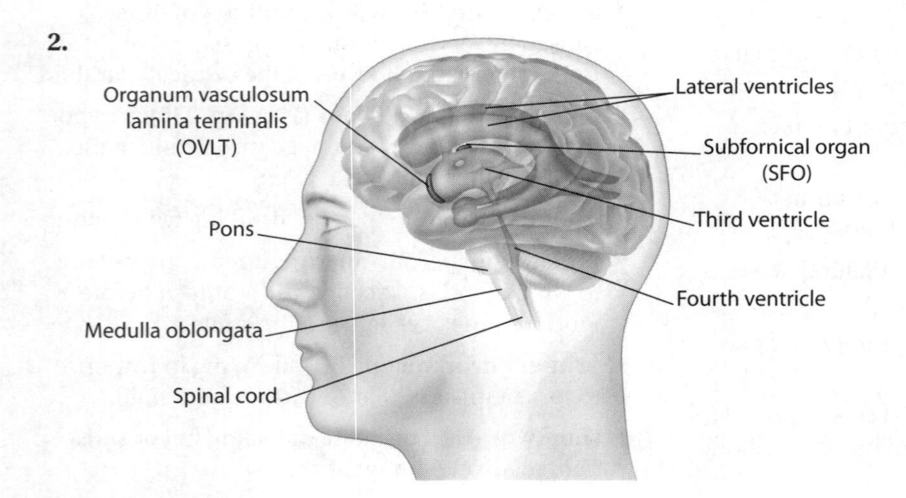

Figure 10.21, p. 376.

CHAPTER 11

Key Terms with Definitions

- **acquired sexual motive** (p. 408): a learned sexual response to a stimulus produced through conditioning.
- **adrenogenital syndrome** (p. 412): a condition resulting from excess androstenedione secretion by the adrenal glands in a genetically female human, producing masculinized genitals.
- **alpha-fetoprotein** (p. 392): a protein synthesized by the fetal liver and present in the bloodstream of both male and female fetuses that binds to and deactivates circulating estradiol.
- **androgen insensitivity syndrome (AIS)** (p. 413): a condition in which a defective androgen receptor protein prevents normal testosterone action, causing a genetic male to develop female external genitals or ambiguous genitals.
- **androstenedione** (p. 398): An adrenal androgen hormone similar to testosterone that affects the sexual motivation of a premenopausal woman.
- **castration** (p. 399): the removal of the testes.
- **endometrium** (p. 397): the inner lining of the uterus.
- **erectile dysfunction** (p. 414): a chronic inability to have a penile erection sufficient to achieve penetration.
- **estradiol** (p. 392): a form of estrogen; a hormone similar to testosterone, thought to be responsible for masculinization of the brain.
- **estrogen** (p. 392): the female sex hormone.
- **estrous cycle** (p. 396): a cycle of changes in the level of female sex hormones in nonhuman mammals.
- **5-alpha-reductase deficiency (5-ARD)** (p. 412): a condition in which testosterone is not converted to dihydrotestosterone in a genetic male because of a deficiency of 5-alpha-reductase type 2 enzyme; the external genitals typically have a female appearance at birth.
- **follicle-stimulating hormone (FSH)** (p. 396): a hormone secreted by the anterior pituitary gland that causes one or several ovarian follicles to grow into a mature Graafian follicle, the egg to mature, and the Graafian follicle to secrete estrogen.
- **gender** (p. 389): a set of culturally defined roles, attitudes, and responsibilities for females and males that are learned, may change with time, and vary among and within societies.
- **heat** (p. 396): a period of intense sexual arousal when estrogen levels peak in estrous mammals; also called estrus.
- **Klinefelter syndrome** (p. 388): a condition in which a person has an XXY genotype and is phenotypically male, but has small external genitals, sparse pubic and armpit hair, and a tendency to be infertile.
- **lordosis** (p. 390): a female copulatory posture in which the hindquarters are raised to facilitate insertion of the penis by the male.
- **luteinizing hormone (LH)** (p. 397): in females, a hormone secreted by the anterior pituitary gland that causes ovulation.
- **medial preoptic area (MPOA)** (p. 403): a group of neurons in the anterior hypothalamus that influences female sexual responsivity.
- **menstrual cycle** (p. 396): a cycle of changes in the level of female sex hormones in humans and some other primates.
- **menstruation** (p. 397): the expulsion of the uterine lining in menstrual animals.
- **Müllerian-inhibiting substance (MIS)** (p. 387): a hormone released by the testes that helps prevent the development of the female reproductive system.
- **Müllerian system** (p. 387): a set of ducts in the human embryo that develops into parts of the female reproductive system.
- **myotonia** (p. 395): the rhythmic contraction of muscles, as in the male and female genital organs during orgasm; also causes erection of the nipples.
- **orgasm** (p. 395): the climax of the sexual response.
- **orgasmic dysfunction** (p. 415): the inability to have an orgasm.
- **ovariectomy** (p. 397): the surgical removal of the ovaries.
- **oxytocin** (p. 401): a posterior pituitary hormone that plays a role in reproductive activities, such as

sexual arousal, orgasm, nest building, suckling, and bonding with offspring.

- **pheromone** (p. 400): a chemical released into the external environment for communication within a species; can be used to signal reproductive readiness.
- **premature ejaculation** (p. 415): the inability of a man to delay ejaculation until his partner achieves orgasm.
- **progesterone** (p. 397): a female sex hormone manufactured by the corpus luteum; with estrogen, it prepares the lining of the uterus for implantation of the fertilized egg.
- **retarded ejaculation** (p. 415): the inability to ejaculate during sexual intercourse.
- **sex-determining gene** (p. 386): the gene on the short arm of the Y chromosome that determines the biological sex of an individual.
- **sex therapy** (p. 416): the psychological approach to treating sexual dysfunction.
- **sexual dysfunction** (p. 414): a chronic failure to obtain sexual satisfaction.
- **testis-determining factor (TDF)** (p. 387): an enzyme that causes the undifferentiated gonads to become testes.
- **testosterone** (p. 389): the male sex hormone that influences the sexual development of the brain and plays a significant role in male sexual arousal.
- **Turner syndrome** (p. 388): a condition in which a person is born with one X chromosome and no other sex chromosome; the female reproductive system develops only partially.
- **vaginismus** (p. 415): a condition in which muscle contractions close the vagina and prevent intercourse.
- **vasocongestion** (p. 395): a dilation and filling of blood vessels that produces erection of the penis or clitoris, nipple erection, and sexual flush.
- **ventromedial hypothalamus (VMH)** (p. 403): the hypothalamic area responsible for the effect of estrogen on sexual behavior.
- **vomeronasal organ** (p. 405): a specialized sensory organ, separate from the main olfactory system, that detects pheromones released by a receptive female.
- **Wolffian system** (p. 387): a set of ducts in the human embryo that develops into parts of the male reproductive system.

Answers to Labeling Exercises

1. Female

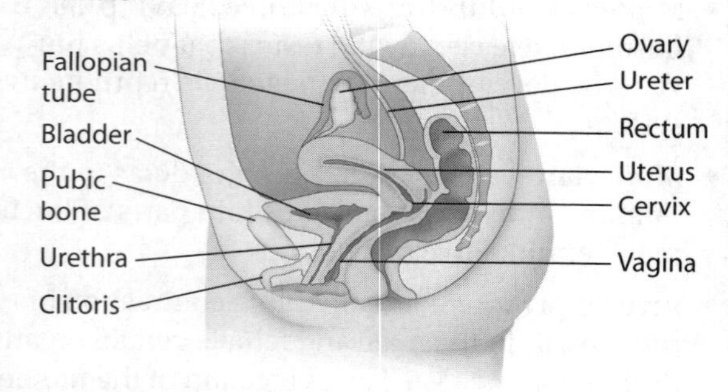

Male

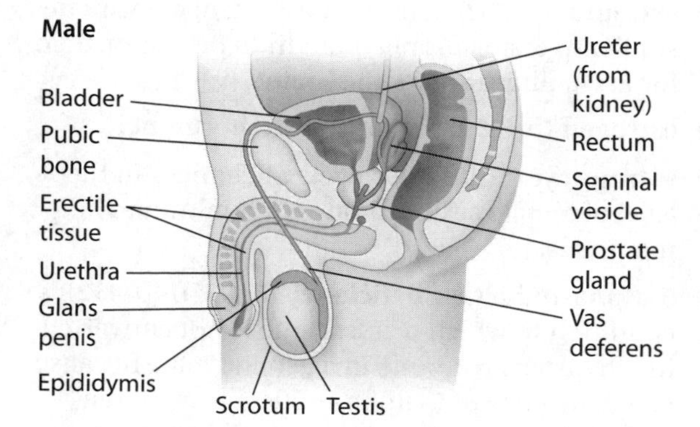

Figure 11.7, p. 395.

2.

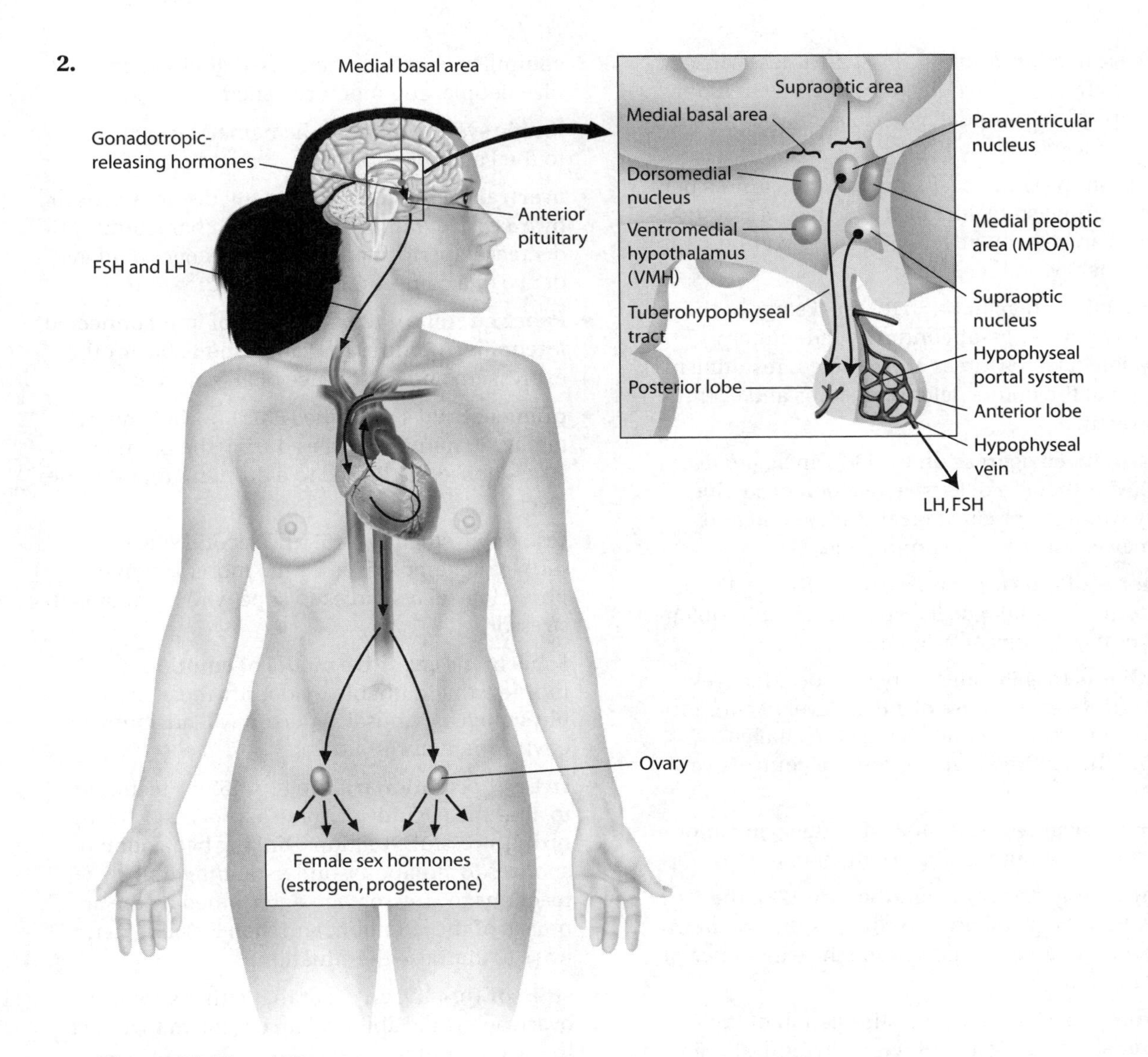

Figure 11.11, p. 402.

CHAPTER 12

Key Terms with Definitions

- **aggression** (p. 431): a behavior motivated by the intent to harm a living being or an inanimate object.
- **alarm stage** (p. 443): the first stage in the GAS, characterized by intense sympathetic nervous system arousal; also called alarm reaction.
- **amygdalectomy** (p. 434): a surgical procedure that treats extreme aggressiveness by destroying areas in the amygdala.
- **Cannon-Bard theory of emotion** (p. 424): the view that an event activates the thalamus, which stimulates the cerebral cortex to produce the feeling component (the experience) of the emotion and, at the same time, the rest of the body to produce the expression of the emotion.
- **cognitive appraisal** (p. 452): a cognitive evaluation of an event to determine its effect on one's life.

- **disease of adaptation** (p. 447): an illness caused by the efforts of the body to cope with stressors; examples are essential hypertension, gastric or peptic ulcers, and colitis.
- **emotion** (p. 422): a feeling that differs from a person's normal state; includes a change in physiological arousal, an affective (feeling) component, and a behavioral response.
- **exhaustion stage** (p. 446): the final stage of the GAS; when a stressor continues indefinitely, physiological resources are depleted, resulting in failure of the body's defense systems and eventually death.
- **fear-induced aggression** (p. 438): an aggressive behavior that is a defensive reaction occurring only when the organism feels threatened and perceives escape to be impossible.
- **general adaptation syndrome (GAS)** (p. 443): a pattern of physiological responses to a physiological or psychological stressor.
- **hardiness** (p. 455): an ability to cope effectively with stressors, because of a high level of commitment, a perception that change is a challenge rather than a threat, and a sense of control over events.
- **irritable aggression** (p. 432): an attack on almost anything without making attempts to escape.
- **James-Lange theory of emotion** (p. 422): the view that the physiological changes that occur in response to an event determine the experience of an emotion.
- **kindling** (p. 426): repeated stimulation of the amygdala, causing an animal to be more susceptible to seizure activity.
- **Klüver-Bucy syndrome** (p. 433): a disorder produced by temporal lobectomy, characterized by placidity, socially inappropriate sexual activity, compulsive orality, a decreased ability to recognize people, and memory deficits.
- **limbic system** (p. 425): the name MacLean gave to the Papez circuit.
- **overtraining syndrome** (p. 446): disorder caused by excessive training by athletes; characterized by decreased performance, mood changes, and evidence of a compromised immune system.
- **Papez circuit** (p. 425): a system of interconnected forebrain structures that are responsible for the expression and experience of an emotion.
- **premenstrual syndrome (PMS)** (p. 437): an irritability in human females during the premenstrual phase, attributed to a drop in progesterone level.
- **resistance stage** (p. 445): the second stage of the GAS, characterized by the mobilization of physiological resources to cope with a prolonged stressor.
- **Schachter's cognitive model of emotion** (p. 427): the view that if unable to identify the cause of physiological arousal, a person will attribute it to environmental conditions.
- **stress inoculation training** (p. 452): a technique to alter the cognitive appraisal process by recognizing stressful situations, linking behavioral responses to situations, understanding that reactions to stressors are determined by the appraisal of the situation, and then learning new ways to appraise the situation.
- **stressor** (p. 442): an event that either strains or overwhelms the ability of an organism to adjust to the environment.
- **type A behavior pattern (TABP)** (p. 454): a set of behaviors that includes an excessive competitive drive, high aggressiveness, and an intense sense of time urgency.

Answers to Labeling Exercises

1.

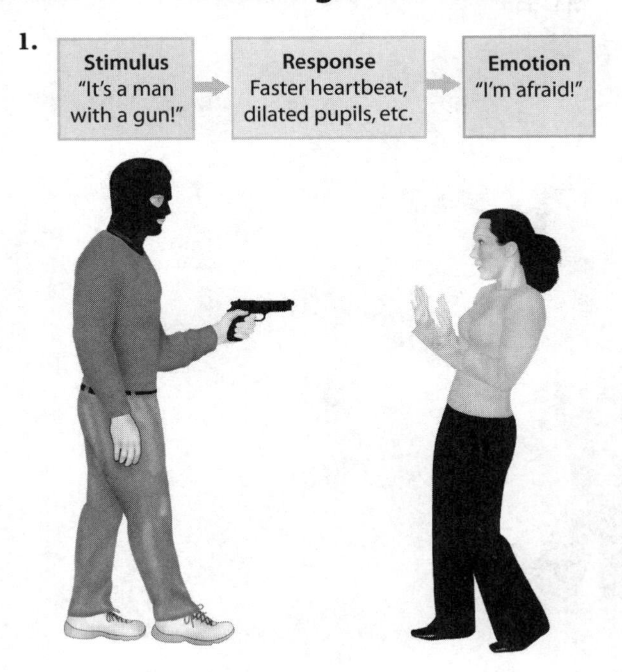

Figure 12.1, p. 422.

2.

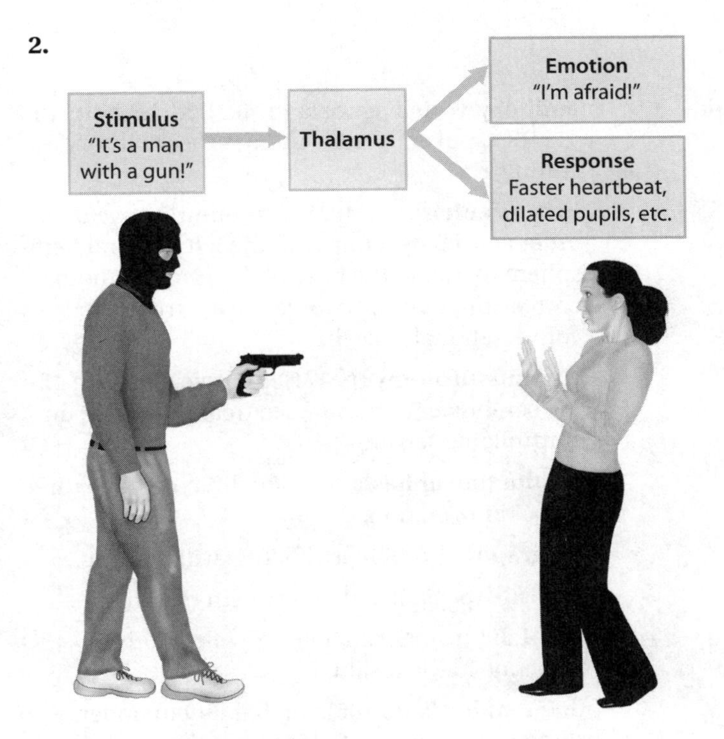

Figure 12.2, p. 424.

3.

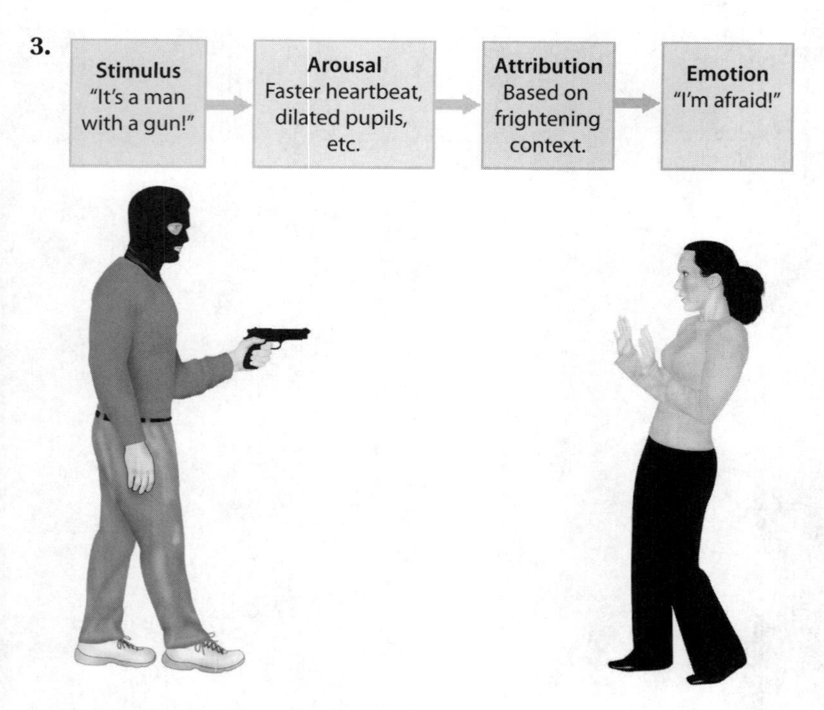

Figure 12.5, p. 427.

CHAPTER 13

Key Terms with Definitions

- **agrammatical speech** (p. 485): speech that is deficient in grammar.
- **agraphia** (p. 491): an inability to write.
- **alexia** (p. 491): an inability to read.
- **angular gyrus** (p. 467): an area of the parietal lobe with connections to Wernicke's area; involved in comprehending written language.
- **anomia** (p. 487): a difficulty selecting the correct word for either written or spoken language.
- **anomic aphasia** (p. 489): a consistent difficulty finding names, and substituting indefinite nouns and pronouns for substantive words.
- **aphasia** (p. 484): an acquired impairment in the use of language.
- **apraxia of speech** (p. 490): an inability to plan and sequence movements for producing speech.
- **arcuate fasciculus** (p. 467): a bundle of nerve fibers in the brain that connects Wernicke's area and Broca's area.
- **auditory-verbal agnosia** (p. 491): an inability to identify spoken words but not other auditory stimuli.
- **Broca's aphasia** (p. 485): a communicative disorder caused by damage to the left cerebral hemisphere rostral to the base of the primary motor cortex; an inability to initiate well-articulated conversational speech.
- **commissurotomy** (p. 471): a surgical cutting of the cerebral commissures to treat otherwise uncontrollable seizures.
- **conduction aphasia** (p. 488): difficulty repeating verbal information.
- **dysgraphia** (p. 492): a difficulty with writing.
- **dyslexia** (p. 492): a difficulty with reading.
- **echolalia** (p. 489): a repetition of something someone has just said.
- **fluent aphasia** (p. 485): an inability to understand the language of others and the production of less meaningful speech than normal.

- **global aphasia** (p. 486): a severe depression of all language functioning.
- **hemispheric lateralization** (p. 469): the differentiation of functions between the right and left sides of the brain.
- **language** (p. 462): a system of words, word meanings, and rules for combining words into phrases and sentences.
- **language acquisition device (LAD)** (p. 465): an innate mechanism that allows children to readily grasp the syntax relevant to their native language.
- **morpheme** (p. 463): the smallest meaningful unit of language.
- **neologistic jargon** (p. 468): a passage of lengthy, fluent, nonsensical speech.
- **nonfluent aphasia** (p. 485): a difficulty producing fluent, well-articulated, and self-initiated speech.
- **paragrammatical speech** (p. 487): speech characterized by the use of inappropriate morphemes.
- **paraphasia** (p. 488): an error in speaking.
- **phoneme** (p. 463): the simplest functional speech sound.
- **phonology** (p. 463): the study of the sound system of a language that prescribes how phonemes can be combined into morphemes.
- **phrase** (p. 463): a group of two or more related words that express a single thought.
- **pure alexia** (p. 491): an inability to read, with no difficulty writing; caused by a separation of the angular gyrus from visual input; also called alexia without agraphia.
- **semantics** (p. 464): the linguistic analysis of the meaning of language.
- **sentence** (p. 463): two or more phrases that convey an assertion, question, command, wish, or exclamation.
- **split-brain preparation** (p. 469): a surgical technique that severs the cerebral commissures and the optic chiasm (only in nonhuman animals), eliminating most communication between the hemispheres.
- **syntax** (p. 463): the system of rules for combining words into meaningful phrases and sentences.
- **temporoparietal cortex** (p. 468): a brain area encompassing the supramarginal gyrus and angular gyrus; involved in language comprehension.
- **transcortical motor aphasia** (p. 486): sparse, self-initiated speech with relatively good language comprehension.
- **transcortical sensory aphasia** (p. 489): fluent speech, poor comprehension, and anomia, along with an unusual tendency to repeat verbal stimuli.
- **visual-verbal agnosia** (p. 491): an inability to recognize printed words, but not spoken words; results from damage that isolates the visual cortex from cortical language areas.
- **Wernicke-Geschwind model** (p. 467): a model of language processing in which language is comprehended in Wernicke's area before messages are passed to Broca's area for speech production.
- **Wernicke's aphasia** (p. 487): a communicative disorder caused by damage to the posterior portion of the superior and middle temporal gyrus and the temporoparietal cortex; an inability to comprehend language.
- **Williams syndrome** (p. 466): a rare genetic disorder in which relatively intact language ability is coupled with mild to moderate mental retardation.

Answers to Labeling Exercises

1.

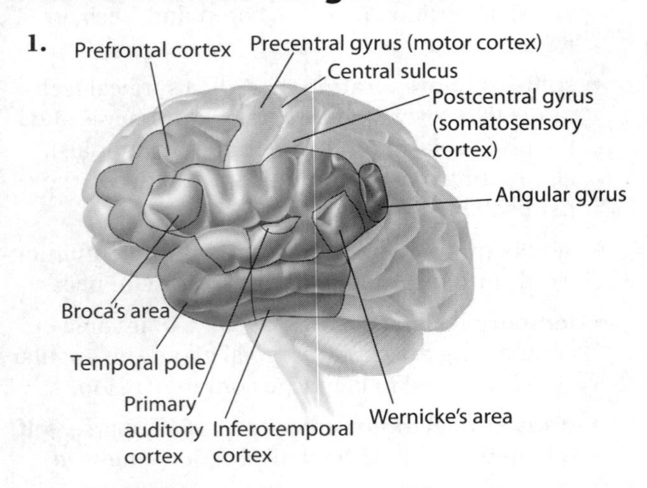

Figure 13.2, p. 468.

2.

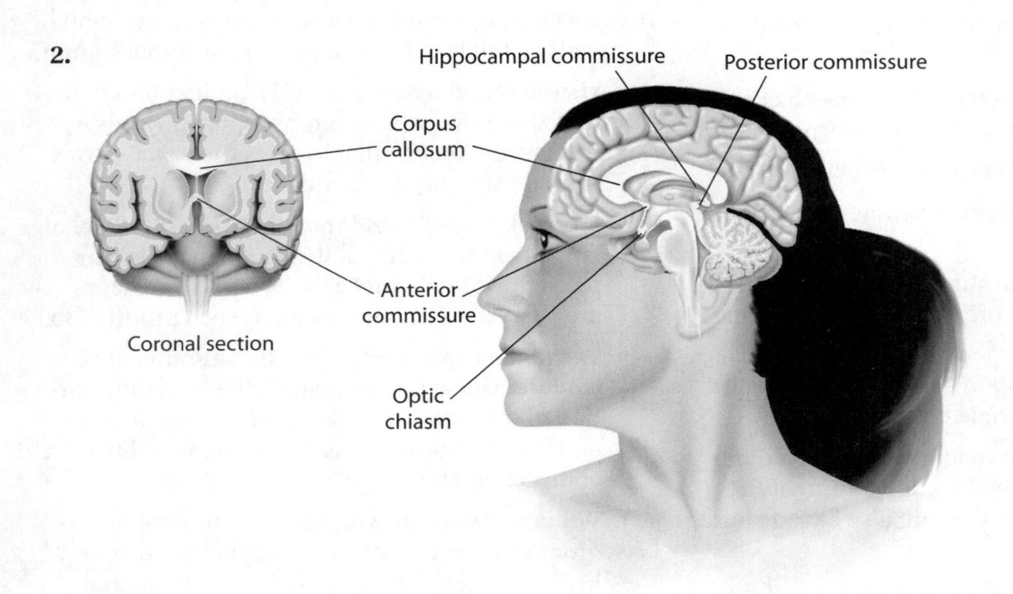

Figure 13.3, p. 469.

CHAPTER 14

Key Terms with Definitions

- **Alzheimer's disease** (AD) (p. 531): a type of dementia characterized by progressive neurological degeneration and a profound deterioration of mental functioning.
- **amyloid beta protein** (p. 533): a protein that accumulates in neural tissue and is thought to cause the degeneration of neural fibers and disruption of neural connections in specific brain areas that are characteristic of Alzheimer's disease.
- **anterograde amnesia** (p. 521): an inability to recall events after injury to the brain.

- **Atkinson-Shiffrin model** (p. 505): a model of memory storage in which an experience is sequentially stored in the sensory register, the short-term store, and the long-term store.
- **cell assembly** (p. 510): a circuit of neurons that become active at the same time; serves as the site of permanent memory.
- **cellular modification theory** (p. 516): the view that learning permanently enhances the functioning of existing neural circuits or establishes new neural connections.
- **conditioned response (CR)** (p. 503): a learned reaction to a conditioned stimulus.
- **conditioned stimulus (CS)** (p. 503): an initially neutral stimulus that eventually elicits a conditioned response after pairing with a UCS.
- **confabulation** (p. 529): a tendency to make up stories to fill in gaps in memory.
- **contingency** (p. 504): the specified relationship between a behavior and its reinforcement or punishment.
- **declarative memory** (p. 509): factual memory, or the memory of specific events.
- **dementia** (p. 531): a loss or impairment of mental functioning.
- **episodic memory** (p. 507): the memory of temporally related events experienced at a particular time and place.
- **habituation** (p. 502): a decrease in response following repeated exposure to a nonthreatening stimulus.
- **interference** (p. 506): an inability to recall a specific memory because of other memories.
- **Korsakoff's syndrome** (p. 529): a severe memory impairment usually seen in chronic alcoholics.
- **interpositus nucleus** (p. 515): the area of the brain central to the conditioning of the nictitating membrane response.
- **learning** (p. 502): a long-term change in behavior as a function of experiences.
- **long-term depression (LTD)** (p. 526): a persistent activity-dependent reduction in synaptic effectiveness.
- **long-term potentiation (LTP)** (p. 524): an increased neural responsivity that follows a brief, intense series of electrical impulses to neural tissue.
- **long-term store** (p. 505): the site of permanent memory storage.
- **medial temporal lobe** (p. 521): a brain area containing the hippocampus and surrounding cortical areas; involved in storing experiences.
- **mediodorsal thalamus** (p. 528): a brain structure associated with profound memory impairment.
- **memory** (p. 502): the capacity to retain and retrieve past experiences.
- **memory attribute** (p. 506): an aspect of an event that can stimulate memory retrieval.
- **mossy fiber pathway** (p. 524): one of the afferent pathways into the hippocampus; intense electrical stimulation of its neurons produces LTP.
- **neurofibrillary tangle** (p. 533): an unusual triangular and looped fiber in the cytoplasm of neurons that is a hallmark of Alzheimer's disease.
- **neuroplasticity** (p. 527): the modifiability of the brain that allows adaptation to changing environmental conditions.
- **NMDA receptor** (p. 525): a receptor that is sensitive to the neurotransmitter glutamate.
- **operant conditioning** (p. 504): a type of learning in which a response either produces reinforcement or avoids punishment.
- **Pavlovian conditioning** (p. 503): a type of learning in which a neutral stimulus is paired with a stimulus that elicits a reflex response until the neutral stimulus elicits the reflex response by itself.
- **perforant fiber pathway** (p. 524): the most widely studied of three pathways into the hippocampus; intense stimulation of its neurons produces LTP.
- **procedural memory** (p. 508): skill memory, or the memory of highly practiced behavior.
- **punisher** (p. 504): an event that decreases the frequency of the behavior that precedes it.
- **rehearsal systems approach** (p. 506): an alternative to the Atkinson-Shiffrin model in which Baddeley argued that memories go directly from the sensory register to long-term storage.
- **reinforcer** (p. 504): an event that increases the frequency of the behavior that precedes it.
- **retrograde amnesia** (p. 512): the inability to recall events that preceded a traumatic event.

- **retrograde messenger** (p. 526): a chemical sent from the postsynaptic membrane to the presynaptic membrane to maintain neurotransmitter release.
- **reverberatory activity** (p. 510): the continued reactivation of a neural circuit following an experience.
- **Schaffer collateral fiber pathway** (p. 524): one of the afferent pathways into the hippocampus; intense electrical stimulation of its neurons produces LTP.
- **semantic memory** (p. 507): the memory of knowledge concerning the use of language and the rules, formulas, or algorithms for the development of concepts or solutions to problems.
- **senile plaque** (p. 533): a granular deposit of amyloid beta protein and the remains of degenerated dendrites and axons; found in large numbers in the brains of people with Alzheimer's disease.
- **sensitization** (p. 503): an increase in reactivity to a stimulus following exposure to an intense event.
- **sensory register** (p. 505): in the Atkinson-Shiffrin model, the initial storage site where a memory is held for a brief time without modification.
- **short-term store** (p. 505): in the Atkinson-Shiffrin model, a temporary site where information is held before storage in permanent memory.
- **Skinner box** (p. 504): an enclosed chamber invented by B. F. Skinner to train an animal through operant conditioning.
- **unconditioned response (UCR)** (p. 503): a reflexive reaction to an unconditioned stimulus.
- **unconditioned stimulus (UCS)** (p. 503): a stimulus that involuntarily elicits a reflexive response.
- **working memory** (p. 506): a system that permits the temporary storage and manipulation of information required for tasks such as comprehension, learning, and reasoning.

Answers to Labeling Exercises

1.

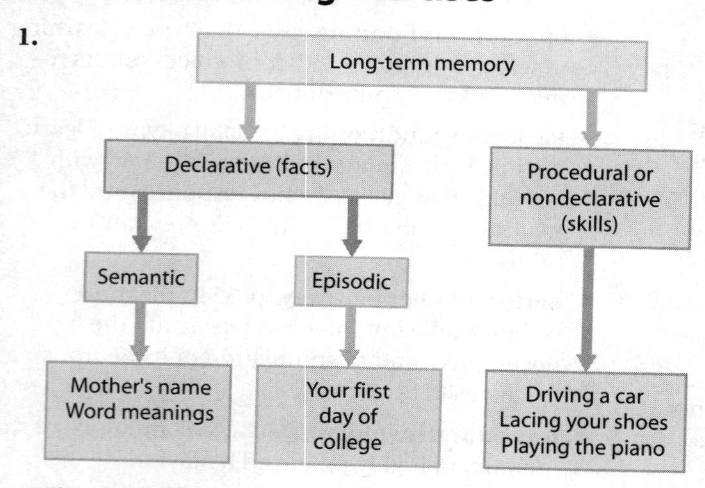

Figure 14.4, p. 509.

2.

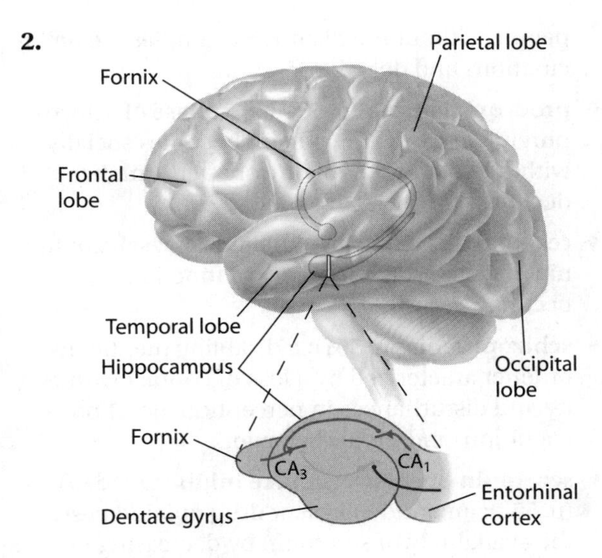

Figure 14.21, p. 524.

CHAPTER 15

Key Terms with Definitions

- **active phase** (p. 564): the phase of schizophrenia in which the more acute symptoms of the disorder appear, such as hallucinations and delusions.
- **affective disorder** (p. 544): a mental disorder characterized by one or both of two mood states: depression and/or mania.
- **bipolar disorder** (p. 547): a type of affective disorder characterized by episodes of mania and depression that typically continue throughout the person's lifetime.
- **concordance rate** (p. 553): the rate at which any characteristic occurs in both members of a pair of relatives.
- **cyclothymia** (p. 547): one of the bipolar disorders characterized by less intense episodes of mania and depression than are seen in bipolar disorder.
- **delusion** (p. 563): a false system of beliefs that a person defends against reality.
- **dementia praecox** (p. 561): Kraeplin's name for the disorder now known as schizophrenia.
- **depression** (p. 544): an affective disorder characterized by an intense, continuing feeling of sadness and worthlessness.
- **depressive disorder** (p. 544): a type of affective disorder in which depression is the only mood state.
- **dexamethasone suppression test (DST)** (p. 559): a test to determine whether the administration of dexamethasone suppresses ACTH and cortisol secretion; many depressed people have an abnormal response.
- **dopamine hypothesis of schizophrenia** (p. 565): the view that an excess of activity in the dopamine system results in the positive symptoms of schizophrenia.
- **dysthymia** (p. 546): a chronic, usually low-level form of depression.
- **electroconvulsive therapy (ECT)** (p. 554): a treatment for depression in which an electric current is passed through the head to induce a seizure.
- **hallucination** (p. 563): a sensory experience in the absence of environmental stimulation.
- **hypercortisolism** (p. 559): an abnormally high secretion (hypersecretion) of cortisol from the adrenal cortex; found in many people with major depression.
- **hypofrontality theory** (p. 570): a theory that the negative symptoms of schizophrenia are caused by decreased activity in the prefrontal cortex.
- **hypomania** (p. 547): a milder form of mania in which occupational or social functioning is not impaired.

- **learned helplessness** (p. 556): a pattern of depression-like behavior produced by repeated exposure to an inescapable noxious event.
- **loosening of associations** (p. 563): a tendency to make sentences containing several disconnected thoughts; a characteristic of people with schizophrenia.
- **major depression** (p. 545): a type of depressive disorder characterized by a depressed mood of at least 2 weeks' duration.
- **mania** (p. 546): an elevated, expansive, or irritable mood and inflated self-esteem or grandiosity.
- **monoamine oxidase inhibitor (MAOI)** (p. 551): a type of antidepressant drug that increases monoamine levels by preventing MAO from degrading excess monoamine neurotransmitters.
- **monoamine hypothesis of depression** (p. 549): the theory that depression is caused by decreased activity at monoaminergic synapses, particularly where serotonin and norepinephrine are the neurotransmitters.
- **negative symptom** (p. 564): normal behavior (e.g., appropriate emotions, desire for social contact) that is absent in people with schizophrenia, as seen in social withdrawal and a flat affect.
- **neologism** (p. 563): a meaningless word created by a person with schizophrenia.
- **positive symptom** (p. 564): a behavior exhibited by a person with schizophrenia but absent in people without the disorder; examples are hallucinations and delusions.
- **prodromal phase** (p. 564): the phase of schizophrenia in which the person becomes socially withdrawn and school or work performance declines.
- **residual phase** (p. 564): the phase of schizophrenia in which some recovery of functioning occurs.
- **schizophrenia** (p. 561): a disabling mental disorder characterized by a loss of contact with reality and disturbances in perception, emotion, cognition, and motor behavior.
- **serotonin-specific reuptake inhibitor (SSRI)** (p. 552): an antidepressant drug that increases the availability of serotonin by decreasing its reuptake.
- **tardive dyskinesia** (p. 567): a motor disorder with facial tics and involuntary limb movements; often appears after long-term use of antipsychotic medicines.
- **tricyclic compound** (p. 551): a type of antidepressant drug that increases brain levels of norepinephrine and serotonin by interfering with neurotransmitter reuptake.
- **word salad** (p. 563): a type of speech with no discernible links between the words.

Answers to Labeling Exercises

1.

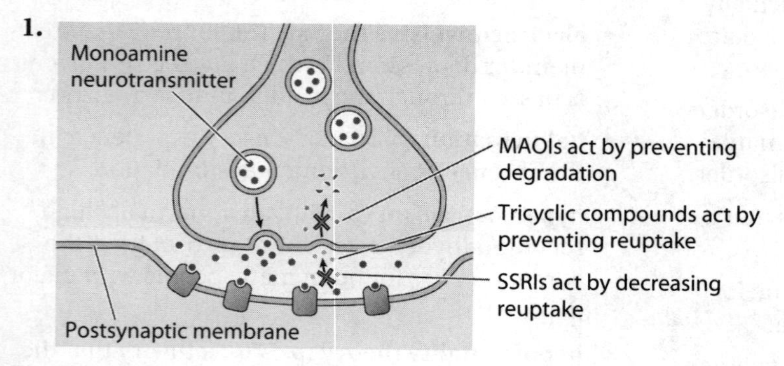

Figure 15.5, p. 551.

2.

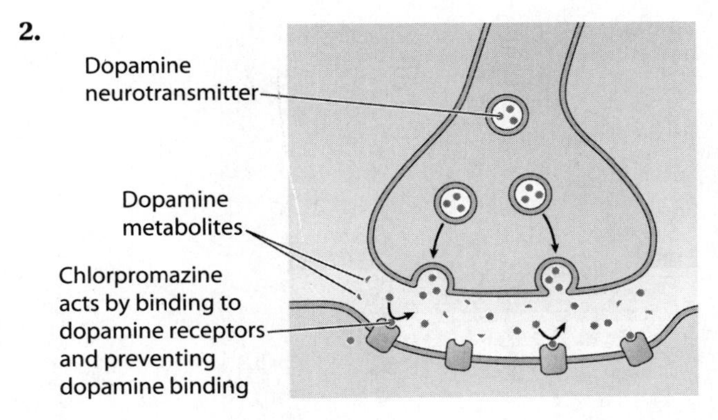

Figure 15.12, p. 565.